HUSH, LITTLE BABY

A Novel By

Deborah M. Piccurelli

Sword of the Spirit Publishing

ISBN 13: 978-0-9838836-2-3
Published by Sword of the Spirit Publishing

www.swordofspirit.net

ACKNOWLEDGEMENTS

I want to express my heartfelt gratitude to everyone who had a hand in bringing this novel into existence. First, to my husband and two sons for putting up with me throughout the writing of this book. To my dear friends, Pam Halter and Sally John, who not only read and critiqued all or part of the manuscript, but encouraged me along the way. To my crit buds, Vasthi Acosta, Lori Chally, and Lydia Tsirozidis, for offering their valuable time, skills and input, which helped make my story the best it can be.

My research for this book began about six years ago, and I interviewed some people who probably don't remember me. I thank Matt and Amy Roloff, who I spoke with before they became famous for their hit TV show, *Little People, Big World*. Matt was president of Little People of America, back then. Mark Crutcher of Life Dynamics, the pro-life organization that conducted the investigation into fetal harvesting by abortion clinics gave me great insight into the subject, which I truly appreciate. Any errors are solely of my making.

I also wish to thank Donald James Parker and Sword of the Spirit Publishing for the wonderful opportunity to turn my manuscript into a book.

And, from the depths of my soul, I thank my Lord Jesus.

CHAPTER 1

She would be working for her sister's killer.

Amber's skin goosebumped as she drove down the town's main highway to the Cedarview Women's Center for her first day on the job. To think the man responsible for Ashley's death, Dr. Albert Hines, would be her employer.

Her foot pumped the extender pedal for the brake, and her Honda Odyssey glided to a smooth stop at the red traffic signal. She sometimes wondered what it would feel like to be five-six instead of four foot tall and able to drive without the extenders, to live a life without the need for *any* adaptive products.

She was about to find out, in part anyway. Her last visit to the clinic for the interview revealed very few accommodations for a little person. Not that she expected there would be any, as they probably never had a dwarf working there before. Despite her size, Dr. Hines had shown her much respect. Because of that surprising courtesy, a tinge of guilt crept in at the thought that he would end up in prison because of her.

Not enough to put her off, though. He had it coming.

Amber pulled the minivan into the clinic's parking lot and watched, mouth agape, as two lines of protestors shouted across an imaginary divide. Some of them resembled snarling cougars ready to pounce at the slightest provocation.

Her heartbeat quickened. Her first day on the job and she had to deal with this? The big question was how to get through that crowd unscathed.

A heavy sigh forced its way through her lips, as she rolled into an empty spot around the side of the simple brick building. Her dry mouth tasted stale. She turned off the engine and sat frozen for a moment. The overcast sky added to her sense of dread and doom.

What am I doing here?

Despite the cold weather, her palms were sweaty, and she rubbed them against the soft wool of her coat. She couldn't go in. Crossing those picket lines could incite a riot. The pro-choicers would think she was on *their* side, and the pro-lifers would think she was against *them*. And what if something triggered Dr. Hines's memory, causing him to recognize her from that long-ago day when she'd come here with Ashley? He hadn't mentioned it, but he could have gotten a glimpse of her. A dozen years, youth, and shorter hair might not make a big difference. But the more time she spent in his presence, the higher the risk. She could well imagine what such a big guy could do to someone as small as her.

She checked her hair in the rearview mirror, and her anxious blue eyes peered back at her. "You're being silly," she told her reflection. She opened the car door to a blast of cold air. She would do this. For Ashley and for the babies. As for the raging bulls around front, she'd leave them to the Lord.

Amber climbed out of the van. She couldn't see the mob from here, but she could hear them: a myriad of voices, some yelling, and some chanting. Sounded like hundreds of people. Could there be that many?

Her hands and knees trembled. She disliked large groups of people, especially hostile ones. They didn't mix well with little people.

Mustering up her courage, Amber strode around the corner of the building and headed for the front door, a mere fifteen feet away. *Fifteen feet!* Her own personal green mile.

There were two separate groups comprised of approximately a hundred and fifty people assembled in front of the clinic.

As soon as she got near, a voice yelled out, "Don't do it!"

"Leave her alone!" cried another. "It's her choice!"

Soon both sides erupted into a crescendo of shouting that threatened to break the sound barrier and closed in on Amber.

As she reached for the doorknob a sudden shove sent her flying sideways, and she hit the concrete like a sack of potatoes. Pain shot up her right arm. A hand yanked her up and ushered her back to the door but others clawed her in the opposite direction. "Murderer!" came a legion of voices, as she was jostled.

Help me, Lord! Why are my fellow Christians behaving this way?

She tried to pull free.

"Break it up! Here, here, now!"

She knew that deep voice. A pair of strong male hands gripped her shoulders and guided her to the door. She cringed at their touch yet grateful for the rescue. As soon as she crossed over the threshold, the door slammed behind her, muffling the angry cries of the people and the sirens of the arriving police cars. She squinted in the brightly lit waiting room from its contrast to the dreary outdoors.

While straightening her clothes, she kept her eyes averted. How embarrassing, having to be rescued by the subject of your investigation. "Uh, thank you, Doctor." Her hair had to be straggled after that scuffle. She patted it into place and winced with the movement of her injured arm. "This happen often?"

"Protests? Yes. But never before has a new employee made quite an entrance as that, Miss Amber."

She might have thought the incident annoyed him but for the twinkle in his forest green eyes. She grinned through her aversion to this man. "It's my mission in life to get noticed wherever I go."

Dr. Hines threw his head back and laughed out loud, his light brown hair fluttering with the gesture. "You're a sassy one." Then, in the next instant, his expression became serious. "Come with me, and we'll get started." He moved toward the back of the clinic.

Dr. Hines's sudden mood shift left Amber with a chill creeping through her veins.

* * *

In her tiny, sparsely furnished office, Amber placed her purse in a desk drawer. As she pushed it closed, she glimpsed a step stool underneath the desk. Just like the one she'd always kept under her desk at *The Tri-County Informer*. The one Evan had kept there while she'd been gone for the past two years.

With a shake of her head, she brought herself back to the present, and the business at hand. Nurse Maggie Bonner had to have left the step stool. Maggie had also been the one to tip her and Evan off about Dr. Hines and arrange Amber's job interview with the doctor by putting in a good word for her. After meeting the nurse that first time, Amber could tell the woman was a caring and kind person.

Marveling at Maggie's thoughtfulness, Amber pulled the stool out and stepped up to hang her jacket on the naked coat tree in the corner. She'd remember to thank her new friend later, she thought, following the alluring aroma to the break room.

Back at her desk, Amber looked forward to a good cup of

coffee after what she'd just been through. She took a sip. *Ugh!* She could fuel her car for a week on the stuff. One thing's for certain, she'd be arriving early each morning to make the coffee herself.

The offensive-tasting liquid relegated to a far corner of the desk, Amber let her eyes peruse the room. Not much to look at. White walls, black metal desk with fake wood grain top, her fabric swivel chair, a couple vinyl visitor's chairs, and the coat tree. If this were her real job, she'd bring in a few personal things to give the office a homier quality.

A nervous shiver rippled through her. Although she'd worked undercover before, this time was different. She'd never had a history with the subject of her piece. Plus, a story of such importance rarely surfaced in this area of South Jersey.

When she and Evan had met last week for the first time since their separation, he'd kissed her cheek. Everything she remembered about him had stayed the same: His warm brown eyes, thick dark hair, and quiet strength. But she was there about a news story, so she had pushed her memories aside and listened to what Nurse Maggie had to say.

Now, her thoughts returned to seeing Evan again, that day, for the first time. A deep sigh escaped her lips.

"Like your office, Miss Amber?" Dr. Hines's voice cut through the fog she'd been in. Stealthy as a panther, he'd crept up without warning. The length of his pristine white physician's coat emphasized his height and leanness as he propped himself against the doorjamb. The warm, welcoming tone in which he spoke oozed over her like heated oil. A smile accentuated his words. "I know it's small, but . . . well, you don't need much room." His green eyes held a mischievous glint.

A grin spread across her lips without any effort on her part, and she hated that his charm so easily affected her. Nevertheless, it made her job a little easier. "Ha-ha, very funny," she said.

"Did you find what I left for you under the desk?"

Amber had to stop and think before the meaning of his words penetrated. The step stool. Maggie hadn't done it after all. She smiled. "Yes, I did. Thanks so much for your thoughtfulness."

"My pleasure." He winked. "Now that you've made yourself at home," he said, nodding toward her coffee cup, "shall we get started?"

For the second time that morning, he seemed to berate her

without actually doing so. "Sure thing, Doc."

Time to get down to business. Amber's stomach clenched along with her hands. Her fingers groped for her wedding band, which always provided a special comfort. There was no comfort, this time. Her ring finger matched the bareness of these white plaster walls.

Dr. Hines walked fully into the office carrying a stack of paper, which he placed on her desk.

"This is what you're to do." After taking a sheet from the pile, he extended his free hand, palm up, and wiggled his fingers. "Give me that clipboard, please." Amber handed him the one on the corner of the desk. He placed the paper under the clip, and then passed the board back to her.

As she read the form, her tongue turned to flypaper. Dr. Hines wanted her to ask clients to donate their fetuses to research.

Her surprise must have shown on her face, because Dr. Hines asked, "What's the matter?"

She looked up at him. "Oh . . . I'm sorry. I—I didn't know this was part of the job. You only told me I was to advise patients, answer questions, or explain procedures."

"Is there a problem?"

She hesitated. "No. Not at all."

"I want you to do everything you can to get our patients to sign that."

"Everything?" She heard the quiver in her voice and hoped he didn't notice.

Amber was cast in shadow by his height as he loomed over her. "Yes, Miss Amber. *Everything.*" The way he said it left no doubt in her mind that she had no choice.

How could she stand doing that? She would be instrumental in the very thing she was trying to stop. Every time she sent a patient into the procedure room with one of those signed consent forms, she would have a part in the same barbaric practice as every other person working at this clinic.

Dear God, what have I gotten myself into?

* * *

Her first patient came in about 10:30 a.m. Amber took a few deep breaths before she entered the reception area.

The young woman sat in one of the padded chairs, leafing through a magazine. Her paperwork indicated she was twenty-six years old. Amber noticed that each of her ears sported four gold hoops hanging in succession from largest to smallest.

"Denise Galloway?" Amber extended her hand. "I'm Amber Blake."

Denise's already large eyes widened even more. A moment of hesitation passed, followed by a warm smile. "Nice to meetcha." The woman pumped Amber's hand, which made the earrings flutter on her lobes and her auburn ponytail bounce. The rank odor of stale cigarette smoke filled Amber's nose, and she suppressed a cough.

"Follow me, please." Amber took Denise to her office. "Have a seat."

Denise slumped into the black vinyl chair positioned in front of Amber's desk, and she looked around the small, austere room. "I like what you've done with the place," she said with a wink.

Amber smiled at that and climbed onto her seat. The words on the form attached to the clipboard blurred as she stared at them, and she wondered how to begin. She cleared her throat. "Denise, do you understand everything about the procedure you're here to have?"

A brief flash of pain flickered in Denise's eyes before she waved a hand in dismissal. "I've had two already, so I'm an old pro."

Amber cringed at the number but rebuked herself for judging. "So a third won't bother you?"

"Nah." Denise pulled a pack of cigarettes from her large handbag and tapped it on the side of her index finger until one popped halfway out. Despite her show of indifference, a wistful expression tugged at the young woman's features as she placed the cigarette between her fuchsia-colored lips.

Compassion erupted in Amber's heart, and she forced herself to resist the impulse to wrap Denise in a comforting hug. "I'm sorry, but no smoking is allowed in here."

Denise shrugged and put the cigarette away.

"So then, you're sure you understand what's involved in this . . . procedure?" Amber couldn't force herself to utter the A-word.

"Yeah, I understand." Denise crossed her long legs.

"Okay. Then I need to ask you another question." She handed the clipboard to Denise.

"Shoot," Denise said, glancing at the form.

"W-would you care to donate your baby to research?" Her tongue lost moisture and stuck to the roof of her mouth.

Denise frowned at her. "You're talking like it's already

born."

"I mean the fetus, of course. Would you care to donate the fetus to research?" She'd have to watch how she said things from now on.

Denise slanted a glance sideways. "Hmmm." Waving her hand again, she said "Oh, heck, it's for a good cause. Why not? It's not like I'll want the thing back." She emitted a mirthless giggle and stuck out her hand. "Got a pen?"

"Yeah, sure." Amber handed over the one that sat on top of her desk, silently refusing to give up.

Denise scribbled her name on the signature line.

"Don't you want to read before signing?"

"Nah, I trust you."

Amber was amazed at how easily this woman consented without really knowing what the whole thing entailed.

"Do you have any questions, Denise?"

"Nope." The young woman uncrossed her legs. "Let's get on with it."

Should she let Denise go through another abortion without ensuring that it's what she truly wanted? If she did, sleep would be elusive tonight. "Are you aware of how the procedure is done?"

"Well . . . it really doesn't matter."

Her heart constricted. She had to get around this without giving herself, and her beliefs, away.

"Haven't you ever read the pamphlets given to you prior to . . . having it done?"

Denise wrinkled her nose in distaste. "I really don't want to know, so I purposely avoid them."

"Why don't you want to know?"

She shrugged. "Because I don't need to." Her hands twisted and squeezed together in her lap.

"What do you think will happen to the fetus once it's being used for research?" A different tack might help. She folded her arms and leaned them on her desk.

"I don't know. I can't think about that," Denise said, a defensive note in her voice.

Amber sighed heavily. Poor girl, to be stuck in such a situation. "Denise, you don't have to go through with this if you don't want to." She spoke gently.

"I have to. I can't be strapped with a kid when I can barely afford to get by on my own. Not without a husband."

Amber fought the urge to ask why she hadn't thought of

that before sleeping around. That wasn't fair. She had once accused Evan of being a snobby Christian, and now she proved guilty of the same. She was the last person to be judging. Silently, she begged the Lord's forgiveness, and His love nudged away her arrogance.

"Are you sure, Denise? You could give your baby up for adoption."

"Yes, I'm sure. I have to work. I can't walk around pregnant or take time off to give birth."

"Are you absolutely sure?" Amber prodded, leaning toward her.

Denise hesitated for a millisecond "Yes," she whispered.

Amber straightened up, defeated, and pulled in a deep breath.

"Okay, Denise. Have a seat out front. Someone will be with you shortly." She felt as though she had led the proverbial lamb to slaughter.

After Denise left, Amber slumped against the desk, exhausted. How could she survive doing this all day, every day?

There was only one person to go to.

Jesus, I know I can do all things you call me to do. I trust you will guide me in each case.

Amber took a deep, cleansing breath. She felt so much better now. Lighter. She got up to call the next patient.

And just outside the open office door stood Nurse Rita Franks, her glare accusing. How long had she been standing there? Had she heard Amber trying to talk Denise out of the abortion?

Amber had met Rita the day of her interview with Dr. Hines. He introduced the two women, and Rita immediately acted cold and distant toward Amber. For what reason, Amber couldn't guess.

Whatever the case, not half a day into the job and already Nurse Franks may have incriminating evidence that could get her fired.

CHAPTER 2

"Amber, will you come in for a second?" Dr. Hines called to Amber as she passed his office on her way back from lunch.

Uh-oh. She had never been discovered the first day of an investigation before.

"Just wondered how your day was going," he said from behind his desk

Whew! Either Rita hadn't overheard her conversation with Denise or she chose not to divulge it.

Perhaps Dr. Hines knew about what happened with Denise Galloway and wasn't letting on. But why? To test her? To bide his time until he found out why she really came?

"To be honest, doing the same thing all day long, is monotonous." If he only knew the truth. Her contribution to his heinous activities made her ill.

She perused the office, trying to absorb everything that might be useful later. A credenza. A door on the back wall, probably a closet. A desk. One entire wall to the right boasted a slew of framed diplomas and certificates. A little show-offey. For now, she preferred to assume Dr. Hines took pride in his accomplishments. On the day she was interviewed she hadn't seen any of these things, because they'd met in the conference room.

That there were no pictures of family members or friends anywhere in his office made her wonder what type of person he really was.

"Hmm." His brows furrowed, and he appeared to be in deep thought. "I'll have to remedy that by giving you some extra duties."

The fax machine sat on his desk. Maggie said daily transmissions came in with the orders for body parts.

She needed to get copies of those orders.

"Like what?" She barely paid attention to the conversation. How was she going to get her hands on those faxes? And how could she make copies of them without getting caught?

"Let me think on it for a while."

"Okay, just let me know." She left the office, eager to figure out her strategy.

Maybe Evan could help.

* * *

Amber reached up to ring Evan's doorbell, questioning the wisdom of showing up unannounced and uninvited.

The door opened before the long musical chimes ended, and he stood there staring, his jaw hanging. He wore gray sweats, his usual choice of attire for relaxing. That hadn't changed in two years.

"You can close your mouth now." She walked past him into the house, resisting the urge to stroke his goatee.

"Sorry, I just never expected you to show up here. Is something wrong?" He closed the door after her.

"Nothing major. Just thought you could help me figure something out."

She looked around. Everything appeared exactly the same as the day she left. The monstrous crystal chandelier hanging from the high ceiling in the entranceway. The oriental runners on tile. The overstuffed blue sofa she could see in the family room off to her right . . .

"I see you haven't redecorated." She was glad. They had bought this house together. She loved it then. Still did. Wonderful, happy memories were made here.

"Well, no. I like what you did after we moved in. I wouldn't change a thing."

She smiled, unable to think of anything to say to that. Besides, speaking might release a torrent of tears, sentimental fool that she was.

Amber noticed Evan checking his watch. "Am I keeping you from something?"

"No. I have an appointment later, but there's still plenty of time."

"Do you want me to leave?"

"No."

"Well, if you're sure . . ."

"Are you hungry? I was just having some Chinese take-out. There's more than enough."

The mere mention of food set her stomach rumbling. "Sure, I could use a bite, but after the day I've had, I'm not sure I can keep it down."

"That bad, huh?" He led the way to the kitchen, where the pungent aroma of the food permeated the room.

"You wouldn't believe it."

"Try me." Like her, Evan used a step stool to collect dishes from the upper cabinets. He grabbed utensils from a drawer, and then carried everything to the table.

"I'm absolutely drained because I have to keep my emotions in check while I persuade all these women to consent to abortions, then sign their fetuses over to research."

"Poor sweetheart."

A shiver of delight ran through her at the familiar endearment. *Sweetheart.* He had always called her that while they were together. Now, as always, pleasure enveloped her at the way his voice deepened when he said it. She quashed the instinct to snuggle into its cozy cocoon.

It was a mistake to come here. Probably a mistake to work with him, too. What had she been thinking?

Except for the clink of forks against their plates, they ate in silence. Amber normally enjoyed Chinese food, but tonight her taste buds wouldn't cooperate. She might as well have been eating plastic, instead of vegetable fried rice.

When he finished, Evan pushed back his plate. "So, what do you need help with?"

"I spotted the fax machine where they get the daily orders Maggie told us about." Though she wasn't finished eating, Amber slid her dish aside, too. "It sits right on Dr. Hines's desk. Getting my hands on those transmissions will be tricky, let alone making copies. I was hoping you'd have some ideas."

"Hmmm." Evan paused. "What do they do with them afterward?"

She shrugged. "They could throw them away, for all I know."

"Now that would be convenient. All you'd have to do is dig around in the trash cans."

Amber remembered her conversation with the doctor after lunch. "Dr. Hines wants to give me extra responsibilities. If only I could offer to do something that involved handling those orders. Thing is, as a new employee, I wouldn't know about them."

"If you offered to do some filing, or something, you might get to find out where they go."

"I don't know." She reached for her fork again and pushed some rice around on the plate. "He has a secretary for that. I guess I could suggest helping her. She sometimes seems a bit overwhelmed."

"Couldn't hurt. Try it."

"I think I will." She dabbed her mouth with a napkin.

More silence . . . until Evan's words cut through it.

"Amber, did you ever consider coming back home? Getting back together?" He rubbed behind his ear with a forefinger. To her, an endearing habit.

She looked at him, taking her time to answer. How she wanted to shout, "Yes!" and leap into his arms. But first she needed to know something. "Have your feelings changed about having children?"

He sighed and looked away.

She had her answer.

"Then there's nothing more to say on that subject." What sense would getting back together make, then? They'd still argue over that, and everything else, just as they had before. They could barely get along. She hopped off the chair and gathered dishes from the table.

"Amber, please. Why can't we talk this out?"

"There's nothing to talk about." She rooted under the sink for the step stool they'd always kept there, and he'd used earlier. "Nothing's changed in two years. What could we say differently now than we did then?" She opened the door to the dishwasher and began rinsing and stacking the dishes.

"But I still love you. I never stopped. I don't believe you stopped loving me, either."

He came to the sink and reached up with one hand, as if to caress her cheek. Amber slapped a dishcloth into his open palm. Evan frowned, then held it under the running water. After squeezing the cloth, he went to wipe down the table. As he moved away, his arm brushed against her back. She stiffened. After all this time, her body was still highly sensitive to his touch. When he came back and chucked the rag into the sink, Amber caught a faint whiff of his cologne. She recognized his favorite scent, one she had always loved. It was called *Attraction*, for obvious reasons.

Before they finished cleaning up, Amber stepped off the stool and grabbed her coat and purse. If she didn't get out of there quick, she might never leave.

"You're going already? Why did you even come? Surely you could have figured out what to do about the faxes on your own."

"I don't know why I came. It was a mistake." She left the kitchen.

"Amber, wait." He followed her out. "Let's talk. Please."

"I have to go. Thanks for dinner." She dug in her purse for the keys to her minivan as she walked. When she pulled them out, a tiny baby doll she used to occupy Melly while waiting in doctor's offices or supermarket checkouts, popped out and fell to the floor. Without missing a step, she reached down and snatched it up.

"What was that?"

"Nothing!"

"Come on, Sweetheart, be reasonable. You can't keep leaving every time the conversation gets uncomfortable for you."

She yanked open the heavy oak door and fled.

Wanna bet?

CHAPTER 3

Again, Evan was left standing alone after Amber ran out on him.

When they'd first split, he thought she would be back in a matter of days. Amber had been hounding him to start a family for a long while before that. He didn't understand. He'd laid it all out for her before they married, vehemently declaring that he never wanted to father any children. Amber swore she didn't mind, so long as they were together. Then years into their marriage, she'd made a complete turnaround.

There was a terrible argument, and they'd both said some terrible things. The worst had been when each of them claimed they weren't in love with the other any longer. With the constant fighting, he really did feel that way, at the time. Amber probably had, too. Seemed as though she still did. At any rate, Evan had stormed out of the house that afternoon to cool off. When he returned home later that night, Amber was gone. She might as well have ripped his heart from his chest, dragged it through mud, and nailed it to a tree.

At first, he'd told himself she didn't mean anything she'd said, and would be back soon. But she hadn't come home, and weeks turned into months. Without Amber, his sanity so abandoned him that he entertained the thought of giving in and starting a family with her. He came to his senses when he remembered how badly he had been treated growing up. Not only by his peers, but by his father, as well. Regardless of whether he fathered a dwarf or an average-sized child, he would not—*could not*—bring a child into the world who would be subjected to ridicule the way he was. Neither did he want a child who might be ashamed of him.

Meanwhile, Amber had left town, and asked her parents not to tell him where she was. She returned five months ago.

Now, just as the first time she left, the deafening quiet of the house wrapped itself around him. As Evan wandered into the living room, he noticed a strand of long blond hair draped across his sleeve. Amber's. He hadn't seen one of those hanging around in a long time. He plucked the silky wisp from his arm and wound it around his fingers, then sniffed, hoping to take in the scent of her shampoo. The dratted thing was too skimpy. He released the fine tendril, watching it float, fairy-like, all the way down to the carpet.

Yep, this house was too quiet. These rooms should be echoing with laughter. Amber's and his.

But the laughter of children? Not likely.

CHAPTER 4

"Mommy!" Melody ran toward Amber when she arrived at her parents' house to pick her up. Her dark little ponytail, sticking up from the top of her head, whipped every which way. She wrapped her arms around Amber's mid-section, and the impact rocked her back slightly. While her daughter was fast catching up to her in height, Amber knew Melly would someday be much taller.

Being Mommy to this child for the past eighteen months had been a total joy for Amber. Without Melly, she didn't know how she would have survived the loneliness following her split from Evan. Having grown weary of the arguments and discord, she left with the intention of moving on. Then she discovered she was pregnant with Melly, and her life had been put on hold. Not that she regretted having Melly. Never. She only wished her husband could share in her happiness, but, as it was, he had no idea their daughter even existed.

"Hello, sweetie. How's my girl?" Amber asked, tucking loose strands of hair behind Melly's ear.

"Be good guwl."

"She certainly was." Ma said. "But then, she always is."

Amber threw her mother a wry look. In her early sixties, Darla Sharpe was still an attractive woman. But what Amber admired most about her mother was how she had always treated Amber as if she were no different than anyone else in the world. Ma never made her feel as though she resented having a dwarf for a daughter. Ever. Because of it, Amber loved her all the more. "Of course she's always good," she said. "Because you give her everything she wants."

"Now, Amber, I don't spoil her." Ma's perfectly-shaped eyebrows arched and reproved.

"Neither one of us does," Dad piped up from his recliner across the room. His reading glasses sat low on his nose, and his sharp eyes peered over the top of the lenses "'Sides, what she wants, and what we give her are never anything harmful." He opened his arms to Melody. Grinning broadly, she ran over to him and he lifted her onto his ample lap. Amber's heart did a two-step at the sight of her baby girl enjoying the same favorite spot she had growing up.

"So, how was your first day, dear?" Her mother's voice held a hint of disapproval.

"Great, actually." Aside from the incident outside the building. Ma didn't have to know everything.

Amber walked farther into the cozy family room and removed her coat. The aroma of strong coffee brewing wafted from the kitchen, as it so often did.

"Really? I'm surprised." Those raised eyebrows, again.

Amber flung her coat onto a corner of the overstuffed couch and climbed up. "The doctor is charming, thoughtful, and kind, as far as I can see." She remembered how he had helped her down from her chair on the day of her interview, mindful of her height difference. She shook her head and continued. "But even so, just being in a place like that . . . Going there every day will be difficult to get used to."

Ma sat down next to her. "It will be tough, but you'll do it."

"Just be careful," Dad said from across the room.

"Don't worry, Dad. I doubt there will be any trouble." She averted her eyes. Guilt crept in for not telling them about this morning's incident. Dad's reaction in no way surprised her, though. He'd always been protective. She knew in the back of both their minds was the nagging reminder that this was the doctor who had performed Ashley's abortion.

"I hope not. But I think this guy could be dangerous," Dad said.

She shrugged. "I doubt it. He's just a doctor who seems to be doing what he believes is a good thing."

"A good thing! There's your first clue." Dad spread his hands, palms up. "And was your sister's death a good thing? I repeat, be careful."

"I will. But just realize that what happened to Ashley was unintentional, not premeditated murder." As soon as the words slipped out, she wanted to snatch them back.

"That hardly makes us feel any better about the whole thing, Amber. But your father's right to caution you. It always made me nervous when you went undercover. I thought that was all over with when you left Evan and especially since you had Melly."

"Please don't worry. I'll be fine." Her voice sounded less confident than she'd hoped. She knew Dr. Hines did some pretty horrific things, but if she buried that thought for the time being, she might be able to focus on his good points. However few there may be.

Ma reached over and tucked a lock of hair behind Amber's ear. "I'll get you some coffee."

"Thanks." She knew Ma still worried. "And Ma?"

Her mother stopped and looked at her with raised eyebrows.

"I'm sorry for what I said . . . about Ashley."

Ma nodded then continued on to the kitchen.

Amber watched as Dad held a book in front of Melly while she flipped the pages and chattered. Her little girl enjoyed spending time with Grandma and Grandpa. Thank God for small blessings, because she'd be doing that a lot in the coming weeks.

How she wished she were in Melly's place now: safe and secure in her father's arms, instead of embarking on this precarious mission.

CHAPTER 5

Thank God for yesterday's demonstration. To ensure his employees' safety, the doctor had given them all a key to the clinic. Now, heart pounding, Amber used hers to let herself in early.

She put away her coat and purse then stood in the middle of her office and took a deep breath to collect herself. She had about an hour to snoop before the others arrived.

Now to search the files. Hopefully, they contained something that could be used as evidence to confirm the fetal harvesting. Maybe they would even lead to whatever else Maggie suspected might be going on.

She grabbed the box of donuts she had brought off her desk, and headed directly for the break/file room. Metal file cabinets lined the walls. A copy machine and a small table, bearing the coffee maker and all the fixings, implied this room had multiple uses. The faint aroma of yesterday's brew produced in her a craving. She struggled to suppress it.

Amber placed the donuts on the round table in the center of the room, and pulled a chair over to a filing cabinet. She climbed up to stand on the seat. Maggie said Dr. Hines kept the faxed orders locked in his desk, so Amber decided to start here, instead. She opened the top drawer and riffled through folders and papers. These appeared to be patient files, containing notes from appointments, records of payment for services, and descriptions of procedures: saline, cranial decompression . . . She winced at the cold, clinical terms.

An abrupt squeak-squeak followed by a thud startled her. The front door! Footsteps thumped in the hall, growing louder with each step. Amber's heart beat in sync. She pushed the drawer closed as quietly as possible and jumped off the chair, hoping the sound of her feet hitting the floor couldn't be heard outside the room.

In a panic, she slid the chair back into position, then darted to the coffeemaker and grabbed the filters.

"Oh!" Rita, Dr. Hines's other nurse stood in the doorway,

hand at her throat. "You scared me."

"Good morning." Amber smiled, then drew in a calming breath through her teeth. She peeled off a paper filter for effect, wondering why Rita had arrived so early.

The nurse's stern gaze threatened to wither Amber's confidence. "What are you doing here?"

Amber scooped coffee grounds into the dispenser and slipped it into its slot above the carafe. "I brought donuts." She gestured toward the table with her chin. "Thought I'd have the coffee ready, too."

Rita had not moved, and the icy claws of her hostility groped at Amber. She remembered how Rita reacted when Dr. Hines introduced them. She and Rita had shaken hands, but when Dr. Hines mentioned Amber would be the clinic's new abortion counselor, Rita dropped her hand like a hot cookie sheet.

"I meant what are you doing in this room?"

Amber walked over and picked up the donuts and held them out to Rita. "Would you like one?"

The nurse merely glanced at them then pinned Amber with a glare that would cut an elephant down to size. The woman's cold gray eyes matched various strands sprinkled throughout her otherwise black hair.

Rita's gaze traveled down then up the length of Amber as an obvious insult. "What makes you think you can come right in here and take over like you own the place?"

With that, Nurse Franks turned on her heel and strode out of the room, leaving Amber to stare after her, mouth agape.

* * *

Amber knocked on Dr. Hines's office door and poked her head in. "Got a minute?"

"I actually have a procedure in a few minutes." He remained at his desk, and glanced at his watch. "But for you, Miss Amber, I'll make the time."

"Thanks." She slipped through the partially open door.

"Have a seat." He motioned toward a blue fabric-covered chair positioned in front of his oak desk, and waited until she climbed up. "Now, what's on your mind?"

"I've been thinking about our discussion yesterday, and what I could do between patients." To help keep her gaze from wandering in the direction of the fax machine, she looked down and fiddled with her tennis bracelet. Evan had given it to her several years ago for her birthday. Since then, she'd worn it often.

"Go on." He prodded gently.

"I wouldn't mind helping Carol with filing or other clerical duties." Amber pushed her hands beneath her knees, as she waited for Dr. Hines's answer.

He pursed his lips, and checked his watch again. "I don't think so."

Her hope deflated like a slashed inner tube.

Dr. Hines cleared his throat and stood. "I've been thinking about that myself," he said, coming around the desk. "I'd like you to help Doug."

Help Doug? But Maggie told me he dissects the fetuses! Amber never formally met the man but only saw him occasionally. He seemed, to her, somewhat enigmatic.

A golf ball formed in her throat. "How do you want me to help him?"

He crossed his arms over his chest. "I would like you to help him with packing up the parts and tissue for shipping to the gift companies. Doing that would free up some time for him to focus on more of the dissecting."

Her face went numb and cold. Dr. Hines leaned down and studied it. "Are you all right, Amber? You're as white as my coat."

Looking into his dark green eyes, she swallowed hard. "I'm perfectly fine, Doc." Appearing weak while undercover could turn deadly.

"Good." He strode toward the door. "I've got to go, but when you have some free time, go to Doug and he'll show you what to do. I've already spoken to him." Dr. Hines rushed from the office, leaving Amber alone.

She released a pent up breath. This had not turned out as planned. If she helped Doug in her spare time, how would she ever—

A loud ringing sound intruded into her thoughts. She looked toward the phone, but that wasn't what caused the noise. The trilling finally stopped, followed by a repetitive mechanical noise, like a robot running in slow motion. A sheet of paper inched its way out of the fax machine. Amber glanced at the open door and carefully climbed down from the chair. She tiptoed around the desk and peeked at each line of the transmission as it printed out:

> Tissue Needed: whole eyes (6—10 per day)
> Preservation: Any media, sterile container
> Gestation: 15—24 weeks

Ship fresh on wet ice by same day courier

The golf ball in Amber's throat grew into a tennis ball. If she helped Doug, would she see these specimens? Would she have to touch or handle them in any way?

Loud throat-clearing nearly sent her rocketing to the ceiling.

"And what are you doing, missy?" Rita Franks loomed just inside the office door, hands on hips.

What could she say to explain herself? She decided the truth was always best.

"Dr. Hines just left, and when I heard the fax coming through, I got curious." She offered a sheepish grin.

Rita impaled her with a forbidding gaze. "You shouldn't be snooping in Dr. Hines's office."

"You're right. I'm sorry." She edged around Rita and left the room, wondering if the woman's untimely appearance was intentional.

"Dr. Hines isn't going to like this one bit," the nurse's voice trailed after her.

CHAPTER 6

Amber and Maggie shared a booth in the fifties-style diner. The zesty odor of fried onions overpowered the other indistinguishable aromas of various cooked foods.

"I'm glad we could both get away from the center for a while, Maggie. I needed this." An unexpected friendship had grown between them since the day the nurse first appeared in Evan's office with her tip about Dr. Hines.

Maggie placed a comforting hand on Amber's arm. "You look distraught. What happened?"

"Dr. Hines gave me a new responsibility, and Rita is really bugging me." She pulled a chrome napkin holder across the Formica tabletop and peered at her distorted image reflected there. Maggie was right, she didn't look good.

"When I saw you go into his office, I wondered what that was about. As for Rita"— Maggie shrugged—"she bugs everybody. What's she doing that gets on your nerves?"

Amber brooded. "I don't know. It's as if she's been watching my every step. She found me in the file room this morning, and reprimanded me for even being there. Later, she caught me peeking at a fax coming through in Dr. Hines's office."

Maggie ran her fingers through her short, brown hair. "Yikes, that's not good. What did you tell her?"

"That I was curious."

"I guess that's as close to the truth as you can get." Maggie pulled a napkin from the holder and polished her utensils with it.

"I just hope she doesn't go to Dr. Hines."

"I can't guarantee she won't."

"Thanks, Maggie, that's comforting." Amber smiled at the waitress, who placed a large salad before her and left.

"Sorry, hon, but it's the truth."

"I just don't understand why she hates me so much."

"Oh, that's easy," Maggie held three French fries dripping with ketchup poised at her mouth. "She thought she had that counseling job in the bag."

Amber clanked her fork down. "I've stolen her job?"

"Not exactly," Maggie said. "There were no guarantees, but Rita thought Dr. Hines would offer her the job when he created the position."

Amber put a hand to the side of her face. "Oh, I feel awful."

Maggie wore a serious expression. "Well, here's something that will make you feel worse—she's also jealous of you because she's in love with Dr. Hines."

Amber jerked back. "Jealous? Of me?"

"Yes, of you. For some reason, Dr. Hines treats you special. We can all see that."

Amber drew up her shoulders in disbelief. "He probably has some strange fascination with me because I'm a little person."

"I don't know." Maggie licked some ketchup off her index finger.

"He's really nice, but I'm sure he's that way with everyone."

Maggie patted her hand. "It's no big deal. Once this is all over, you'll never see Rita again." She took a hearty bite of her burger.

Amber couldn't let it go. "So, she thinks he's interested in me romantically?"

Maggie nodded as she chewed and swallowed.

"Do you or Doug feel this way?"

"Doug made one little comment the other day, but he's a man of few words. I take the fact he said anything at all to mean he's noticed something." Maggie wiped her hands on a napkin. "As for me, yeah, I think there's something there."

"What makes you think that?" Amber glanced down at her salad. Her appetite gone, she pushed the plate back.

"Little things, like his nickname for you. *Miss Amber.* The way he stares at you when you're not looking. And not because you're a little person. He looks at you like any guy looks at a woman he's interested in."

"No way." Terrific. Now she'd feel awkward around him.

"I wouldn't worry about it." Maggie's expression was sympathetic. "It will probably work in your favor." She straightened in her seat. "Now tell me about this new responsibility."

* * *

Amber stopped in front of Doug's door. She squared her shoulders, took a deep breath and rapped three times. Then she turned the knob.

As soon as the door opened half way, the stench hit her

like a knockout punch. Chemicals mingled with . . . the thick, acrid smell of fresh blood. Amber gagged. The faint of heart would not survive here. She clenched her teeth and strode into the room.

"Can I do something for you?" Doug stood in front of a table and looked down at her. His scrubs and latex gloves were spattered with deep red stains. A shiver ran down Amber's neck, as she remembered the fax and what Doug would need to do to get those eyes.

He held some sort of cutting instrument that she didn't recognize. Blood ran down the length of the blade, and she felt her own draining from her head.

"Dr. Hines said I'm to help you." She forced herself to look straight into Doug's eyes, not wanting to see what might be lying on the table before him.

"Oh, yeah. He told me." Doug put down the instrument, peeled off the gloves and deposited them into a large, red, plastic container marked "biohazard." "You'll be working over here."

Doug walked toward the other end of the large room. Amber followed, keeping her gaze cemented to the backs of his shoes.

He led her to an area where cabinets and countertops lined the wall. Several glass tubes of various sizes sat on the laminated surface, the contents unrecognizable, jumbled masses. But knowing those containers actually held body parts, or fetal tissue, caused Amber's limbs to weaken. She steadied herself against the lower cabinet doors.

"You'll pack the specimens in these." He opened a bottom cabinet and pulled out a flattened cardboard box. Doug took the sheet of paper resting on the countertop and handed it to Amber. "This will tell you where and how to ship them."

As she read, recognition socked her in the chest. In her hands was one of the faxes requesting body parts!

This was better than helping Carol with filing. Working with Doug would provide the vital information and proof of Dr. Hines's questionable practices.

If she could manage to keep her stomach from protesting.

The document she now held revealed the location to one of the companies the clinic supplied. She had to find an opportunity to photocopy these orders.

* * *

Everyone else had gone for the day. Amber made her way

to Doug's workroom. Earlier, he'd told her to leave all of the faxes together on the counter, and that he would make sure to get them back to Dr. Hines. They still sat there in a small pile. She grabbed them and dashed to the copy room.

The machine had been turned off for the night. She pressed the power button and waited for it to warm up again. Her foot tapped out a rhythm on the linoleum floor, as she fought to keep from screaming, "Come on!"

The stack of papers she held now was thicker than when she'd set them aside earlier. Of course, Doug would have taken care of some packaging before and after those that she'd worked on. But at least she had a good amount to take to Evan.

Finally, the "ready" light illuminated. Amber placed the first page on the glass, closed the lid, and pressed the green button. She did this several more times. With only two faxes left to copy, she stopped holding her breath.

Amber lifted the lid to make another duplicate.

"Just what do you think you're doing?"

That familiar voice never failed to fray Amber's nerves. Especially when she hadn't heard Rita Franks enter the room.

Amber deliberately ignored the nurse and finished making her copies. What was she doing here, anyway? She had definitely seen Rita leave at closing time.

"Well?" Nurse Franks demanded.

Amber gathered her papers into a stack, executing each move with careful precision. She walked toward Rita, using slow, exaggerated steps. The best defense, in her opinion, was to turn the tables. She stopped in front of the woman, standing very close. This was one of those times she wished she were an average-sized person. Intimidation was minimal when you had to look up at your adversary. But she'd give it her all, anyway. "Why are you always sneaking up on me, Rita?"

"Looks to me like you're the one doing the sneaking."

Amber pinned Rita with the coldest, hardest stare she could muster, while searching her brain for what to say next.

"I asked you what you were doing." The words dripped with venom.

Amber waited a beat. Then in a quiet but firm voice, she said, "My job." She pushed by Rita and strode directly to Doug's room. She deposited the original documents on the countertop then went to her own office. Hyperventilation threatened with each quick, shallow breath. After snatching up her purse, she stuffed the copies inside, grabbed her jacket, and headed for the door.

Too late. Footsteps pounded behind her in the hall.

"Get back here, Missy!"

She kept moving, left the building, and darted straight to the Odyssey. Once inside, she dialed Evan's cell phone while zipping out of the parking lot. A glance in the rearview mirror showed Rita's silhouette just outside the clinic door, hands on hips.

That woman's untimely appearances unnerved Amber. So did her attitude. But Amber felt sorry for Rita. The disappointment of loving someone you couldn't have made a person crazy. She should know.

In any other situation, Amber would have used such common ground to form a friendship. Not this time. Revealing personal details would render her vulnerable, and she couldn't afford that. Rita couldn't be trusted, especially since she viewed Amber as a threat. She already had a few things to hold over Amber's head.

Well, she'd make sure Rita never got the chance to use them against her.

CHAPTER 7

"So what have you got for me?" Evan asked, as Amber entered his office.

"Oh, just these," she sang. With a kittenish grin, she reached into her handbag, then handed him the folded stack of papers.

Evan studied each one. Amber shifted her weight from leg to leg, fiddled with her coat buttons and tapped her foot on the thick carpet. Another minute and she'd be yanking out her hair.

"Well?" she demanded.

Evan glanced up at her. "Oh, sorry. This is excellent! Disgusting, but excellent. How did you get them?"

Amber huffed a breath on her fingernails and buffed them against her shoulder. "I'm good, aren't I? But I'll never tell."

"Come on, you little minx, stop teasing and tell me."

Somberness replaced her giddiness, as she thought of what she had done a good part of the day to actually procure those documents. She climbed onto one of the visitor chairs across from Evan, and stared at her clasped hands. "I—I had to help the technician pack body parts for shipping."

"You what?" Evan sprang forward in his chair. "How did you manage that?"

Amber looked up at him. "I didn't do a thing. It was Dr. Hines's idea."

Evan got off his chair and came around to stand beside her. "Sweetheart," he whispered, "how did you . . . Were you okay with that?"

He caressed a lock of her hair, and a delicious shiver ran through her. "I tried not to look at those tubes filled with fetal tissue." She shifted in her seat. "Pretty hard when you're packing them, so I pretended they were flowers. That's what they are, you know." She stared down at the floor. "Beautiful little flowers that never got their chance to bloom."

After a slight pause to regroup, she took a deep breath and continued. "All of the orders go to Doug to fill, then the whole stack goes back to Dr. Hines. If he does anything else with them besides keeping them locked in his desk, I couldn't tell."

"Well, you got them. That's the main thing." He moved away from her, taking his warmth with him.

"Yes, so now what will we do with them?"

"That's easy. It's my turn to do a little undercover work."

"Undercover where? How?"

"At the gift companies who send these orders." He returned to his seat behind the desk and squinted at one of the faxes. "This one's called Life Gifts. I'll start there."

"What will you do there?"

"I'm not sure, yet. All I know is that I want to meet the people who run these places, and find out how their minds work."

A sudden sadness enveloped her. That meant he'd have to go away, because most of those companies were in other parts of the country. That shouldn't bother her at all. But it did and she struggled not to show it.

"I'm going to book a flight to Wisconsin tomorrow. I'll call you from there and let you know how it's going."

"How long will you be gone?" She tried to sound casual.

Evan's eyelids lowered to half-mast, and his lips spread into a sly smile. "Why? Will you miss me?"

Heat crept into her cheeks. He knew her too well. "No, I just wondered in case I came across something important."

His expression still hadn't changed. "I'll just be a phone call away."

"Right." *Jerk!* You'd think after two years without Evan she'd be able to control her emotions.

"How about a kiss goodbye?"

Her whole body snapped to attention. "No! Are you out of your mind?"

"Yeah. When it comes to you, I'm completely crazy."

He got up and came around the desk. His eyes locked with hers, and he moved toward her with purpose. Not sure what to do, Amber hopped off the chair and backed away. His kiss would have been wonderful, she knew, but caving in now would prevent her from moving on.

"Stop, Evan."

"Why? You don't really want me to."

"Yes, I do."

Only inches away, he reached out and grasped both her upper arms. "I don't believe you," he whispered, and leaned in.

"Evan, I'm filing for divorce," she blurted.

He went still, his gaze penetrating.

Shrugging out of his grip, she said, "I decided a couple weeks ago. The day Maggie came to the office about the story."

His eyes filled with pain. "And you're just telling me now? When did you see a lawyer?"

She lifted her chin, and straightened her sleeves. "I haven't seen one, yet."

Evan's face relaxed and he went back to his chair. "Good. You really need to think about this, Amber. You're making a big mistake if you go through with it."

"I *have* thought about it. I'm sorry, Evan. I've got to do what's best for me and—" She'd almost mentioned Melody.

"For you and who?" He looked worried.

"You."

"Me? How could you know what's best for me?"

Amber stepped closer to the desk. "Don't you want to get on with your life?"

"Yes. With you in it."

"Have you forgotten we don't want the same things anymore?"

"Have *you* forgotten that you were the one who changed?"

"People do. They mature. But you haven't."

"Sorry to disappoint you, but I call it 'keeping your word.'"

She sighed and shook her head. "As usual, this is going nowhere. I'm tired and I'm going home."

The last thing she heard as she walked out the door was Evan's defeated plea. "Please, Amber. Think before you act."

Her breath caught in her throat, as she raced through the newsroom. Once outside, she leaned against the building pulling in long gulps of air. The look on Evan's face ripped her heart to pieces. She hadn't meant to tell him about the divorce just yet. The temptation of his kiss was almost too excruciating to resist. She was glad she hadn't given in. Evan would think she'd gotten over their disagreements. He would think it meant they could go back to the way they were.

Now that she told him her decision to see a lawyer, she would have to actually go through with it.

* * *

Amber stepped through the front door of her parents' home. "Ma? Dad?" A warmth settled over her at the familiar sight of the earth tone décor in the neatly-kept living room. "Where is everybody?"

"We're in here," Ma called from the family room.

Amber strode toward the large room at the back of the

house. Dad sat in his overstuffed recliner and Ma on the Early American sofa holding Melly, who appeared drowsy.

Ma smiled. "Hi, hon."

Amber walked over and lifted Melly from her mother's lap.

"Mommy!" She curled her arms around Amber's neck.

"Hello, my sweet girl." Amber kissed Melly's soft, chubby cheek, then hugged her. "I missed you soooo much!"

"She's in her jammies and ready for bed." Ma reached over and gave Melly an affectionate pat on the rear.

"Thanks for taking care of her. I know I'm late, but I had to drop something off to Evan."

Her parents shared a hopeful glance. They weren't fooling her. They'd do anything to help her and Evan get back together. Ma and Dad loved him like the flesh and blood son they never had.

"That's okay, honey," Dad said. "We love having Melly. In fact, anytime you're going to be awfully late, just give us a call. She can even stay the night."

"That's right." Ma raised her eyebrows meaningfully. "We have everything she needs here. Extra clothes and pajamas."

"Okay, you two, I know what you're trying to do. But I couldn't impose like that, anyway. You do so much already."

"It's no imposition." Ma playfully pinched the tip of Melly's nose, making her laugh.

"Hopefully there will be no need." Amber grabbed Melly's fluffy pink jacket from the loveseat.

"You just remember our offer if there *is* a need."

"I will, Dad." There surely would not be the type of need her parents referred to, no matter how much they hoped.

Amber sat a yawning Melly on the couch; then she slipped the jacket around her. She lifted Melly into her arms and took the tote bag her mother held out.

"Say goodnight to Grandma and Grandpa, Melly," Amber spoke in a soft tone.

"Night, Gamma, Gampa."

Dad stood and kissed Melly's head. "Goodnight, Peaches."

"Goodnight, darling girl," Ma said, and kissed her granddaughter's cheek.

"Thanks, again, both of you." Amber kissed her parents. Since childhood, she never went anywhere without kissing them goodbye. Now that little tradition would be passed down to Melly.

A lump formed in Amber's throat along with the realization that Melly might never have the privilege of kissing her own daddy.

* * *

Melly had fallen asleep on the way home, and Amber struggled to unlock her apartment door while holding both her child and the tote bag.

"Soon you'll be too big for Mommy to carry," she whispered to her slumbering daughter. Once inside, she dropped everything by the door, and took Melly straight to bed.

Melly woke slightly while Amber removed her coat, but drifted off again within seconds. Amber sat on the edge of the low, bunny-shaped bed, staring at her daughter's profile in the shadows cast by the colorful, carousel night lamp. Her heart inflated like an inner tube. Sometimes, she just couldn't believe the blessing the Lord had poured out on her through Melly. Her thoughts turned to Ashley, as she remembered that her sister had given up such a blessing, and much more.

Amber reached out and stroked Melly's hair. "Aunt Ashley would have loved you, sweetie," she whispered.

"Ash-ee?" Melly said in a tiny voice, her eyes still closed

Amber laughed softly. She hadn't realized Melly could hear her.

"Good night, Sweet Pea," She leaned over to kiss her. But Melly's deep breathing indicated she was already sound asleep.

CHAPTER 8

On Evan's first night out of town, Maggie asked Amber to meet her for dinner. Even though it meant she'd have to give up precious time with Melly, she accepted. She liked the nurse and wanted to know more about her. Besides, Evan would probably imagine her waiting around and dashing for the phone with every ring in anticipation of his call. He would be right, had she not removed the temptation by going out with Maggie.

They agreed on a popular Italian restaurant and shortly after their arrival, a hostess showed them to a small table. The roomy chairs matched the high gloss of the table and glided smoothly on casters. Climbing onto the seat proved difficult for Amber. Maggie reached over and clamped her hand on the armrest to keep it from rolling back while Amber settled into it, then wriggled to the edge, leaving her legs to dangle.

"Thanks, Maggie."

"Sure thing." Maggie glanced around the crowded room, as some of the patrons stared at Amber. "Nothing like having an audience just to get into a chair," she said, loud enough for those close by to hear.

Wow, her new friend had stood up for her! How humbling. "Don't sweat it, Maggie. I'm used to it. This is nothing compared to some of the stares and insults I've endured in my lifetime."

The waitress appeared and took their orders, then left.

Maggie placed a hand on Amber's arm. "It must be hard for you with achondroplasia." Her eyes glistened as though she fought back tears.

Amber crossed her arms and leaned them on the table. She wasn't surprised Maggie knew the term for the most common form of dwarfism. "It's tough, sometimes, yes. But you get used to it."

Maggie tilted her head as she looked at Amber. "What's it like?" She blinked her eyes, and looked away. "I'm sorry. I'm not trying to pry or patronize you."

"No, really." Amber patted her hand. "I don't mind, at all. I'd rather have honesty and questions, than people staring at me as though I'm a freak, or judging me by the way I look."

A shy smile adorned Maggie's face.

"So you want to know what it's like. I guess I could give you a vague description." She squinched up her face and tapped a forefinger on her chin. "Hmm. Where do I begin?"

The waitress came back with a huge bowl of salad and a basket of warm garlic bread. She distributed small plates and beverages.

"Thank you." Amber smiled at the girl, who couldn't be more than eighteen. The waitress smiled back then turned to leave.

"You were saying?" Maggie inclined her head.

Amber sent up a quick, silent blessing over their meal before answering. "Since everything in this world is made to accommodate the average-sized person, we have a lot of adjusting to do. There's constant use of step stools. Also lots of peering over high counters and desks, a lot of climbing for items way above our head, like in cabinets and in grocery stores. Although, I must confess, I sometimes ask customer service to provide me with help when I shop."

Maggie shook her head. "I just can't imagine." She scooped up a bunch of lettuce with the salad tongs and tilted her chin toward Amber's plate, indicating she should hold it up.

Amber lifted her dish. "It's something you just learn to cope with. Like a paraplegic, for instance. They have to adjust to life in a wheelchair. It's no different."

"I suppose." Maggie speared some lettuce with her fork. "But I'm sure there's some prejudice. You mentioned the things you've had to endure. What were they?"

Amber thought for a moment. "I once had a college professor tell me I'd never make it as a journalist. He said that 'my kind of people' were only good for carnivals and side shows."

Maggie's face registered shock. "What a cruel man! If that were me, I would have tried to get him fired."

Amber shook her head. "I couldn't do a thing like that. He said it out of ignorance, plus he had a family to support."

"Amber, you are too kind."

"Not really. But everyone deserves forgiveness. It's what I would want for myself, because I'm not perfect. I blunder lots of times.

"What about family? Are your parents little people? Do you have any brothers or sisters?"

"No, my parents are average. I had a twin sister. She was

average, too." Amber picked up the basket of bread and held it out to Maggie, who chose a piece.

"Was?"

Amber mentally kicked herself for blurting that out. She looked down at her plate. "Ashley died when we were in our twenties."

Maggie sucked in a breath. "I'm so sorry, Amber. I shouldn't have pried."

"No, really, it's okay. That was a long time ago." But it still hurt sometimes.

Maggie's eyes looked moist and sympathetic. "Do you mind if I ask how she died?"

Amber swung her legs to and fro under the table. She wasn't ready to talk about it to Maggie.

"I'll tell you about it sometime, but not right now. I hope you understand."

Maggie smiled. "Of course I do."

After the meal and before ordering dessert, Amber excused herself to use the ladies room. She passed through the lobby of the restaurant, weaving her way through the waiting crowd.

Upon exiting the lavatory, Amber heard a familiar voice.

"Well, well, Miss Amber. Fancy meeting you here." Dr. Hines's words rang out. Several people turned to look her way as she approached him.

"Hello, Doc. Hope you're not too hungry. Looks like you have a long wait."

"Actually, we're close to the top of the list." He indicated the crowd with his hand. "Most of these people arrived after we did."

Beside Dr. Hines stood an attractive woman whose height almost matched his. So did some of her features.

"I'd like to introduce you to my sister, Jasmine. Sis, this is Amber Blake. She's our new counselor. Just started working at the center this week."

Jasmine bent to shake Amber's hand. "I'm very pleased to meet you. I know Al has wanted to add a counselor to his staff for some time."

"It's good to meet you, too. I'm very fortunate to be working for your brother."

Jasmine simply smiled in reply. A smile that didn't reach her eyes.

"Are you here alone, or did you come with someone?" For some unknown reason, Dr. Hines's expression seemed hopeful.

"I'm here with Maggie."

"Why don't you two ladies join us?"

"Thank you, but we've finished our meal, and will be leaving after dessert. We wouldn't want to impose, anyway."

Dr. Hines reached down and patted Amber's shoulder. "You wouldn't be imposing, but since you're way ahead of us, we'll catch up another time."

His icy-hot touch penetrated her clothing and reached clear through to her bones. Although Dr. Hines never exhibited anything but respect and kindness toward Amber, his attention still made the hair at the back of her neck stand on end.

Sometimes, though, he almost made her forget Ashley died because of his carelessness.

"Sure, Doc. See ya." She returned to her table.

"Guess who's waiting in the lobby?" Amber climbed onto her chair while Maggie automatically steadied it.

Maggie returned to studying the dessert menu. "Who?"

"Dr. Hines, with his sister, Jasmine."

"Oh, yes. Jasmine. I've met her. A stunning woman."

Just then, a hostess walked by their table, trailed by the subject siblings. Dr. Hines waggled his eyebrows and waved, while Jasmine looked straight ahead. Amber threw him a half-hearted smile, and Maggie gave a brief wave.

"I've never seen him act quite so silly, before," Maggie observed. "I think you bring that out in him."

Amber clasped her hands to her chest. "Ah, the desire of my heart: to make a man act silly."

"Very funny," Maggie said, looking heavenward.

Evan used to act silly just to make me laugh.

A memory caught Amber off guard. She and Evan were young. They went rollerblading together for the first time. Evan soared ahead like he'd been doing it all his life. But Amber couldn't quite get it right and kept falling on the ground. He came back and skated beside her. The next time she fell, he made himself fall too, flailing his legs and arms wildly and letting out a goofy yell. He looked so ridiculous, she laughed out loud. After such a display, how could she remain dejected about her inability to skate?

The waitress came and took their dessert orders. After she left, Maggie frowned at Amber.

"What?" Amber demanded.

Maggie shook her head. "It's obvious Dr. Hines has certain feelings for you that go beyond the employer-employee relationship."

Amber shook her head. "Maybe, but it's just too weird. Besides, I don't want that. It would complicate everything."

"It might, but it could also turn out to be useful."

The waitress returned and placed a plate of tiramisu and a cup of coffee before each of them. Amber took her fork and sliced through the smooth custard and spongy cake. In her mouth it felt like silk, and the espresso flavor enhanced its richness. She and Evan had always ordered this same confection whenever they came here.

She shook herself. If she continued to reminisce about the past her night with Maggie would be ruined.

"Heavenly." Maggie's eyes were dreamy.

"I have to agree with you there." Amber stuffed another forkful into her mouth.

Maggie's expression became serious. "Getting back to our conversation, I'm just pointing out the possibility of Dr. Hines's interest in you so you can use it, if you need to."

The thought of having any other relationship with Dr. Hines besides a professional one made her blood turn to ice. On the other hand, it could certainly be beneficial. "I guess you're right, but it's not likely to happen."

Maggie let out a sigh of frustration. "And why not?"

Amber shrugged, and wrinkled her face. "I don't know. I mean, it's just not very common for an average-sized person to pursue a little person."

"It happens, though."

"Yes, it happens."

"Haven't you ever dated anyone tall?"

She swung her legs again. "No. I never dated anyone other than Evan. He was my first boyfriend and my last."

Maggie nodded, looking thoughtful. "I see." She dragged out the last word, giving her statement an air of intrigue.

"It's hard to believe someone like Dr. Hines would be attracted to me."

Maggie's eyes bored into hers. "I'm telling you it's possible. Just keep it in mind."

Amber observed Maggie's body language. Her serious expression and tone implied more than what she actually said. She glanced around to Dr. Hines's table. He raised his glass to her in a mock toast.

A sense of foreboding gripped her by the throat.

CHAPTER 9

Evan sank onto the lumpy mattress. Hotels always had low beds, easy to get on and off. Not like his bed at home. With that, he needed a step stool. He and Amber had laughed like a couple of kids the first time they'd used it. Even with the stool, they had to dive onto the bed if they wanted to get any sleep that night.

They were young and carefree then. How he wished they could recapture those days.

He had arrived in Wisconsin late in the afternoon. The sun had already begun to dip behind the tree clusters across from his hotel. Just enough time had remained to contact the director of Life Gifts, and make an appointment for the following day. With nothing much to do before dinner, he reached into his pants pocket for the cell phone and speed-dialed Amber at home. She was probably having her evening meal right about now.

After four rings, her voice mail picked up.

"It's me. I arrived at the hotel about an hour ago. It was late, so I just made an appointment for tomorrow. I'll call again after the meeting." A brief thought flitted through his mind, so he added, "I'm going to call your cell phone, in case it's turned on."

After hanging up, he quickly pressed the number for Amber's wireless. She picked up after three rings.

"Amber? It's me."

"Oh, hi. How was your flight?"

A hum of background conversation and clinking of dishes could be heard, and he guessed she was out somewhere. The picture in his mind of her waiting at home for his call vanished. "Long. Look, I won't keep you, it sounds like you're with friends, or something. Just listen to the message I left on your home phone to find out what's on tap for tomorrow."

"Okay." She grew quiet; then he heard a low murmuring that seemed closer than the rest of the background noise. "Maggie says 'hello'."

"Maggie?"

"Yes. We're having dinner out."

"Are you with anyone else?"

"No, it's just the two of us." He was about to breathe a sigh of relief, when she added, "But we did run into Dr. Hines and his sister, Jasmine. Small world, isn't it?"

"Oh, yeah, small world. Too small." *Hines is just the person I'm worried about.* She mixed with those clinic people as if they were her regular circle of friends. He'd have to talk with her about that when he got back. Working at the center was enough. She didn't need to spend off-hours getting chummy with them. Maggie was a nice lady, but she worked there, too. And that Hines character was a whole different breed. If Amber spent too much time with him, or other workers from there, she could easily slip up and blow her cover. "I'll let you go, then. We don't want to be rude to Maggie."

"She just left for the restroom. I guess I'll hear from you sometime tomorrow, then?"

"Right. Goodnight, Amber."

When she didn't respond immediately, he thought she wanted to say something else. But she didn't.

"Goodnight, Evan."

He flipped the phone closed and rested it on the bedside table. Scrubbing his hands over his face, he wondered just how good of a night he *would* have. After seeing Amber in his office with Maggie that first day, she'd been consistently on his mind.

None of his nights had been good since.

* * *

The next afternoon, Evan entered the posh restaurant. He gave his name to the hostess, a tall, slender woman, chic in a mid-length black dress, stockings, and shoes.

"Follow me, Mr. Blake." She showed him to a small private room boasting a table set with elegant china, crystal and silverware. The woman padded across plush, royal blue carpeting, and laid a menu by an empty place setting. A man sitting at the table offered her a smile. His dark hair offset the fake, orange-hued tan of his skin.

Evan reached into the side pocket of his suit jacket and discreetly pulled out a recorder. The man stood up. His face briefly registered surprise then quickly reverted to a pleasant expression. Leaning down slightly, he extended his hand. "Mr. Blake? Glad to meet you." His shake was firm and short.

"My pleasure, Mr. Wharton."

"Call me Michael."

"All right, Michael, I'm Evan."

Michael motioned to the chair opposite him. "Have a seat."

He waited for Evan to climb up. "Just ask me whatever it is you'd like to know about Life Gifts."

"Would you mind if I record our conversation? It's so much easier than taking notes or remembering the details."

Michael hesitated for a second. "I guess that's okay."

"Thank you." Evan switched the recorder on. He cleared his throat, leaned forward, and clasped his hands in front of him on the table. "Why don't we start with your telling me how Life Gifts operates?"

"Sure. We provide researchers with human tissue—"

"Michael, if you don't mind my interrupting, to what type of researchers are you referring?" As if he didn't already have an idea.

Michael smiled through his teeth. "That's quite all right. If you're thinking of investing in Life Gifts, then you've got to have your questions answered. Interrupt whenever you find it necessary."

"Thank you. Go on."

A waiter entered the room and asked for their lunch orders. After he left, Evan eyed Michael. "Go on, please."

"Yes. We provide tissue, organs, other body parts, to universities, pharmaceutical companies, hospitals—anyone, really, who contacts us with requests. Much of it is harvested from freshly aborted fetuses. Sometimes we pay rental fees for space in abortion clinics, in order to have a technician on site to dissect said fetuses and ship the freshest body parts possible to our clients."

Maggie had already told them most of this. He needed more. "How do these facilities know about your company in order to make such requests?"

Michael offered a smug grin, as he raised the index finger of one hand. He lifted a briefcase from the floor and popped the locks. Reaching in, he took one of many colorful brochures, closed the case and replaced it beside his chair.

"We advertise." He handed the pamphlet to Evan. "These are sent to various institutions across the country. When we get a positive response, we send a technician out to that particular facility to do the harvesting."

Evan stared down at the words, and they bled together, but not before his brain processed the cold, blatant sales handle:

If you require exceptionally fresh fetal tissue,
Life Gifts can accommodate all of your needs.

His nostrils flared, and he almost didn't care if the scumbag across from him noticed. *You'd think they were selling a common can of paint!* A price list following the offensive promo line added to the furnace in the pit of his stomach. They charged $175 for livers, $1,205 for brains, and $750 for whole cadavers!

"Why do whole cadavers cost less than brains?" he asked. "You could get an intact body, as well as the brains for less than the brains alone."

"Ah." Michael nodded, as if he were used to being asked. "No brains included with those."

Evan's stomach turned.

Going further down the list was out of the question. He put the brochure aside and snatched up his glass of water. It did nothing to douse the flames burning up his insides.

Imagine! The unborn were being reduced to commodities. Whatever happened to respect for human life? People fight to save the whales or crocodiles or any number of animals headed toward extinction. They are angered over the cruel procedure used on harp seals in order to obtain their furs. Why in the world do they allow babies to be chopped up and their body parts sold like packaged poultry?

The waiter returned with their food, and Evan was grateful, because it afforded him time to regroup. That advertisement had thoroughly disgusted him. Chicken cordon bleu stared up at him from the plate, but the images he couldn't erase from his mind rendered it unappetizing. He pushed the dish back from the edge of the table.

"Do you mind if we continue while you eat?" Evan asked Michael.

"No problem." The man had already stuffed his mouth with food. Seemed the graphic nature of their discussion hadn't affected his palate.

"What about getting consent to donate the fetus?"

"That's in the hands of each facility's staff. We provide them with forms printed on their own letterhead. We put in lots of medical and legal jargon, it sounds good to the patients, so they sign."

Evan just nodded. He was afraid to open his mouth for fear he'd blast this barbarian.

Michael crammed a roasted potato into his mouth. "Food here is delicious, isn't it?"

"Yes, I guess." Evan continued the questioning. "How do you know you're going to be able to obtain all of the parts your customers need?"

Michael put his fork down, folded his arms on the table and leaned forward. He spoke in a conspiratorial tone. "See, that's where it could get a little tricky."

"Tricky?"

Michael's eyebrows knit together. "Sometimes we have to tell the abortionist what method to use and what term the patient should be. The procedure needs to be changed in order to meet the specifications."

"Changed how?"

"For a late-term abortion, the usual method is a D&E, or Dilatation and Evacuation, which involves dismembering the fetus. But then the organs and body parts wouldn't meet the researchers' requirements. Instead, a partial-birth must be done."

The back of Evan's neck prickled with moisture. "Partial-birth—but isn't that illegal?"

Michael smiled. "That law is never enforced. There's so much back-and-forth about it."

Evan sat back in his chair. He'd had enough. *This meeting is over.* He made a show of checking his watch. "Look at the time, will you?" He glanced up at Michael. "I have to get going, but I think we've pretty much covered everything. I'll meet with my associates to discuss our conversation and then get back to you." Evan jumped off the chair, snatched the brochure and recorder from the table, and headed out of the restaurant.

"You haven't even touched your food," Michael called after him.

Evan wanted to pretend he hadn't heard and keep walking, anxious to leave the company of that Neanderthal. But that would look suspicious. "You can have it," he threw over his shoulder, and raised his hand in a quick wave without looking back.

* * *

Two nights later, Amber clicked off Evan's tape recorder. "It's outrageous. I just can't believe it. I can't believe this *guy!*"

They sat on the couch in Evan's living room. Amber stared down at the brochure Wharton had given Evan. She shuddered at how this unfeeling savage made his living. "I'm speechless, Evan. I don't know how you sat there and listened without wanting to bash his face in."

"It wasn't easy, believe me."

She rested back against the cushions. "Well, you've got some pretty incriminating stuff, here. It will help to validate what we report about Dr. Hines."

46

Evan pinned her with a chastising gaze. "Speaking of Dr. Hines . . ."

Amber knew that look. "What did I do now?"

Twisting his mouth into a grimace, he glanced away and then back. "I don't think it's a good idea to socialize with him, or other staff, when you're not working at the center."

Where was this coming from? "I never socialized with Dr. Hines."

"He was at the restaurant the other night while we were on the phone."

"I was there with Maggie when I ran into the doctor and his sister. It's not like we went together, or agreed to meet there."

"And should you be associating with Maggie? She's employed by the very person we're trying to expose."

Amber jumped to her feet. "Maggie? I like her. We've become friends. She's not like the others."

Evan got to his feet, too. "She's the enemy, just like the rest of them."

"Enemy! How can you say that? She's the one who brought this story to us in the first place."

He stood very close, pushing his face into hers. "She's one of them," he said in a dangerously quiet tone. "And she participates in abortions."

Evan was confusing her. "I try not to think about that part, but she's on our side. Besides," she added, "whatever happened to loving the enemy, praying for, and doing good to them?"

He had to admit to himself that she had him there. He'd reached that level of faith. But to Amber he said, "That has nothing to do with this." Before she could protest, he laid a finger against her lips. "Listen, Amber. I just think you should be careful. You don't want to blow your cover. You never know what could happen."

"You're just being too cautious, Evan. They all seem to like me a lot." Sometimes, she almost believed she really worked at the center. Everyone there accepted her into the fold. Well, except for Rita, but Maggie had enlightened her about that situation.

She had nothing to worry about.

CHAPTER 10

As she robotically packed body parts in boxes, Amber numbed her mind to the reality of the task. She snapped to attention when the door creaked open. Rita entered carrying a bucket.

"Here you go, Doug." She plunked it down at his feet, then spun toward the door. "You know what to do."

Doug looked down into the bucket and swore under his breath. "Rita, c'mon! I'm really getting tired of this." He gave the container a light kick, and it moved a few inches. "Man!"

Amber wondered what he went on about. "What's the matter?"

"Aw, it's the same old thing."

She waited, but when it became apparent he had no intention of elaborating, she prodded. "What is it? What's the same?"

"Come over and take a look."

Amber crossed to the other side of the large, laboratory-like room and peered into the bucket. Nothing could have prepared her for what it contained: a live fetus! A tiny intact baby, jerking and twitching and gasping, as if it were fighting for its life! She sucked in a sharp breath, and for a second, she didn't know what to do or think. Just stood there staring down at the poor little being.

Oh, Lord, oh, Lord, oh, Lord! The mantra reverberated throughout her innermost parts. She raised her eyes to Doug's. "What are you going to do with him?"

He heaved a frustrated breath. "What they want me to do."

"Which would be . . .?"

Without a word, he bent to lift the handle and carried the bucket over to the sink.

If Doug was doing what she thought . . . But then she remembered Maggie telling her and Evan that sometimes the abortion process didn't quite work. That some of the babies were born alive. But she never imagined she'd witness a . . . killing.

Amber rushed over to the sink where Doug had turned on

the faucet. "No!" Unable to reach the faucets, she pushed him away.

"Stop it, Amber. I've got to do this." He grasped both her upper arms and placed her aside.

The water would be getting dangerously high, by now. "Please, Doug, let me have him! I'll take him to the hospital. Maybe they can save him. I'll—"

"No, Amber. It's too late, anyway." He jerked his chin toward the sink. "It's filled up now."

She backed up, one hand over her stomach, the other over her mouth. Salty tears seared her eyes, and spilled over her lashes. The room spun, and she felt faint. "I can't stay here."

Amber burst through the door and into the hall, running so fast, she tripped over her own little legs, and tumbled to the floor. For a second, she just lay there, sprawled facedown on the carpet. *God, please help me! Where do I go?* Slowly, she pulled herself up, then plodded to the lavatory. Once there, she entered a stall and vomited into the toilet. When finished, Amber lowered the lid, flushed and sat down on top.

A nightmare. That's what it was! She would wake up any minute. She waited. When it didn't happen, Amber lowered her head to between her knees, hoping that would quell the dizziness. But nothing could remove the vision of that sweet, innocent child, whimpering, its tiny arms flailing, as if to reach out to her for help.

Why was she torturing herself by being here? She could end this anytime she wanted. Evan wouldn't blame her. In fact, he'd be relieved. But she wasn't a quitter. Someone had to expose this . . . this butcher. Amber had begun to warm up to Dr. Hines and his winning, easy-going ways. It saddened her to admit that that's how she would think of him from now on. A butcher.

The tears itched her cheeks. She ripped off a piece of tissue to wipe them away then reached into her skirt pocket for the cell phone. Evan would want to know what she'd seen today, and she needed to hear his voice, right now. She speed dialed his office number.

"Amber?" She reveled in the sound of his voice, and its welcoming quality.

"Evan, I—I hope I'm not interrupting anything." She didn't realize her speech would sound so shaky.

"You sound terrible. What's up?"

"I just had a little upset, is all. I'm fine, though." Her voice echoed in the empty restroom, and she toned it down a notch, imagining what it must sound like to anyone passing by in the hall. "I'll stop by after work and tell you about it."

"Come by the office. I'm working late tonight."

"Sounds good. See you then." She flipped the phone closed.

Just as she got to her feet, she heard the door swish open, and a woman's voice call out to her.

Rita.

"I'll be right there." she answered.

"I saw you run by in the hall. Is there something wrong?"

As if she needed Rita's questions, right now. She lifted the toilet lid, threw in the tissue and flushed again. "I'm okay."

"Are you sure? Does it have anything to do with that specimen I brought to Doug?" Rita no longer sounded concerned. Suspicion laced her inquiry.

How could she answer without sounding idiotic?

Amber exited the stall. "It's just . . . the first time seeing that . . . well, it took me by surprise."

Rita stood in the doorway, one arm pressed against the door, holding it open. She glared at Amber for a moment, then her eyes softened slightly. "That happens sometimes." She walked away leaving Amber dumbstruck.

* * *

Later that day, Carol, the receptionist, poked her head in Amber's office. "The next patient is ready."

"I'll be right out."

Amber put down her pen, and closed the file from the last patient. She always went out to greet the women, rather than have Carol show them to her office. For one thing, she wanted to make them as comfortable as possible. Herding them from one room to another, one person to another, only served to emphasize the cold, impersonal machinations of the clinic. If she couldn't persuade patients to change their minds, then she would at least show them some kindness and respect.

Carrying a completed form, she entered the reception area. A distraught-looking teen, cheeks shiny with tears, sat in one of the cushy blue chairs. Next to her sat a middle-aged woman, face pinched and unyielding.

Amber read the name on the paper. "Tracie Perry?"

The young girl looked at her but didn't move. Her face crinkled up as more tears welled up.

The woman stood. "Let's go, Tracie. It's time." She

yanked the girl out of the seat by her arm and dragged her toward Amber. "I'm Tracie's mother, Mrs. Jen Perry."

Amber offered her hand. "Hello, I'm Amber Blake, the counselor."

Mrs. Perry ignored Amber's gesture. "What does she need to talk to a counselor for?"

"If you both follow me, we'll discuss that." She turned and headed toward her office, the girl and her mother lagging behind.

Once they were in the office, she shut the door behind them. "Have a seat, please." Amber indicated the chairs in front of her desk. Then she climbed into her own chair.

"What's this all about?" Annoyance fringed Mrs. Perry's tone. "Why can't we just get on with it?"

The woman had obviously forced her daughter to come here. Amber wanted to choke her for it.

"All patients must meet with me first. It's the doctor's policy." She cleared her throat. "Tracie, have you ever had this procedure before?"

The girl's eyes, rimmed with smeared, black eyeliner, registered indignation. "No!"

"Okay." Amber's heart went out to the girl. She fixed her gaze on the girl's mother. "Mrs. Perry, Tracie clearly does not want this, and shouldn't be pushed into it."

Before the woman could respond, Tracie piped up, "There, you see, Mom?"

"Quiet, Tracie. I'll handle this." She impaled Amber with a hateful glare. "Ms. Blake, you have no right to get involved. The decision is ours to make."

"It seems you're doing all the deciding, and what Tracie wants doesn't matter." She should be more careful. If she continued with this, her position here would be jeopardized. But the sullen look on the poor girl's face tore her heart to pieces.

Mrs. Perry's eyes widened, and her mouth formed an "O." "How dare you! This is none of your concern. I don't give a fig for the doctor's policy. Just let us get on with it!"

"Calm down Mrs. Perry. I'm thinking of what's in Tracie's best interest. I'm sure you want that, too." Amber looked pointedly into the woman's eyes.

Mrs. Perry's stare wavered. "This *is* in her best interest. If she doesn't do away with it, her life will be ruined."

Never mind that her grandchild's life would be snuffed out. "If Tracie goes through with the procedure against her will, she will be emotionally scarred for life."

Mrs. Perry looked away.

Amber directed her question to Tracie. "Do you really want to do this, or are you doing it to please your mom?'

"I'm doing it because my parents say they're ashamed of me," she said, her voice sullen.

Amber shook her head. "Tracie, you don't have to do it. It's up to you. If you can't keep the baby, you can give it up for adoption. Find a good home with loving parents."

The girl looked down at her hands and mumbled, "I don't know if I want to keep it or give it up, yet. All I know is I don't want to do this."

"Tracie!" Mrs. Perry jumped to her feet. "Young lady, you are not keeping that baby. You must have the abortion."

Tracie looked up at her mother, more tears streaming. "I can't, Mom. I just can't!" She stood. "This will be your first grandchild. Suppose someone had tried to talk you into aborting me? Would you have been glad to be rid of me?"

The woman's hands shot to her hips. "Of course not! How can you say such a thing?"

"Because that's what you're asking me to do." Tracie snatched a tissue from the box on Amber's desk and blew her nose.

Mrs. Perry sank back into the chair, voice softening. "Tracie, this is different. I was married to your father. We planned on having you."

"Well, maybe I didn't plan this baby, and I'm not married, but it's a part of me, and I don't want to kill it!" The girl broke into noisy sobs.

"You're not killing anything. It's not a baby, yet!" Mrs. Perry stood again, her anger rekindled. She looked to Amber. "Tell her. Tell her it's not a baby."

Amber remained silent.

"Enough of this nonsense, I want to talk to the doctor!"

Before she could protest, the woman jerked Tracie out of her chair and dragged her into the hall, yelling about counselors trying to talk women out of abortions and calling for the doctor.

Shocked, Amber remained at her desk, unable to move even a toe.

Dr. Hines's voice could be heard in the hall. "Here, here, what's all the commotion?"

I'm sunk.

* * *

Amber avoided contact with Dr. Hines for the remainder

52

of the day. At closing, she shot out the door with the speed of a road runner. She wanted to get away without any chance of a confrontation and give herself time to regroup.

Reaching her minivan, she popped the lock and scrambled inside, pulling out of the lot in a matter of seconds.

Heaving a sigh of relief, her thoughts turned to Tracie Perry. That poor young girl. After Mrs. Perry dragged her daughter out of Amber's office, and loudly summoned the doctor, they'd spent a good amount of time shut up in his office. Afterward, Tracie had given in and had the abortion.

Tears sprang to Amber's eyes at the thought. For both mother and baby. She pulled a tissue from her pocket and quickly dabbed them away.

She suddenly craved the sound of her own child's voice. One hand on the steering wheel, she dug the other into her purse for her cell phone, then speed dialed her parents' number.

"Ma? Let me talk to Melly."

* * *

Amber reached the newspaper office around 5:30 p.m. Even though darkness wouldn't settle for almost half an hour, she felt shrouded by a different kind of darkness. One that penetrated every ounce of her being.

"Ah, my favorite reporter," Evan remarked, when she entered his office.

Without uttering a word, she tromped over to what used to be her desk, climbed onto her comfortably familiar chair, and flopped into it.

"Hard day?" he asked.

She closed her eyes. "Yes, but I don't want to talk, right now. I just want to sit quietly for a few minutes."

"Be my guest."

While resting, Amber listened to Evan fiddling around at his desk. Opening and closing drawers. Clicking keys on the computer. Whistling. All familiar sounds that reminded her of happier days. Curiously, this brought her comfort. She remained still for a time, absorbing it all.

Gentle tapping on her shoulder and the whisper of her name pulled her from slumber. Her eyes came into focus on Evan's a few inches above hers. A breath caught in her throat, then she smiled and stretched lazily. "I'm sorry. I didn't mean to fall asleep."

"No problem. But the food's been delivered, and I thought you should eat."

At the mention of food, she became aware of the rich, homey aroma of roasted chicken. Then a snippet of what she'd seen today flitted through her mind. "Oh, Evan, I don't think I can eat anything."

"Are you sure? Look, I got all the trimmings." One by one, he placed containers on his desk. "Mashed potatoes with gravy. String beans. Baked apples." He opened up a small sack and peered in. "Oh, and biscuits."

Touched that Evan remembered exactly what she liked, a tingle ran up her spine. But flutters invaded her stomach. "I appreciate the trouble you went to, but I just can't."

"You know what? I'm not much in the mood to eat, either." He put everything back in the bags, and laid them aside. "Care to talk about it, now?" Evan asked her.

She sighed. "I guess." Combing her fingers back through her bangs, Amber got up and paced the small area behind her chair. Talking about the things she'd experienced today would be painful. Her emotions were on overload already, but Evan needed to know, and she needed to tell him.

"I—" She puffed out a frustrated breath then began again. First, what happened in Doug's room spilled out. Once she'd started, the words spewed forth like a fountain. Everything. The born-alive baby. Her encounter with Rita in the restroom. Finally, that whole fiasco with Tracie and Mrs. Perry. By the time she finished, tears poured down her cheeks, and she'd sunk to the floor, resting on her haunches, and cupping her hands over her face.

Evan came over, knelt down, and wrapped his arms around her. "Oh, Sweetheart, I'm so sorry you had to go through all that."

Amber leaned into his embrace. Nowhere else could she draw the comfort she craved at this moment.

"I don't want you going back there. We've got enough on the guy. This investigation is finished." He stroked her hair.

Amber jerked away from Evan's arms. "No! We need more."

"But look at you. You're a wreck. How much longer can you take it?"

His arms were still inviting, so back she went, laying her head against his shoulder. "I *have* to finish this. Remember Maggie said there was more going on than she was able to tell us? We still have to find out what that is."

He pulled back and looked at her. "I do remember

Maggie saying something like that. But nothing is worth this pain."

"I knew what I was getting into."

Evan let go of Amber and went back to his desk. She wished he hadn't, because all comfort and security went with him, along with a piece of her heart.

"Okay. We've got the faxed requests; we've got your witnessing of the baby drowning. The brochure and tape from the gift company. I think that's enough."

"I don't, and I just want to make it clear that I make my own decisions about whether to end it, or not. About whether it's too much for me to handle or not. Understand?"

He took a deep breath, let it out heavily. "Perfectly."

"Good, then I continue." She gathered up her coat and handbag. "I've got to go. I want to make notes for the file about everything that happened today."

Evan came around the desk and pulled his jacket off the rack by the door. "It's late. Let me walk you to your car."

They walked out of the building and through the parking lot. There were a few vehicles scattered throughout, since the paper went to press overnight. Yet, an atmosphere of desolation surrounded them. A cold breeze ruffled her hair.

"I see you've gotten a new set of wheels." Evan peered through the driver side window.

Praise God, she always removed the car seat when dropping Melly at her parents' house.

"Yes, it was time."

"But why a minivan?"

"I like riding high and the extra room."

"Did your dad install your pedal extenders or the dealer?"

"I paid the dealer to do it. For someone Dad's age, it's difficult to crawl under the dashboard."

Evan nodded. She knew he was thinking that he would have done it for her had they still been together. He'd taken over that chore once they'd gotten married. But not this time.

"You'd better get going," he told her. "Call me when you get home."

His concern brought her pleasure. "Okay. Sure."

She dug into her handbag for the keys. Evan held open the door until she climbed in. He made a circular motion with his index finger, indicating she should roll down the window. When she did, he stood on tiptoes, pulled her head down, and planted a quick, gentle kiss on her lips.

"Talk to you later," he said softly.

Once again, he swept her away. "Uh-huh," she mumbled.

Evan loped off toward the building, leaving her sitting in the Odyssey, fingertips pressed against her mouth where it still tingled from his touch.

* * *

After putting Melly to bed, Amber called Evan at home.

"Is everything okay?" He sounded agitated.

"Yeah, why?"

"I thought you were going to call when you got home. You were in such a state earlier, I was beginning to worry."

She'd never even thought about that. "Oh, I'm sorry! I forgot that I had to stop at my parents' house."

"Okay. Well knowing that makes me feel better. Just let me know next time."

"I'm really sorry."

"Forget it. You're home now, and everything's fine."

"Right. Nothing to worry about."

"I guess I'd better let you go, then."

"Yeah. I have those notes to do before bed."

"Right. Well . . . goodnight."

She didn't want to let him go. "Evan?"

She had barely finished saying his name before he responded. "Yes?"

"Thank you."

"For what?"

"For being there. For what you did tonight. It really helped." Her traitorous voice had automatically taken on a more intimate tone.

"I'll always be here for you, Sweetheart. Whenever you want me." Evan's voice had also dropped an octave.

Whenever I want him. If he only knew how much I want him.

"Thanks. Goodnight, Evan."

It hurt so much to be apart. Maybe she should tell him about Melly. Maybe he wouldn't be mad. Maybe he would love and accept their child and not feel betrayed.

And maybe she would become queen of the universe.

CHAPTER 11

On Tuesday morning, Amber skimmed through the parking lot in the pouring rain. No hat, no umbrella. A warm front had moved in resulting in unseasonably high temperatures for February, but the promise of a miserable day remained—in more ways than one. The rain she couldn't help, but she would do her best to avoid Dr. Hines.

Soaked and chilled through all the layers of her skin, Amber pulled off her wet coat, and left it slung over a chair in her office. She dashed down the hall to the coffee room to pour herself some of the steaming brew. Her hands absorbed warmth from the cup as she carried it back to her desk.

Intending to keep herself behind a closed door for most of the day, Amber slipped into the room, and screeched to a halt, almost spilling her coffee. Dr. Hines sat at her desk, methodically bouncing a pencil on its surface like a see-saw. Eraser. Point. Eraser. Point.

Thunder crashed and rumbled across the sky outside.

"Good morning, Miss Amber," he said, his speech devoid of its usual jocular tone.

Her throat constricted. She worked its muscles to force out some sound. "Hello, Dr. Hines," she finally croaked. He stared at her for a moment. A droplet of water dripped from her bangs onto her cheek and trailed down to her jaw. She could stand the silence no longer. "Would you like me to get you some coffee?"

"No, that isn't necessary."

Again, silence. His eyes never left hers. She shifted from one foot to the other, then faking bravado, placed her hot drink on a corner of the desk. "Well . . . is there something I can do for you?"

He stopped bouncing the pencil and leaned forward. "Perhaps." More silence, then he gestured to a chair in front of her desk. "Close the door, and have a seat."

As she turned to do so, she caught a glimpse of Rita lingering in the hall. Probably to overhear Dr. Hines chewing her out. Amber shrugged, pushed the door shut and climbed onto the chair.

Dr. Hines continued staring and sighed deeply. "Amber, I'm disappointed with the way you handled our patient yesterday. On your first day here, I informed you of our policy and rules, correct?"

"Yes, but—"

"Then why did you try talking Tracie Perry out of an abortion?"

"Doc, that girl was very distraught. It was clear to me her fragile emotional state was caused by her mother forcing her into a decision."

"That's not our concern." His tone remained even, non-threatening.

Amber couldn't say what she really thought. "I realize the position I've put you in and I'm sorry."

"What do you think usually happens to an employee of mine who blatantly breaks the rules?"

Fixing her eyes on his, she said, "Tell me."

"I have zero tolerance for people who deliberately go against my wishes. I usually fire them on the spot." He sat back in the chair, his expression implying no one should dare to cross him.

If Dr. Hines fired her now, she'd never find the key ingredient to stopping him for good.

She realized he expected her to plead with him, but she wouldn't give him the satisfaction. "I hope that won't be the case with me, Doctor. I've done a fine job in the two weeks I've been here. And as a counselor, I've always sought the best interest of the patient."

Dr. Hines came around the desk and sat in the chair next to Amber. The one where her sodden coat lay draped. He leaned back against it without flinching. Ignoring the dampness seeping into his white dress shirt, Dr. Hines impaled her with a piercing gaze. "You know, I might be persuaded to keep you on."

The statement caught her off guard. She'd been expecting a set-down, not a bargaining chip. If she didn't go for it, she'd look suspicious.

Swallowing hard, she looked him in the eye and forced out the words. "What can I do to persuade you?"

He cocked his head and smiled. "Go out with me."

Another thunderbolt shook the building, jolting Amber like an electric current. If his previous statement caught her off guard, this one totally knocked her into orbit. "You're joking, right?" She hardly believed Dr. Hines needed to resort to coercion in order to get a date.

"Nope."

"But why?" Even though Maggie had warned her, Amber never took seriously the idea that Dr. Hines liked her.

He spread his hands. "Isn't it obvious that I'm attracted to you?"

To actually hear him say it brought the world around them to a standstill. She moved her mouth, but no sound came out.

"Can I take that as a 'yes'?" Dr. Hines's humor had apparently returned.

Amber shook her head. "I . . . Please, I need some time to think."

He sauntered back around the desk, sat down, and began bouncing the pencil again. "What's there to think about? If you like me, the answer is 'yes.'" He stopped the pencil, balancing it between his knuckles. "You *do* like me, don't you?"

He asked as if challenging her. *Daring* her to turn him down. How to answer? She chose her words carefully. "Dr. Hines, I do like you very much. But I'm not sure the timing is right. I've been through a lot of things lately, and I wouldn't want that to affect a possible relationship in any way."

His gaze pinned her to the chair, as he again remained silent for a moment. "Okay, I'll give you some time."

A great sigh of relief escaped her, and he frowned. Realizing she'd failed to hide her true feelings, Amber thought she'd better make light of the situation. "Is this how you get all your women, Doc?" Actually, she did wonder.

He grinned. "Not usually, but I somehow got the feeling that with you, I'd need an edge."

That made her laugh out loud.

He glanced at his watch. "Gotta get to work. I'll expect your answer tomorrow."

Tomorrow! "But—"

"Tomorrow, Amber." He stood and strode out of the room, displaying a large wet spot on the back of both his shirt and his dark pants.

Oh, man. What should she do? She couldn't stand the thought of going on a date with the man responsible for Ashley's death. That would be stepping over the line. And what would Evan say? Even though they didn't live together, they *were* still married.

Maybe it was time she did something about that.

* * *

Evan called just after she walked in the door.

"Just wondering how you made out with Dr. Dread today."

She wasn't ready to talk to him, yet. She and Melly hadn't even removed their coats. Plus, she looked forward to spending time with her baby before bedtime. Hoping he wouldn't be angry, she said, "Can I call you back in a little bit? I'm in the middle of something, and I want to be able to talk to you without interruption."

He sighed. "Okay, but try to be quick."

She punched the *end* button and tossed the phone on the couch. "Come on, sweetie. Let's get your coat off."

Within minutes, Melly happily splashed around in the bathtub. A stiff, dark tuft of hair Amber had sculpted with shampoo lather stood straight up on top of her head. Laughter echoed through the room, as the two flicked water in every direction.

What a pleasure to spend this special time with her daughter. If only Evan could experience such joy. Would that change his views on parenting?

After tucking Melly into bed, Amber went into the living room, and called Evan on the cordless phone.

He answered on the first ring. "Yo."

"I promised I'd call back."

"And you're a woman of your word. So how'd it go?"

She hesitated. "Well, he wasn't mad."

"Okay, that's good. But what did he say?"

There was no avoiding it. Amber took a deep breath. "First, he chastised me for going against his policy. Normally, anyone who does that is fired on the spot."

"Well, I know he didn't fire you, because I'd have heard from you sooner. I was itching to call you all day, you know."

Amber suddenly felt warm and headed for the bedroom. "Hold on a minute, I've got to open the window."

"In February?"

Balancing the receiver between her shoulder and ear, Amber unlocked the window and slid it open a few inches. "This apartment sometimes gets over warm. If I don't open the window a smidgen, I'll suffocate in bed all night."

"Hmm. You ought to have the super do something about that. So, anyway, what did Hines say?"

Amber went back to the living room and curled up in a

corner of the overstuffed sofa. "He said maybe I could do something to persuade him to keep me on."

"I don't like the sound of that. What does he want?"

Lifting her eyes heavenward in a quick silent prayer, Amber took a deep breath. "He wants me to go out with him."

"What! You've got to be kidding."

She could hear him breathing through the earpiece. She knew what was coming, and nothing she could say would stop it.

"Amber, you're not thinking of doing it, are you?"

"I might." She squeezed her eyes shut, waiting for the expected outburst.

"I'm coming over there."

She shot to a sitting position. "What?"

"I'm coming over. We have to talk."

"No!"

"Yes. I'm leaving now."

"But you can't!"

"Why not?"

"I don't want you to." Spurred into action, she raced around the room, picking up toys. What should she do? If he came, there would be shouting. Then Melly would wake up. She wasn't ready for him to know.

"Why, is somebody there with you?" An accusatory tone.

"Of course not! Would I be on the phone with you if there was?" She carried an armload of stuffed animals, dolls, and a play telephone toward her bedroom. At the same time, her foot kicked a ride-on toy along in front of her.

"Look, I'm coming." The line went dead.

Amber stood still, unsure what to do.

Oh, my. No good could come of this. She'd call her parents. No. Eight-fifteen was too late to bother them. Besides, they'd never get here in time to pick up Melly and avoid running into Evan. Not to mention Melly would have to be taken from her bed and out of a sound sleep. She couldn't do that to her.

Praying Melly stayed deeply asleep during Evan's visit provided her only hope.

God, I'm counting on you.

She threw the toys into her bedroom, not caring where they landed, and closed the door. Pictures! Zipping around the apartment, she snatched up photos of Melody posing with her, her parents, and alone, and shoved them into a desk drawer. More had to be torn from the walls, leaving bare hooks behind. The groupings she had created looked unbalanced, but there was no time to rearrange them. Next, she sped to the kitchen to hide further evidence that a child lived there.

* * *

Amber opened the door, and Evan stormed right through.

"Won't you come in?" she said, to the empty space before her.

"Shut the door, Amber, we have to talk." He tore off his jacket, and threw it onto the sofa, looking like a volcano about to erupt.

She walked toward the kitchen. "I made a pot of coffee. Would you like some?" Even though this would prolong his visit, she didn't want him getting suspicious if she didn't act as she always had.

"Why not?" He followed her. "Nice place you have."

"Thanks," she threw over her shoulder.

"Hey, wait."

Amber turned to see Evan staring at the wall where she'd just removed the pictures of Melly.

Oh, no!

"What's the matter," she asked him, trying to sound nonchalant, and not pulling it off.

"You've got picture hangers on the wall, but no pictures. It seems unfinished. Not like you at all."

Amber scrounged for an excuse. "Oh, yeah. I'm going to switch some for newer ones."

That seemed to satisfy him, and they continued into the kitchen.

After they were both seated at the table with mugs of coffee and supermarket Danish—all Amber had to offer on short notice—Evan's dark mood returned. She wondered how he'd react if he knew his little girl was asleep just a couple rooms away.

"I'll get right to the point." His brows furrowed. "You can't do it."

Typical of Evan to think he could boss her around. Crossing her arms, she leaned back in the chair and glared at him. "I thought we already discussed this."

"Discussed? You just told me, how could we—"

"I mean," she interrupted, "we agreed that I make my own decisions about what I can or can't do."

He gulped some coffee. "But this is different."

"How?"

"Because it's dangerous. *He's* dangerous."

Her coffee had too much sugar in it. She pushed it away. "Come on, Evan. He's a doctor, not a murderer." Even before Evan had a chance to shoot her a look, she realized the irony of her statement.

"See what I mean? He's got you so hoodwinked, you've forgotten what he does."

True to some degree. Sometimes, Dr. Hines charmed the socks off her and she'd forget all about his gruesome acts. "Okay, from our standpoint, he *does* kill babies. In all fairness, though, he believes what he's doing is good. There's no malice there."

His cold stare slapped her in the face. "Oh, I guess he has no intention of hurting those babies while he's tearing them limb from limb or sucking out their brains."

She flinched at his words. "No need to be so graphic. But you know what I mean."

"And have you forgotten how he botched your sister's abortion, causing her death?"

She looked at him and blinked. Hard to admit, but sometimes she did forget about that too. *Oh, Ashley, I'm so sorry!* Unsettled by that reality, she slipped off the chair and moved toward the living room.

"Don't walk away! This is serious." He followed her out of the kitchen.

"Ssshhh!" Amber put a finger to her lips. "I'm not walking away; I just want to sit comfortably." She climbed onto the puffy, olive green sofa, and nestled into the corner, her favorite spot.

Evan settled into a matching armchair. "You're not seriously going to do it, are you?" His voice had lowered a notch.

"I haven't decided definitely, but I'm leaning toward accepting."

"Why, for heaven's sake?"

"Because maybe he'll come to trust me and open up a little."

He sat quietly for a few moments, brooding. "I just don't like it. I can't see how you could want to go out alone with that . . . that . . ."

She leaned forward, clasping her hands between her knees. "It's not that I *want* to be alone with him. Believe me, that's the farthest thing from the truth."

"How about if I tail you?" He looked hopeful.

Amber's eyebrows drew together, and she waved her hands in front of her. "No, no, that won't do. He's a smart man.

He'll see you and figure it out."

Evan pouted and punched the chair arm.

Honestly, to know Evan was somewhere nearby watching would make her feel more comfortable. But with the way he behaved now, she couldn't trust him not to blow it. And she wouldn't underestimate Dr. Hines. "Look, everything will be fine. I promise."

He studied her for a moment. "You've just decided to go ahead with it, haven't you?"

Amber nodded. "What choice do I have? He'll fire me if I don't. Then we won't know what else he has up his sleeve."

Evan dipped his head, covering his eyes with one hand. "I can't believe this." Looking up again, he said, "There's nothing I can say to make you change your mind?"

"No."

He stood up. "I guess I'd better be going, then." Anger and defeat tinged his voice.

Amber followed him to the door.

He turned and gently grasped her shoulders. "Do what you have to do, but just remember that we *are* still married."

She thought about reminding him they were married in name only, but his tender look rendered her speechless.

"I worry about you, you know," he whispered.

"I know, but don't. I can take care of myself."

Before she could say or do anything else, he pulled her to him and kissed her long and sweet. Her knees reacted as they always did: weakening, buckling. She wrapped her arms around his neck, losing herself in his masculinity, the feel of him so close. His tender embrace made her feel protected, treasured. She conveyed her acceptance of it by running her fingers through his hair, which only served to heighten their passion. She wished it would never end.

Evan broke the kiss, breathing heavily, and pinning her with an intense gaze. His dark eyes seemed to be saying, *"There. I've left my stamp on you. You're mine. Now and always."*

How she wanted to believe that.

"Promise you'll tell me when, where, how—everything about your dates, every time. I want to know before, and I want to know after."

Still dazed from their kiss, she could only nod.

Without another word, he walked out the door.

* * *

Amber plodded into her office on Wednesday morning, and found Dr. Hines sitting at her desk again.

Relentless bugger.

"Well, have you made up your mind?"

She hadn't even taken her coat off, yet. "Yes, I have." Placing her purse on a chair, she continued. "I'll go out with you."

"Good." He stood and came around to her, gently placed his hands on her shoulders. Surprisingly, the gesture did not feel totally unpleasant. "You'll be glad you accepted. Be ready at seven o'clock Saturday evening." At the door, he turned to look at her. "And get dressed up." Then he left.

Amber clicked her heels and saluted at the spot where he'd just been. "Yes *sir!*"

After removing her coat and putting away her things, she went to get coffee. As she poured the steamy brew into a Styrofoam cup, Rita entered the room.

Things are going to change right here, right now. A smile spread across her lips. "Good morning, Rita."

The nurse did a double-take. "What?"

"I said good morning."

"Oh." Rita snatched a cup from the stack. "Morning," she muttered.

This wasn't going to be easy. Amber leaned against the small, round table, as she sipped. "I like your hair. Is it a new style?"

"Huh?" Rita absently reached up and patted around her salt-and-pepper head.

"It looks good on you."

"It's . . . not new. But thanks." She cast Amber a puzzled look.

Amber smiled as Rita whisked off. That went better than she expected. Amber hoped that by showering Rita with kindness, she could chip away at the wall the bitter woman had built around herself.

CHAPTER 12

Which looks better?" Amber held up a dress in each hand for her mother's scrutiny. Ma stepped back, looking down at each one. "Hmm, let's see." She paused. "Black is always a good choice." After studying each garment a moment longer, she added, "But royal blue isn't bad, and the high collar beats a scoop-neck in February." Ma frowned at Amber. "*And* for a first date."

Amber tsked. "C'mon, Ma, you know I don't see it as a real date." She padded across the plush bedroom carpet to the closet and hung the black dress on a low bar.

"It sure seems like one, if you ask me. Getting all dolled up and acting jittery as a schoolgirl." Ma's arms flew up. "I can't believe you're going out with this man! Need I remind you who he is?"

Amber couldn't believe it, either, and no, she needn't be reminded who he was: the man responsible for Ashley's death. She still felt that strange emptiness without her twin sister, like half of herself was missing. No one would ever understand what it took for her to endure a night out with Dr. Hines.

Sucking in a breath and straightening her back, Amber went to the dresser and rummaged for make-up in a small top drawer. "You and Dad had better take Melly out of here. You never know if Dr. Hines will arrive early."

Ma pressed her lips into a thin line and sighed. "All right, honey. You stay and get ready. We'll let ourselves out."

"Tell Dad goodbye and thanks for me."

"I will." Ma kissed her cheek. "*Please*, be careful." She left the room.

After a few muffled murmurs from Melly and her parents, Amber heard the front door close. A sigh rushed from her lips. Having her parents take Melly meant she had one less thing to worry about.

Standing back, Amber inspected her make-up with approval. She took off her robe and donned the flowing, royal blue dress. Gold hoop earrings and black leather pumps completed the ensemble. Next, she removed the jumbo rollers that gave her hair lift and bend. She smiled. Evan used to tease that the rollers made her look like she was taking off for the moon.

Amber grabbed a brush and tugged it through her hair with quick, deliberate strokes. Evan. If only *he* were the one taking her out this evening.

She studied herself in the full-length mirror on the closet door. *A little pudgy in the rear, but not bad.* Evan had never seen this dress. If she wore it for him, he would tell her how beautiful she looked and playfully suggest they stay home from wherever they were supposed to be.

Amber shook herself to stop her musings, then glanced at the clock on the nightstand. At least another fifteen minutes before Dr. Hines would arrive. A yearning to hear Evan's voice rose in her. She felt like she was sacrificing herself at the altar. If she could speak with him, this date wouldn't seem so difficult to bear. He did ask her to call *before* and after the date.

Speed dial was a wonderful thing. Within seconds, she heard Evan's "Yo."

"It's me."

"Hi, me. Aren't you supposed to be somewhere tonight?"

"I'm ready early. Just wanted to kill time while waiting."

"Is that all I am to you? A time-killer?" His voice oozed indignance.

"No, I was just teasing. You asked me to call before I leave, remember? You know me, Evan. You had to know I'd keep my promise."

"Do I? I'm not sure I know you at all, anymore."

A great sadness crept into her soul at his words. She *had* changed since they'd been apart. She didn't much like the change in herself, either.

"Regardless of your feelings about me, Evan, I really need your support tonight. Can't we call a truce?"

His answer was what she interpreted as a sigh of resignation.

"Thank you."

"Sure." The distant tone in which he spoke unnerved her, but she couldn't expect more, right now.

She walked into the living room and, despite the dress, got up onto the sofa in a lady-like fashion.

"I'm nervous, Evan. What if I mess up?"

"You'll do fine."

This time, he spoke comfort and assurance, and she wrapped herself in its warmth. "Thanks."

"What are you wearing?"

His words plucked her from the warmth and plunged her into a sea of icy water. "What?"

"What are you wearing?"

Looking down at her outfit, she shrugged. "Just a dress."

"It's not low-cut, is it?"

"Evan! You're talking crazy, and I'm going to let that remark pass." She might sound offended, but in reality, she liked knowing he cared enough to be a little jealous.

"I'm sorry, I just don't trust the guy. You don't want to entice him, or anything."

She suppressed a chuckle. "I doubt he'll be enticed by a collar that's up around my neck."

The release of a pent-up breath sounded through the phone. "Good choice."

The door bell rang.

"I guess you're on," Evan said.

She stood. "Guess so." Her heartbeat accelerated.

"Good night, Sweetheart. Be careful." Sadness crept into his voice.

"I will. Good night." As if they had said their last good-byes, tears threatened to surface, and Amber blinked them back. The door bell rang again. "Coming," she yelled.

Sending up a silent prayer for strength and protection, she strode to the door and pulled it open.

"Hello, Amber." He stood tall and majestic in a dark suit and tie. Her mouth dropped open. *Does he have to be so good-looking?* Recovering, she answered his greeting.

His intense gaze appraised her. "You look captivating."

She could almost feel her eyes sparkle at the compliment. Even if it did come from the lips of her worst enemy. "Thank you." Stepping aside, she said, "Come on in."

Hands behind his back, he sauntered in a few steps and presented her with a bouquet of red roses.

She drew in a sharp breath. "They're beautiful. Thank you." Her fingers caressed the velvety petals, and she buried her nose in a scarlet bloom, sniffing. "I'll put these in water." She closed the door and turned toward the kitchen.

"Wait."

His command stopped her in mid-stride. She turned back to find him holding out a box of very expensive chocolates.

"Thought you might like these, too."

Flowers and candy? Did men still do that? Reaching out, she said, "I'm a woman, and this is chocolate. You're spot on."

He smiled.

"Thank you, Dr. Hines."

His face screwed up, and he cringed. "Since we're not at the center, call me Albert or Al."

"All right . . . Al." His name felt foreign to her tongue. "Let me take care of these roses, and we can be off."

He nodded and sauntered farther into the living room.

Amber went to the kitchen, found a vase in a low cabinet, filled it with water, and placed the flowers inside. Returning to the living room, she set them on the coffee table in front of the sofa. "Perfect."

"Yes, perfect." Dr. Hines did not look at the floral arrangement, but at her. His gaze sent creepy crawlers up her spine.

Amber cleared her throat. "Shall we go?"

Dr. Hines took her black velvet wrap, which had been draped over the back of the sofa, and held it out low for her. As he folded it around her shoulders, his hands lingered on her upper arms longer than she would have liked.

What was she getting herself into? This was a side of Dr. Hines she'd never seen, and probably never would have if she hadn't agreed to a date. But she had, and now she'd have to tough it out. She hoped she didn't need to use the mace she'd placed in her evening bag earlier.

Outside the building awaited another surprise. Amber sucked in a breath as she eyed the sleek, black limousine parked there. A uniformed driver stood stiff and proud by the gaping passenger door, inviting her to enter the cozy interior. She climbed into the beige, leathery softness, and Dr. Hines followed, sitting beside her.

"Where are we going?" She hoped her outfit was appropriate.

"To see an opera at the Academy of Music in Philly."

"The opera! I've always wanted to see one."

He spread his hands, indicating their elegant surroundings. "So, what do you think?"

Amber forced a smile. "I think you really know how to treat a lady." Except for the poor ladies he coerced into donating their aborted babies every day. Babies he used as money-makers.

He grinned back and the whiteness of his teeth seemed to glow in the darkness of the car. "Thank you. I try my best." Then he took her hand and held it between both of his. Swallowing hard, she gently disengaged it, opened her purse, and pretended to be searching for something. Pulling out a pack of gum, she offered a stick to Dr. Hines.

* * *

Dr. Hines, or Al, as he preferred to be called, had procured balcony seats. He sat very close to Amber and occasionally whispered into her ear about some facet of the performance. Throughout the whole opera, she fought the urge to flick his breath away like an annoying mosquito.

On the way home, the limousine couldn't ride fast enough. Every minute felt like torture. Even worse, the conversation never approached a direction where she could question him about the trafficking.

When they finally arrived in front of Amber's apartment building, she couldn't wait to get inside. Relief spread through her knowing she didn't have to ask him up since the limo had to be returned. *Thank you, Lord.*

Her thoughts were interrupted when the driver yanked open the passenger side door. She alighted from the vehicle, and Al followed. He quietly walked with her to the door of the building.

"Thank you for a wonderful, evening, Al. I truly enjoyed it." She pushed the words out.

He took her hand, bent and kissed it, his lips ice against her skin. She shivered.

"As did I." Releasing her hand, he said, "See you Monday."

"Right." She slipped inside the building and rushed to the elevator.

Up in the apartment, Amber stepped out of her pumps and carried them to her bedroom. Fatigue overtook her, and she longed to shed the restrictive evening clothes. As she undressed, the events of the evening rolled by in her mind's eye like a movie trailer. Dr.—er Al displayed nothing but polished, gentlemanly manners throughout their time together. Yet, whenever he touched her in any way, no matter how innocent, on instinct, she'd shrunk back. Praise God he hadn't seemed to notice.

The whole situation would have been worth enduring had she been able to find an appropriate opening to ask about his work. But it would probably be best to wait until she gained his trust. She sighed. Maybe on their next date.

That thought made her wince.

Now in her nightclothes, Amber climbed onto her downy bed and rested her head against propped up pillows. She spied the cordless phone on the nightstand.

Should she? Nah, he was probably asleep. Maybe not, though. He'd always been a night owl.

Before she lost her nerve, Amber snatched the phone and dialed Evan's number.

"Yo."

His voice wasn't as upbeat as usual, but not sleepy, either. "Did I wake you?"

"No, I'm in bed watching television." He paused briefly. "So how'd it go? I've been waiting for your call."

"Not very well."

"Didn't you find out anything?"

She twirled a lock of hair. "No, actually. It was difficult to have conversation during the opera."

He let out a frustrated breath. "What about in the car?"

She hesitated. "I couldn't find a way to bring up the subject of work. It would have been out of place."

"I'm sure you could have thought of *something*. Don't tell me you were so smitten with Dr. Dread that you couldn't think straight."

Why did she always end up having to defend herself to Evan? "Look, this is going to be a process. I can't expect him to just lay everything out there on the first date. When he gets to know and trust me, he'll open up without much prodding."

"Did he . . . try anything?"

"He was a perfect gentleman."

A short silence. "You didn't let him kiss you, did you?"

Amber reached over and turned off the lamp. The dial pad of the phone illuminated the darkness. "On the hand, but not on the mouth." But if he had wanted to she wasn't sure how she would have handled it. Nor how Evan would have taken it.

"But what will you do when he does expect a kiss?"

"I'll deal with it then." She hoped. A yawn crept up her throat. "It's late. I have to go."

They said their goodbyes, and she replaced the phone in its base. She lay there in the dark and thought about her evening with Dr. Hines. Not really so bad, she had to admit in hindsight. His dating skills were superb, though, and his attentiveness left much to be desired in other men. At least, going on what she'd heard from other women throughout the years.

But this was not how she should be reacting, considering the man was responsible for Ashley's death. Thank God she hadn't forgotten that while she'd been with him. She also needed to remember the unspeakable things he did at the clinic.

If only he hadn't been so charming and good-looking.

CHAPTER 13

On Monday afternoon, few patients were scheduled, so Amber helped Doug. Though it still made her ill knowing the contents of those tubes and other containers she packaged, she became adept at going through the motions with little thought.

She glanced over at Doug. Funny how when she first started here, she'd associated him with his job description, and, therefore, thought him creepy. But working together had given them an opportunity to become acquainted. Amber discovered he wasn't as macabre as she'd supposed.

"Doug?" Her voice ricocheted around the large room. The distance between their work areas made it difficult to have a quiet conversation, but she wasn't going down to his end if she didn't have to.

"What?" His eyes never left his work.

"Do you like what you do for a living?"

"I don't think about it. It's just a job," He still didn't look at her.

"Do you want to do this for the rest of your life?"

He shot a quick glance her way. "Of course not."

A fax transmission stated what needed to be packed. She put the paper aside and chose two glass tubes. "What do you want to be? What kind of career goals do you have?" Placing the tubes on a sheet of bubble wrap, Amber folded and rolled it around each one.

"I'm going to be a lab tech. This job is just a stepping stone." He cast a furtive glance toward the door.

"That's terrific. Any prospects?"

Doug stopped working and pinned her with a purposeful look. "I don't want to talk about this anymore, Amber." He turned away, continuing the task before him.

"I'm sorry. I don't mean to be nosey. Just making conversation." She laid the wrapped tubes in a container of ice, then placed the container in the box. Next, she pressed a "Refrigerate on arrival" sticker, together with an address label, on the outside of the package and set it aside.

The door opened and Maggie entered carrying a container of . . . *ugh*, Amber didn't even want to imagine what it held. The nurse's features looked strained, and it seemed as though she purposefully averted her eyes from what she held.

Maggie set the plastic pan by Doug. "Here you go." She threw Amber a wistful smile on her way to the door.

Amber waved her over. "Maggie, can I talk to you for a second?"

As Maggie approached, she shook her head. "It gets harder each day to pretend everything's okay," she whispered.

Amber touched Maggie's arm and offered a silent expression of empathy, then said in a low tone, "Let's have lunch together tomorrow." The center was closed one hour each day for the midday meal, so they would be free to leave together.

"Sure, hon. Love to."

"Good. I'm going to ask Rita, too."

"Why, after the way she treats you?"

"Because it wouldn't hurt for me to show her a little kindness."

Her friend sighed noisily as she walked away. "Okay, whatever you say."

Later, as Amber headed toward the lavatory, she spotted Rita in the break room. Slipping in before she could lose her nerve, she greeted the nurse.

"Hi, Rita."

The woman looked up and gave her a curt nod, then resumed filling the coffee pot from the water cooler.

Amber took a calming breath of the java-scented air. "Listen, Maggie and I are going out to lunch tomorrow. Would you care to join us?"

The question must have been too much for her, because the pot almost slid from her hands. Rita whipped her head around to glare at Amber. She could taste Rita's bitterness toward her, like vinegar on her tongue.

"What did you say?"

"I asked if you wanted to have lunch with Maggie and me tomorrow."

Rita placed the carafe on the heating element and flipped on the switch. "Oh, uh, I don't know . . ."

"C'mon, it'll be fun."

Fluttering her eyelids, she looked around the room, as if searching for an excuse. "But Dr. Hines might need me to stay around."

"Nah, he'll be at lunch, too. C'mon, what do you say?"

"I—I—I—"

"Good, we'll all meet at the front door at noon." With a brief wave, she flitted out before Rita could protest.

She'd be praying all day and night that lunch would go well tomorrow.

* * *

Evan pressed his foot down on the extended gas pedal. He had just finished a meeting with a company right over the bridge in Philly that ordered fetal tissue from Dr. Hines. He'd found it among the faxes Amber had given him from the clinic. This time, he had posed as a potential client.

The proprietress, Jasmine Tate, had appointed him the time of 10:00 a.m. She acted nothing like that savage, Michael Wharton, but possessed a certain degree of coldness. In no uncertain terms, she'd warned him not to be late.

Her office reflected the impression he'd gotten of her personality when he'd spoken with her over the phone: cool. Muted blues and grays with just a touch of green were the colors of choice. The large cherry desk held only a few items on its glossy surface. Completely pristine. Judging by the way she spoke, her own efficiency and no-nonsense approach caused her to expect the same from everyone else.

The Tate Company did not rely on colorful flyers with catchy phrases for advertising, but only a listing in the local business directory and a clean, to the point website.

But after the appointment, the thing that remained on his brain the most was her vague familiarity. Her tall, slender frame. That air of classiness.

He forced the image to the back of his mind and concentrated, instead, on his relationship with Amber. They hadn't had as much contact as he originally thought they would. And now that she was seeing Dr. Dread, they wouldn't be able to meet as often as he'd planned.

While Amber was wined and dined and having a grand old time, he stewed at home in his own stupidity. But what could he do about it?

Hmmm. There might be something . . .

* * *

Amber, Rita and Maggie slid into a booth at the fifties-style diner. The other two women sat together across from Amber. The hostess handed out menus and left.

Rita was quiet, and Amber wanted to make her feel more

comfortable.

"See anything you like, Rita?"

"Not so far, but I'm sure I'll find something." Her eyes never left the menu.

"Ooh, I know what *I'm* getting," Maggie said. "I love their big, juicy burgers smothered in Swiss cheese and mushrooms."

"Mmmm, sounds delicious." Amber looked at Rita. "Are you up for it?"

The woman flashed a smile for the first time since they'd met. "Yes. I'm going to have that, too." She nodded once, forcefully.

After the waitress left with their orders, quiet settled over the three of them, emphasized by the clatter and murmur of the other patrons. This was not good. Amber searched for a conversation starter.

"Have you ever eaten here, Rita?"

"I've been here a time or two."

Talking with Rita proved difficult. Like when Amber tried talking to Melly while her daughter studied a new toy or zoned out in front of the television for *Blue's Clues*. Amber would work hard to coax every word out of that child's mouth. Well, Rita wasn't a child, and she'd do her darnedest to garner more than one-word answers or short sentences from the woman.

Rita's hands rested on the table, and her artsy fingernails drew Amber's attention.

Now, there's *something to talk about.*

"Oh, Rita, I love your nails!" She grasped the woman's hands, fascinated. The nails were sculptured with tiny, colorful plants and flowers painted onto a white background. They resembled an oriental garden. "Who does them?"

Rita pulled her hands free. "I went to the place over at the Towne Center Strip Mall for the first time this weekend."

Maggie then grabbed Rita's hands, much as Amber had, peering at the nails. "Oh, yeah, I know the place. But this just doesn't seem like you, Rita. I never would have thought." She nudged the woman's ribs with her elbow. "I'll bet there's a free spirit hidden under that straight and narrow façade."

"Yeah, Rita. But those are mini-masterpieces!" Amber said.

Maggie winked at Amber. "And you're an expert on all things little."

"Ha-ha, very funny."

The waitress brought their food and placed the platters

on the table. All three women quieted and took their first bites of the succulent burgers.

Amber swallowed, then ventured a new subject. "Have either of you seen a good movie, lately?" Amber's eyes shifted from one woman to the other.

"Yes, I saw the latest Tom Hanks movie." A mouthful of food muffled Maggie's words.

"Really? How was it?"

She offered a dismissive wave of her hand, and swallowed. "Oh, you know. All Tom Hanks movies are good." Maggie turned to Rita. "Have you seen it?"

"No." She lowered her eyes and sipped her beverage.

Another one-word answer. "What was the last movie you saw?"

Leaning her chin on her palm, Rita looked toward the ceiling. "Oh, gee, I can't remember. That must have been at least two years ago. I don't have many people to go with, and I wouldn't go alone."

Poor Rita. Did she keep to herself because she had no friends? Or was it the other way around?

She had an idea.

"Why don't we all go see a movie together?" Evan wouldn't like this, judging by how he'd condemned her for going out to dinner with Maggie while he was in Wisconsin. Well, he'd just have to deal with it.

Rita's face lit up, reminding Amber of the sun rising at dawn. Despite her graying hair and severe features, she could be more attractive. If only the woman smiled more. "That's a terrific idea! How about Saturday?"

Amber felt her facial muscles sag. "Sorry, I can't. I have plans."

"Another date with Dr. Hines?" A sly grin stretched Maggie's lips.

If it was possible for Amber's face to fall completely off, she knew she'd be able to look down and see it lying on her plate. She risked a glance at Rita. Hurt mingled with anger blazed in the woman's eyes, and unshed tears pooled there.

"Excuse me." Rita stood and headed toward the ladies' room.

As soon as she'd gone, Amber lit into Maggie. "What are you trying to do? You know how she feels about the doctor. Why would you say a thing like that in front of her?"

"She has to find out sometime. Better to hear it now, and

from us, than through the grapevine."

Suddenly, Amber wasn't hungry and pushed her food away. "I disagree. And it shouldn't have been done in such a cruel manner. Everything was going so well. She was opening up, and being *nice* to me."

Maggie shrugged and stared at her plate.

"Why do you like to see her squirm?"

Her eyes met Amber's. "I don't know. Sometimes that woman just grates on my nerves."

"I think you're too hard on her. She didn't deserve what you just did."

"You're right. I'm sorry."

She hoped Maggie meant it.

Rita returned to the table with red-rimmed eyes.

"Rita, let me explain—"

"This lunch is over. I'm leaving." She snatched her purse off the table and stalked out of the diner, leaving her food and the bill to Amber and Maggie.

She'd never be able to fix this. If only she could explain to Rita her real reasons for dating Dr. Hines. But then would that solve anything? Probably not. Since Rita participated in his gruesome activities, she likely wasn't bothered by them.

They returned to the center, which remained silent and perfunctory for the rest of the day.

Amber hated that she'd trampled Rita's feelings in the process of investigating Maggie's claims. She hoped to someday make it up to the woman.

CHAPTER 14

Saturday night arrived much too fast for Amber. Even though she'd agreed to see Dr. Hines, enduring an entire evening in his company anchored her like a weight to the ocean floor, while she struggled to swim to the surface.

They occupied a small table in a corner of the high-end restaurant, the dim lighting creating an intimate atmosphere for patrons. Amber watched eerie shadows caused by the candle centerpiece frolic on Dr. Hines's—er, *Al's* face. To call him by the latter was difficult. In her mind, he would always be "Dr. Hines."

Hoping to hide her nervousness, Amber asked him questions about his career choice.

"What made you become a doctor, and ultimately open the center?"

He popped a forkful of strawberry cheesecake into his mouth, studying her as he chewed, as if trying to determine whether to trust her.

"You've met my sister, Jasmine," he finally said. Amber nodded. "While we were both young, she became pregnant. She wanted to abort, but my mother wouldn't let her. Didn't believe in it." A muscle in his jaw twitched. "Mother forced Jas to birth and raise a child she didn't want, and barely had feelings for."

Amber shook her head. *That poor, innocent child.*

"That baby, my nephew, grew to resent her indifference. As soon as he came of age, he moved out of the house, and out of the state. Not doing very well, from what I hear. And two lives were virtually a mess all those years because of my mother's ethics."

"How sad." Amber said this more for the young man's sake. What child could grow up a stable, content human being without experiencing mother love? Or the love of a father, for that matter?

That thought forced her to admit to herself that she could be depriving Melly of her father's love. If he indeed *would* love his daughter. She just had no way of knowing for sure.

Al reached across the table and covered Amber's hand

with his, like a blanket of ice. Suppressing the urge to pull away, she smiled stiffly.

"I vowed to make a difference in situations like that. No woman should ever have to raise a child she couldn't love, and no child should have to grow up without that love."

He drew curlicues on the top of her hand with his forefinger. To Amber, it was a daddy-long-leg spider scampering across her skin.

She shuddered.

A slow, lazy smile spread across Al's lips, and Amber realized he thought she reacted with pleasure.

Oh, my!

When Amber could take Dr. Hines's touch no longer, she disengaged her hand from underneath his. "Excuse me, for a moment?" she croaked. "I need to use the ladies room."

He nodded and smiled. "Sure thing. Go powder that pretty little nose."

Amber headed out of the dining room, toward the alcove where the lavatories were located. As she put out her hand to push through the door, a firm grasp on her other arm spun her around.

"Evan! What are you doing here?"

His eyes darkened and his brows furrowed. "I might ask you the same thing."

She surreptitiously cast her eyes around. "I told you we were coming here. I—"

"I'm not talking about that. What do you think you're doing by letting him touch your hand like that?"

Who did he think he was, asking her such a question? He no longer had any claim on her. "What do you suggest I do, Evan? Jump up and run out? I'm supposed to act like I'm interested in him, remember?"

"But you looked like you were enjoying it." Anger flared in his dark eyes, as his voice seemed to reverberate through the alcove.

"Sshh. Are you going to let the whole restaurant know what's going on?"

He glanced around. "Okay, I'm sorry for raising my voice." His dark eyes pierced her. "You *were* enjoying it, weren't you?"

Crossing her arms, she glared at him. "And what if I was? We're not together anymore. You have no say in who I see."

A woman exited the restroom, shooting them an annoyed

look.

Evan stepped closer, backing her up against the wall, pinning her there without so much as a touch. "You're still my wife." His voice ran deep and low. "And you're the one who left. Not me." Turning abruptly, he strode away.

Amber stumbled through the lavatory door, exhausted after that interchange. Standing before the pink vanity sink, she stared at her reflection in the spotless mirror. Sometimes, she just didn't understand herself. Like how she'd goaded Evan out there. She loved him, so why did she want to hurt him? The answer bubbled to the surface from deep inside: because he'd hurt *her*, and she still hadn't fully forgiven him.

Okay, so most of it was her fault. She did marry him under false pretenses, thinking that after several years he would change his mind about not wanting children. He didn't. But then she became pregnant with Melly. In an attempt to feel him out, she broached the subject of starting a family. He exploded and they argued. Amber left without ever telling him about the pregnancy.

Figuring she'd been away from their table long enough, Amber quickly used a stall, dusted blush over her cheekbones, and returned to Dr. Hines. As she approached, an air of impatience radiated from the general direction of his seat. He strummed his fingers on the table, and checked his watch.

"Well, there you are," he said.

"Sorry to take so long."

"No problem." He gave her a wry, sidelong glance. "Only half the evening's been wasted."

A tiny smile twitched at her lips, even though she knew he partially meant what he said. He most likely considered stating his mind in a joking manner an art form.

Dr. Hines motioned for the waiter to bring their check. He placed his credit card inside the navy blue case and handed it to the young man, who walked away. He checked his watch again. "It's still early. Could we go back to your place? I have something I'd like to talk about."

"We can talk here, can't we?" She smiled to soften her attempt at a refusal.

He glanced at the diners around them. "I'm afraid not."

Was it important enough for her to let him into her apartment? Maybe he would reveal something about his clandestine activity connected to the fetal harvesting or something equally significant. She wrung her hands under the table. "Okay, I guess," she said through tight lips, thinking Evan would flip if he found out.

"Let's go, then."

Dr. Hines helped her into her little fur jacket. As they left the restaurant, Amber scanned the room for any sign of Evan. He was gone.

* * *

Evan waited in the restaurant's parking lot until he saw Amber and Dr. Dread leave. When the doctor's fancy Lexus pulled out, he slowly moved his vintage Mustang a good distance behind them. He'd get the dirt on this date face-to-face tonight. No phone conversations about it whenever Amber saw fit to give him a buzz.

After about ten minutes, the Lexus reached her apartment building. Evan pulled into an obscure spot where he could see when the doctor left.

He watched as the couple exited the car, and strolled to the building together. Phft! He might have known Dr. Dread would be the type to beguile a woman with some Don Juan-ish technique like escorting her to the door.

But they didn't stop at the door. They went inside.

Together.

* * *

Up in the apartment, Dr. Hines helped Amber out of her jacket. "Why don't you have a seat while I put this away," she said, taking the jacket from him. She headed for the bedroom to hang it up, thinking how out of place he looked, here, in her apartment.

When she returned to the living room, Dr. Hines had the TV on, but muted. He'd removed his suit jacket, and left it slung over the back of the armchair.

"Would you like something? More coffee, or a cold drink?"

"No, I'm good." He lowered his tall, lean frame to the couch, and patted the cushion next to him.

Hmm.

Amber eased herself onto the spot next to him, careful not to settle too close, like lovers. "So, what did you want to talk about?"

He shifted his body so that he faced her. "There's something you should know about me."

Here it comes. This is the big secret. "Go on."

Dr. Hines looked down at the sofa cushions and twisted

his mouth, as if chewing the inside of his lips. He didn't answer for a few moments. Then he looked up, meeting her eyes with his. "I was married before."

Amber considered this bit of information for almost a minute. Not what she expected to hear, but she wasn't surprised. The doctor was a personable, good-looking guy. "I see," was all she could think to say.

"There's more. I also had a young son."

"Had?"

Dr. Hines nodded, keeping his eyes down. "He . . . he died from complications of Duchenne dystrophy." Obviously seeing the question in Amber's eyes, he explained. "It's the most common form of childhood muscular dystrophy."

She laid her hand on his arm. "I'm sorry, Al."

His only response was to cover her hand with his own in acceptance of her sympathy.

He had never seemed as vulnerable to her as at that moment. The expression on his face indicated he still mourned his son. Understandable. Amber would never stop grieving if she lost Melly.

"What happened?" Her voice came out soft, and she was surprised to find she wasn't pretending. Maybe because her heart had begun to soften toward him, as well.

"He was only seven when he died. I wanted so badly to help him, to find a cure." His hands rested on his thighs and he curled them into fists. "I was a surgeon, and I couldn't do a thing."

Tears pooled in Amber's eyes, causing them to blur. "Al, I'm sure you did everything in your power, as would everyone else involved."

He pinned her with an intense gaze. "I always felt there was more that could have been done. Especially by me. There's a cure out there somewhere. I know it. I can feel it."

"You're probably right. I'm sure someone will discover it very soon."

Dr. Hines took Amber's hands in his and looked deeply into her eyes, a strange gleam in his own. "Sooner than we think."

At that moment, a thought occurred to Amber. She had to ask. "Al, I'm a little confused. Earlier, you said your sister's situation inspired you to open the center, yet you just told me you were a surgeon. When was that?"

"That was before, but it's true that what happened to Jas

led to my opening the center later."

"What happened in between?" She knew that question bordered on nosey territory, but hoped he'd answer anyway.

Efficiently evading the question, his tone brightened. "No more sad talk. I see you have a DVD collection. Let's watch a movie."

"Sure." Amber tilted her chin toward the stand boasting an array of choices. "You pick." And she knew the subject was closed until he felt the need to open up again.

Dr. Hines chose a disc from one of the shelves and inserted it into the machine. He returned to the sofa and clicked the play button on the remote. His arm lay across the back of the sofa, and the faint sour odor of perspiration drifted from his armpit.

A short cough escaped her lungs, as she turned her attention to the television. He'd chosen a black-and-white Hitchcock flick with James Stewart. "Ah, I see you like the classics, Al."

"Yeah, they outshine the movies of today. Did a fine job without all the explosions, car chases, and all that computer generated stuff."

For a few moments, silence hung thick in the air, like fog on a London night. A weird feeling crept up Amber's spine, and she reached back to scratch it. Only that didn't help.

Then, Dr. Hines's hand gripped her upper arm and pulled her toward him. "Come closer, sweetheart."

Amber cringed inwardly. Even though millions of men used the term of endearment, it just didn't sound right coming from Dr. Hines. *Sweetheart* was Evan's special name for her.

Amber gradually became aware of Dr. Hines's stare. She resisted a look and suffered the pressure of his gaze. His arm around her shoulders kept them close, causing his breath to graze her cheek. Certain he waited for her to turn his way, she ventured a glance and a half-smile.

When she shifted her attention back to the movie, he caught her chin in his hand, and gently pulled her face around. Their eyes met point blank.

His expression conveyed a definite purpose.

Oh, no! He wants to kiss me!

The sight of his lips closing in paralyzed her.

CHAPTER 15

Evan slapped the steering wheel. He should have known Don Juan wouldn't just leave Amber in the hall. He'd gotten inside that apartment. And what was he doing in there? He could be making advances. Or worse, Dr. Dread could be trying to force himself on *his wife*! Maybe he should go up there, intervene.

But then intervention might not be needed. Maybe Amber *could* take care of herself. She always had before. Of course, she'd never been in this type of a situation.

On the other hand, Amber could be welcoming any moves the doctor put on her.

Craziness set in, and all sorts of scenarios flickered on the movie screen of his mind, ending with him busting the door down and yanking Dr. Frankenstein off his wife, landing a few well-placed punches, then shoving his elegantly clad butt out the door.

The temptation got to him. He popped the door open and stepped one foot down—then caught himself. He must be insane. He could cause Amber serious harm by blowing her cover.

Be cool, Blake.

Closing the car door, he settled back into the seat. His hand rested on the steering wheel while his fingers drummed a beat. It could be a long wait. He crossed his arms against his chest to ward off the chill seeping into the car, and shifted to a more comfortable position.

Lord, please keep my Amber safe.

He hoped his prayer would be answered despite his neglect of all things spiritual over the past two years.

* * *

Amber blocked Dr. Hines with a hand laid against the steel wall of his chest. He barely seemed to notice.

She pushed hard. "No, Al. Please."

He glared down at her. "Why not?"

"I'm not ready. I've been through a lot of things recently,

and I can't even begin to think about a serious relationship."

He released an annoyed sigh, and removed his arm from her shoulder. Silence reigned for a few minutes, while he brooded.

"I'm sorry. I don't mean to hurt you. Couldn't we continue as we are without taking it to another level, just yet?"

He smiled wistfully. "I guess I misread the signals."

Amber nodded.

"All right. I won't be overbearing. We'll take it as slow as you like."

She grinned, relaxing. "Thanks. I appreciate your sensitivity to my feelings." Whatever else he might be, Dr. Hines was still a gentleman.

As they both turned back to the TV screen, Amber wondered how long she'd be able to put him off.

* * *

Evan woke with a start. And a stiff neck. Rubbing away the soreness, he gazed at the spot where Don Juan's car had been parked. Good, it was gone. He illuminated his watch face. Twelve-thirty. He wondered what time they'd called it quits. Couldn't have been long ago.

He went up to Amber's apartment. She hadn't even bothered to call him as she'd promised. He had the cell phone with him and it never rang. His finger poked the doorbell with more force than necessary. When she didn't answer the door immediately, he pounded on it, not caring who heard.

Just as his fist went up to pummel the door again, it flew open. There stood Amber, sleepy-eyed and soft-looking in a satiny robe. Her hair was mussed, too.

A breath stuck in his throat, as his eyes drank in the sight of her.

Beautiful.

She rubbed one eye with her fist. "What's going on, Evan?"

For a moment he'd forgotten why he was there. "Huh?"

"What's gotten into you? You keep showing up unexpectedly."

Now he remembered. "You didn't even call me. You promised."

Amber walked away, leaving the door open. "I tried, but your phone must have been turned off."

He strode in and pushed the door closed with his foot. "Turned off! I always keep it turned—" He dug into his pocket, looked at the phone. It was dead. "Oh. It ran out of charge." Amber folded her arms across her chest and nodded, as if to say, "Of course." This wasn't the first time. He had a tendency to let the charge run out of anything that needed recharging. Now would be a good time for the floor to swallow him up.

"Forget that for now. When he didn't come out of the apartment, I worried you might be in trouble. Why'd you even let him in?"

She turned back on him like a boomerang. "What do you mean 'when he didn't come out'? You were spying on us?"

"No."

"Then how did you know he didn't come out? That he was here, in the first place?"

He raked a hand through his hair and scrounged for an answer. "I—I—was waiting for him to leave, so I could come up and see how it went. I was worried about you."

She shot him a look that said she didn't believe him.

"Honest. I fell asleep waiting." His train of thought switched tracks. "What time did he leave, anyway?"

"A while ago. As you can see, I've already been to bed." Her arms spread, indicating her state of dress.

He couldn't suppress a tiny smile as he drank her in again. This time, with no need to hide his gaze. "I can see, all right."

Her face registered anger. "Why are you smirking, like that?"

He shrugged. "No reason." Better change the subject. He sat down on the sofa. "So what's the scoop?"

She sighed, perching herself on the couch about a foot from Evan. "He did tell me why he does abortions." She explained what happened to Dr. Hines's sister and nephew. "To him, it's a noble cause."

That last statement made him cranky. "He should be knighted, then."

"Stop it, Evan."

"That all you got?"

"No, and this will answer your rude question of a few minutes ago. Before leaving the restaurant, he asked to stop in because he wanted to tell me something. Since he'd already begun to open up, I thought he might reveal something important."

"And did he?"

"You could say so. He told me he was married before and

had a son who died from complications of Duchenne dystrophy at the age of seven."

Evan thought for a moment. "Hmm. Could have something to do with why he sells the fetal tissue."

"Yes. He became very emotional when he told me. I could see he's still mourning the loss of the boy. He also said he was a surgeon at the time it happened."

Amber looked uncomfortable, like she might regret having to disclose something so private. Evan hoped a special bond hadn't formed between Amber and Dr. Hines. "Did he tell you what happened between that time and when he got into the abortion business?" His voice sounded gruff.

"No. He changed the subject and when he does that, it's impossible to persist. Gaining his trust will be a slow process."

"Right." He stood. "No doubt you'll be enjoying the process, too."

With a stern face, Amber got up and strode to the door. She pulled it open. "I've had enough of your snide remarks. You'd better go."

"I'm going." He sauntered by her. "Must've hit a nerve."

The door nearly smacked his behind when she slammed it shut.

Standing there in the chilly hall, he shook his head. What happened that made him so nasty toward Amber? He didn't believe any of the mean things he'd said to her, yet he said them anyway. Even at the restaurant. Whenever he saw her, frustration took over. Frustration that she was right there in front of him, yet just beyond his reach. Frustration that another man had the pleasure of her company. Frustration that—all he wanted was to get her back!

Trudging out of the building, he got into his car and drove home.

To his big. . . empty. . .house.

* * *

On Monday afternoon, as Amber passed Dr. Hines's office on her way to Doug's room, a loud bang, a noisy clatter and a few choice curse words jolted her out of a midday slump. Curious, she knocked on the partially open door and poked her head in.

"Everything okay, Doc?"

He stood by his wood grain desk picking through wet, dark-stained papers. "Spilled my coffee on some important documents." His expression was stormy, and she wondered what he could be so angry about. Spilt coffee wouldn't provoke such a reaction from the "in control" Dr. Hines.

Amber walked over to the desk and righted the tipped-over Styrofoam cup. "I'll get some paper towels."

When she came back, she blotted up the excess coffee from the desk, and then the papers, some of which were stapled together. The words "Plaintiff" and "Defendant" caught her eye. Her glance slid to Dr. Hines. His gaze met and held hers.

"A former patient claims I punctured her uterus and it resulted in a hysterectomy. She's suing me." The anger of a few minutes ago had gone, but worry flickered in his eyes for a fraction of a second. He lowered himself into the cushiony chair, cradling his head in his hands as if he had a monster headache.

No need to question the truth of the charge. She remembered the circumstances of Ashley's death and wondered how she could have felt guilty the other night revealing personal things about Dr. Hines to Evan.

Nevertheless, to stay in character, Amber went around the desk and placed a comforting hand on his back. "Oh, Al, I'm so sorry." She was sorry, all right. Not for the doctor, but for the woman who had lost her natural ability to conceive.

He straightened up, now, oozing stoicism. "That's okay, Amber. It happens."

A pretty nonchalant approach. But did he mean groundless lawsuits just happened, or punctured uteruses?

"What are you going to do?"

"I guess I'll have to hire an attorney. Know any good ones?" A wan smile broke through.

"No. Sorry," she was glad to say.

A broad grin now split his face. "No matter. I've been through this before, but I don't think I want to use the same lawyer. I lost the suit." He reached over and curled his hand around Amber's free one. "Thank you for trying to comfort me. It really helps to know you care."

Just then, Rita burst through the door. "Albert, I—oh, uh, excuse me, I didn't—" She glared at Amber's close proximity to the doctor and their joined hands. Amber pulled hers away and pretended to scratch her nose with it.

"Can I help you, Rita?" Dr. Hines asked.

"No. I'll come back later." She stood there a moment longer, as if waiting for him to ask her to stay.

"All right." He turned his attention back to Amber, but she wished he hadn't brushed off the nurse so coldly.

Now she had another strike against her in Rita's eyes.

* * *

"How are you and Evan getting along?"

Amber zipped up Melly's coat. "We're not, and I don't want to talk about it, Ma."

"Oh, honey, I'm sorry."

"Me, too." She took the tote bag Ma held out, then grabbed Melly's hand. "Say goodbye to Grandma and Grandpa, Sweetie."

"Bye-bye." Melly waved with her other hand.

Ma and Dad both said goodbye and kissed Melly.

Amber's cell phone rang.

"Oh, hold on a minute." She slipped the phone out of her coat pocket. A glance at the screen told her it was Evan. Puffing out an annoyed breath, she answered.

"Got a minute?" Sounded like he wanted to get straight to the point.

Holding up a finger signaling to her parents she would take the call, she handed the bag back to her mother and strolled down the hall to the kitchen. Wanting to punish Evan, and prolong his anguish, she remained silent.

"Well, at least you didn't hang up. Listen, I wanted to call sooner, but thought I'd give you some space." When she didn't comment, he continued. "I'm really sorry, Amber. I didn't mean anything I said."

"Then why did you say it?"

He released a frustrated sigh. "I don't know. I just get so angry at the thought of you being with someone else, I lose all reason. Will you accept my apology?"

She would, but she'd make him squirm, first. "I don't know, Evan. You were pretty mean." She remembered the terrible things she'd said to him outside the restroom at the restaurant. She was no better than he.

"I know. I promise to make it up to you."

"How?"

"I'll think of something." A pregnant pause about to give birth squeezed between them. "So, will you?"

"I don't know." She dragged out those three words for effect.

"C'mon, Amber."

"I guess so. Just don't forget you promised to make it up to me."

"Um, have you seen that lawyer about a divorce, yet?"

This change of subject took her off guard. "No. I haven't had the time. But as soon as this is all over—" Her parents and Melly came out of the family room and started down the hall toward the kitchen. She'd have to hang up before he heard Melly's voice. "I've got to go, Evan. I'll talk to you soon."

"Sure. And thanks, Amber."

"No problem." She hoped her voice overrode that of her family's.

"Will I see you tomorrow night to work on the story?"

"Yes. Good night." Flipping the phone closed, she turned to Melly. "Ready to go?" Poor Evan. Guilt sunk its nasty claws deep into her heart. If only she could tell him.

"Who was that, Amber?"

Considering a lie, she glanced at her dad. No. She couldn't. "It was Evan."

That conspiratorial look passed between her parents.

"I've got to get Melly to bed. Thanks, again, for helping me out. As soon as this is over, I'm treating you guys to a huge dinner at a great restaurant."

"You don't have to repay us, honey, you know that."

I know, Ma, but it will make me feel better for imposing so much."

"Stop that!" Dad ordered. "You're not imposing. We've been over this before, so let's put it to rest, shall we?"

"Sure, Dad." If only the issues between she and Evan could be resolved so easily.

CHAPTER 16

At the end of work on Tuesday, Amber slipped into her coat, and headed down the hall to Dr. Hines's office to say good night. She stopped outside his door at the sound of voices.

"I've seen to the chambers, Albert, so you needn't worry." A door inside his office closed and keys jingled.

Chambers?

"Thank you, Rita. Appreciate it." It sounded as though he was barely paying attention to the nurse, answering by rote.

"I'm happy to help out. Is there anything else you need?"

She heard paper rustling before he answered. "No, I'm good. See you tomorrow."

Amber shook her head. Another brush-off. She hated to see him do that to Rita.

Footsteps approaching the door alerted her to move. So that she'd look as though she were just approaching, Amber tip-toed backward as many steps as she could before the door flew open.

"Good night, Rita." She smiled at the nurse, as they passed in the hall.

"'Night." A mumble without eye contact.

Amber poked her head into Dr. Hines's office. "Just wanted to say good night, Doc."

He looked up from his desk. "Have a good one, Miss Amber."

She headed out of the building to meet with Evan.

But what are "chambers"?

* * *

Evan opened the door still wearing his suit and tie from the office. He was as handsome today as the day she met him.

"Hi." She handed him the bag of takeout food she'd promised to pick up on her way over.

"Thanks. Let me pay you back." He reached into his pocket.

"Don't worry about it. My treat." She took off her jacket and hung it together with her handbag on a low hook of the coat tree by the entrance. "I'm starved!"

"Then let's get to it before we start working."

After a quick meal of cheese steak sandwiches, they retreated to the home office. Amber automatically climbed into the seat at the desk and rested her hand on the computer mouse. They had always worked this way. She did the typing, he paced or looked over her shoulder at the screen or sat in the comfortable easy chair in the corner of the room.

But things had changed.

"I'm sorry, Evan. Would you rather sit here?"

He stopped the pacing he'd already begun and looked at her with a confused expression. "What?" She could tell he had already been in deep concentration. "Oh, no, this is fine."

"Okay, if you're sure." She clicked open the word processing program and found the file containing all of their combined notes. They'd emailed everything to each other, so both had a complete, up-to-date file. Having the information readily available afforded them the choice to work at either Evan's or Amber's. Although, because of Melly, she usually found a way to avoid using her apartment.

Amber opened the file and sifted through the documents. They discussed some of the key elements they'd collected, then Amber opened a blank document.

"How about this?" Evan stopped moving and stated his idea for an opening line, while Amber's fingers danced over the keyboard.

She studied the screen. "Nah, I think we should start in a different place."

"Got anything?"

She thought for a moment. "Okay, try this." She clicked away at the keys, and Evan came to read as she typed. He stood just beside her chair with his hand resting on its back. Her stomach did a somersault, and she missed a key. The program automatically corrected the misspelled word. Evan leaned closer as he studied the screen. His arm touched her back, and an involuntary reflex propelled her upper body forward in the chair, as if she'd been burnt. Her nerve impulses still sprang to life at his touch. Even more so, after all this time. She missed it. Longed for it. Keeping on her toes around Evan exhausted her. Maybe just this once, she could let her guard down.

Amber relaxed back in the chair, against Evan's arm. Closing her eyes for a few seconds, she savored the sensation. *Familiar. Comforting. Home.*

"Are you okay, Amber?"

Her eyes flew open at the sound of his voice close to her ear. She turned to look at him, his dark eyes filled with concern. "I'm . . . I'm just tired." This happened to be true, but if only she could tell him how she felt otherwise.

Evan patted her back. "We don't have to do this tonight if you're not up for it."

Her heart fluttered. "No, I'm all right. Let's keep at it." Did he realize what that did to her?

After about two hours of intensely focused work, fatigue set in. Amber's fingers and wrists felt ready to snap off like dry twigs.

"That's enough for tonight." Evan lay sprawled across the seat of his chair, sans jacket and tie, his back leaning against the armrest. "E-mail that to your computer, and we'll both review it as time allows.

Amber transferred the document to an e-mail, clicked the "send" button, and then climbed off the chair. Walking toward Evan, she rocked her head from side to side. "Wow, I thought we'd never finish." The stiff neck was painful, and her numb fingers couldn't apply enough pressure to rub it away. She flexed them several times. "I need a long soak in a hot bath."

"Here, why don't you let me try?" He tapped his hand on the small area of the seat cushion in front of him. "Sit here."

Did she dare?

She did.

Perching herself on the edge of the seat, Amber closed her eyes and dipped her head, as Evan gently gathered her hair, and arranged it over one shoulder. His strong hands began kneading her neck and shoulders. When they were together, he did this for her frequently. Losing herself in the sensation, she allowed a movie trailer in her mind to replay those times, how they always relaxed her, and what they inevitably led to . . .

Her eyes flew open, and she stiffened.

Evan's hands fell away. "What's wrong?"

"Wrong? Nothing." *Beside the fact that I still love you, and I so want to be with you? That I don't trust myself alone with you?* She fought for control, determined not to go through life afraid of caving in where Evan was concerned. For now, she wanted to enjoy what he offered: a simple massage. She relaxed. "Please. Don't stop. I really need this."

"Sure." His hands resumed working their magic.

* * *

Evan didn't know how long he could go on before he lost it and made love to Amber right there on the recliner. When she'd presented herself before him, so sweet-smelling and soft, it was all he could do to keep himself together. Then she'd lowered her head to allow him to move her hair, and he thought he'd go insane. Lifting the golden locks, he'd caressed their silkiness. They were softer than he remembered, and it took all he had to keep from burying his face in them.

And now Amber had him rubbing her neck and shoulders. Did she realize the danger she put herself in with that one small relenting gesture?

He stared at her neck as he rubbed. He'd always loved kissing and nuzzling it. But he wouldn't allow himself to become so distracted and ruin the harmony they'd found tonight. Their relationship, at this moment, was tenuous at best.

Oh, but that beautiful neck. Agony overtook him, and he couldn't resist. Slowly, he moved close and pressed his mouth against her smooth skin. She tensed up, and he let his lips linger there a moment before gliding them back and forth in light, butterfly strokes. It sounded as though a sigh poured from Amber's lungs as her body relaxed. Encouraged, he trailed feathery kisses around to the curve between her neck and shoulder, on the side opposite to where he'd laid her hair.

"Stop, Evan." She didn't sound too convincing.

"You don't mean it, Amber," he mumbled between nibbles.

"Yes, I do." She stood and faced him. "Why does it have to come to this? Can't we work together without ending up in either a fight or an embrace? Is there no in-between?"

Evan sighed deeply. She was right. It seemed whenever they were together his foremost thought was taking her to bed. "I'm sorry, Amber. I just . . . lost it. It won't happen again."

She shot him a disbelieving frown.

"I mean it." He held up three fingers, curling the thumb and pinky together. "Scouts honor. From now on I'm on my best behavior."

"And I'll keep at a safe distance away."

Evan nodded even though he knew no safe distance existed.

CHAPTER 17

Saturday night, Amber and Dr. Hines sat together in the darkened movie theater. He had dressed casually, this time, in blue jeans and a sweater over a turtleneck. His casual attire unsettled her. The suits and other more formal clothing he normally wore fit her perception of him from back when Ashley had her abortion. Cold, distant, and untouchable. But seeing the doctor this way somehow made him real, approachable. That scared her.

Leaning closer, Dr. Hines whispered in her ear. "Would you like more popcorn?"

"No, thank you." She couldn't put another morsel in her mouth. They'd enjoyed huge, sloppy burgers, fries, and milkshakes at a fast-food restaurant before coming to see the movie. She hadn't eaten like that since her college years. Had to admit it tasted good for a change.

Dr. Hines curled his arm around her shoulders and pulled her closer, which put her in an uncomfortable position. The armrest between the seats dug into her ribs. Amber tried to concentrate on the show and stayed that way until she could stand it no longer. Squirming in her seat, she said, "I hope you don't mind, Al, but I have to straighten up."

"Something wrong?"

She rubbed her rib. "It's just that the armrest is poking me."

"Oh, sorry. Didn't realize." He lifted his arm from around her, then slid lower in his seat. "Movie's almost over, anyway."

Amber nodded and turned toward the screen.

* * *

Watching himself in the huge wall mirror, Evan executed a kick he'd just learned. He had been taking private martial arts lessons for some time, but had slacked off lately. Tonight he came back. It was a good way to work off steam after seeing Amber.

"Evan, you've got to lift your leg higher," his instructor, Sifu Jun Yu said. "I know it is difficult, but you must try, otherwise the kick does not work." He crossed his arms over his chest, as he studied Evan, his dark eyes serious.

Evan tried again, but his foot shot just below the line Jun Yu had marked on the mirror. He turned to the younger man. "I'll never get it, Sifu. My legs are just too short."

"Nonsense, Evan. You may have to be closer to your opponent, but you will get it. Keep practicing." He left the spacious room.

Evan shook his head and tried again. And again. As he did so, over and over, his thoughts turned back to Amber. Each time they'd been together weakened his resolve a little more. He wanted her back. But Dr. Romeo occupied most of her spare time with his dates. Despite the fact that Amber was his wife, Evan wished he could date her himself.

Then an idea flashed through his mind. He *could* date her. Whenever she wasn't with the doctor. If they had plans for an evening, Evan would take her out during the day, and vice versa.

As his enthusiasm ballooned, and he made mental notes of how he would court his wife, Evan's kicks began to strike closer to the mark on the mirror. He then noticed the reflection of a young boy watching him from the doorway with interest. Probably curious about his dwarfism. He turned around, ready to answer a slew of questions about his height.

"I'm sorry, mister, I didn't mean ta stare. It's just that I been trying to learn that move for a while."

Relieved he hadn't drawn attention to himself for what he first thought, Evan smiled. "That's okay, Sport. I'm just learning it myself. It's a tough one for us little guys, isn't it?"

The boy nodded solemnly.

Evan's heart lurched. He understood exactly what this kid was going through. "What's your name?"

"Cody."

"Well, Cody, would you like to practice together?"

Cody's face beamed. "Would I!" He tromped across the mat-strewn, hardwood floor toward Evan.

Side by side before the mirrors, they took their stance.

"Ready?" Evan said.

"Ready," Cody said with a huge grin, and together they began executing sidekicks.

* * *

On the way home in Dr. Hines's Lexus, Amber sat quietly, contemplating the movie they'd just seen. What a coincidence that one of the characters had been pregnant, and considering an abortion.

Dr. Hines glanced at her. "You're awfully quiet tonight."

On impulse, she decided to enter precarious territory. "I've been thinking about the movie. You know the pregnant girl who decided to keep the baby?"

He nodded, keeping his eyes on the road.

"I was glad she didn't have the abortion." Expecting tension, at least, Amber turned her head and watched his features. No pulsing jaw muscle, no narrowing of eyes. He didn't even white-knuckle the steering wheel.

"You're allowed to feel that way, Amber. Just because I perform abortions doesn't mean you have to be all for them all of the time. I don't think they're always the answer myself."

She gaped at him, wide-eyed.

"Surprised?" He glanced at her again, then back at the road.

"To say the least." When he didn't respond, she delved deeper. "What type of a situation would you feel that an abortion isn't the answer?"

Dr. Hines cleared his throat. "If the patient already had multiple procedures. I think you get to a point where it's too dangerous to go any further."

Amber nodded, but wondered if he'd been referring to the danger to himself, or to the patient.

Dr. Hines parked the car and walked with Amber to the door of her apartment building.

She stopped on the top step and turned to him. "Thank you for a fun evening, Al."

"My pleasure." He stared at her, as if expecting her to say something else, but she didn't. "Do I get to come up tonight?"

She took a deep breath. He would gradually want more and more. She needed to hold off as long as possible. "Not tonight. I'm exhausted and I've got a lot to do tomorrow."

His steely gaze met hers with intensity, and he studied her for a moment. "Okay. For now." He grabbed her hand. "Come with me."

"Where?"

"Just over here." He led her to the edge of the top step, and he descended a few, until they were almost eye-to-eye, he still being somewhat taller.

"What are you—?"

Before she could finish her question, Dr. Hines cupped her chin, then dipped his head to plant a soft kiss on her lips. Taken completely aback, Amber's arms dropped to her sides, and her purse slid from her shoulder, hitting the concrete with a loud thwack.

Dr. Hines paid it no mind and deepened the kiss.

Amber remained stiff, at first, but his gentleness quelled her apprehension, while everything about him tonight filled her senses. She allowed her arms to coil around his neck. Confused, and surprised at herself, she did not feel repulsed at the kiss. Nor did she cringe when his arms surrounded her in a tender embrace. Especially after he'd let his guard down a little on the ride home. Could it be this man was not the villain she imagined all these years?

Forcing a return to reality, Amber broke the kiss, and stepped back. "Goodnight, Al."

A slow, teasing smile made its way across his lips. "Goodnight, Miss Amber."

After snatching up her purse, Amber rushed up to her apartment and leaned against the closed door, breathing hard.

Now she was repulsed. Not by Dr. Hines's kiss, but by *herself.*

* * *

Lying in her bed in the dark, Amber realized just how taxed she'd been lately. Not only physically, but also emotionally. Always trying to stay one step ahead of both Evan and Dr. Hines regarding Melly's existence, on top of dealing with the horrors at the clinic, caused her to collapse into bed every night. Except, once there, no matter how tired, sleep evaded her.

And now she had one more thing to worry about. *That kiss.* She hated herself for her weakness. How could she let herself get romantically involved with the man responsible for Ashley's death? And how could she even *think* about kissing another man if she still loved Evan? Despite their differences they were still married, and in her mind, kissing someone else paralleled cheating.

Disgust for herself shuddered throughout her whole body. She'd given in so easily. What a hussy.

One thing was for sure, she couldn't go on acting as if nothing had changed.

CHAPTER 18

After dropping Melly at the church nursery on Sunday, Amber walked into the auditorium. She loved this church with its huge stained-glass cross cut into the front wall and the soft blue carpeting throughout. Looking around at the people she'd come to love like family, she wondered if they could see her sin. She imagined the word "hussy" pasted across her chest. Her own scarlet letters. Most people in today's society would not consider kissing someone other than your spouse as sin, but to the people of this church, the act equaled adultery. It did to her, too. Jesus was the one who said it, and everyone here, including Amber, took the Bible seriously.

Amber waved to Mrs. Gardner across the way, but the woman didn't return the gesture. She'd probably only *thought* Mrs. Gardner had been looking at her. Sometimes that happened and then you felt like a fool. Amber always tried not to let that kind of thing bother her, because there really wasn't anything to be embarrassed about. She had extended a friendly gesture. If the recipient hadn't seen it, no big loss.

But maybe Mrs. Gardner somehow knew what Amber had done last night, and couldn't stand the sight of her. The rest of the congregation would find out, the pastor, too. No one would want anything to do with her.

She couldn't bring herself to mingle before the service, as she usually did. She slid into a pew at the back corner of the auditorium, bowed her head, and closed her eyes. No one would stop and talk to her if they thought she was praying.

Her mind revisited the night before. Dr. Hines had certainly surprised her by his openness regarding her position on abortion. Of course, he didn't know the half of it. But if he did, perhaps his reaction wouldn't be what she expected. He continually amazed her.

Then he kissed her. And she amazed herself by allowing it to happen. By almost *enjoying* it. The man caused Ashley's death, yet she could like him. Laugh with him. Kiss him. What did that say about *her*?

There was Evan, too. She'd hurt him once when she left him. Unbeknownst to him, she'd hurt him a second time by not telling him about Melly. Sure, he'd hurt her in a way two years ago by refusing her a child. Sometimes, she longed for revenge. Now she had something she could use, and nothing about it felt good. Evan had warned her things could get sticky. She hoped he could forgive her.

Her parents. She'd already pierced their hearts by even beginning this fiasco. She'd be driving the stake deeper if they knew she felt anything more than indifference toward the doctor responsible for their daughter's death. Oh, they'd forgiven him long ago, but they wouldn't want him cavorting with their only other daughter.

She needed to do something to make things right. But what? There was no way to go back. She'd crossed the line into dangerous territory.

* * *

On Monday, Amber stepped out of the attorney's office and leaned against the door. Squeezing her eyes shut, she waited for her heart to stop pounding and wondered if she'd done the right thing. Although she'd told Evan she'd planned on doing it, in her heart, she hadn't really wanted to. Back then, she'd only said it to protect herself from getting hurt again. Now she did it to protect Evan, who despite everything, had been true to her. He would no longer have to be tied to a wife with a divided heart and mind. He deserved that much and she wanted him to have it as soon as possible.

Amber checked her watch. Ten minutes remained of her lunch hour. She'd better get back to the center.

In less than a week she'd have the prepared divorce papers in her hands.

And then she'd have to force herself to give them to Evan.

* * *

Evan picked up his cell phone from the end table beside the couch where he sat. At eight o'clock on a Monday night, Amber ought to be home. He stopped short of dialing, finger poised over the keypad. He had to be crazy to consider such a thing. Amber was his wife, not some innocent schoolgirl. And he was no school*boy*. Courting her? Absolutely insane. But deep in his spirit, he knew this is what he needed to do. Despite his blatant neglect of God since the day Amber left, he'd prayed about this. First, he asked forgiveness, then praised and

101

worshipped, and then he asked the Lord for confirmation. And got it big-time.

Before he lost his nerve, he pressed the number for Amber's speed dial. Her phone rang. *No turning back now.*

"Hi, Evan, what's up?"

What's up. How about I love you? Come home? "I, uh, need to ask you something."

"Shoot." Strangely, she sounded sad.

"Will you be seeing Hines this weekend?"

"Why?" Her question rifled through the phone like a bullet.

"I'd like to see you."

"Why? Is it something about the article? Tell me now, and I'll see what I can come up with to fix it before then. Free you up for the weekend."

He sighed in frustration. This was not going according to plan. "No, it's not about the article. I just want to see you."

"Whatever for?"

He got up off the couch and paced. Amber never made anything easy for him. "I want to take you out. You know, to dinner, maybe a movie."

"Take me out? You mean, like . . . a date?" He detected a tiny quiver in her voice.

"Exactly."

Silence.

"Amber? Are you still there?"

"I'm here." A tiny murmur he could hardly hear.

He must have shocked her. He'd shocked himself, that's for sure. "Well, how about it?" *Please, say yes.*

"No, Evan, that's not a good idea." That quiver in her voice again.

His heart dropped to his stomach like a brick. "Why not?"

He heard her puff out a frustrated breath. "Just because."

This conversation was leading nowhere. Would he have to beg? "Amber, don't you think I deserve some of your time?"

"Of course, you do. This is not about you, it's about me."

He sat back down and rubbed his eyes with the fingertips of one hand. "I'm asking again. Can I see you this weekend? It'll be fun. I promise."

Her apprehension seeped through the phone and clutched his throat. "All right, I guess," she finally said, still sounding unsure. "Dr. Hines hasn't asked for Saturday, yet, so how about then?"

"Terrific. I'll pick you up at seven. We'll start with dinner."

After he hung up, Evan jumped up from the sofa. "Yes!" He did a little dance around the living room, then turned his face toward the ceiling, closed his eyes, and clasped his hands together. "Thank you, thank you, thank you!"

* * *

Confusion permeated her life, Amber thought, sitting in the passenger seat of Evan's car as it cruised along the expressway. First, she filed for divorce, then she agreed to go out on a date with Evan. Not to mention, just about every weekend seeing the doctor who caused Ashley's death. Crazy. She'd never had such a full social calendar in her life, either.

She turned to Evan. "Where are we going?"

He spoke without glancing at her. "Atlantic City. A nice little place called the Rainforest Café. Ever hear of it?"

"No. Have you been there?"

"Not yet, but Dave's review expounded on its virtues. Now I have a reason to go."

She remembered Dave, their staff restaurant critic. Nice man. Married, with two kids. His wife had been diagnosed with Multiple Sclerosis just before she and Evan separated. And Amber thought *she* had problems. "How are he and Dee doing?"

Evan glanced at her. "Okay. The medicine she takes helps some, but they've had to make some changes in their lives to accommodate her illness."

"I'll bet."

"Anyway, I think you'll like this place."

He couldn't have been more right. The delightful atmosphere made Amber feel she had been dropped into the middle of an actual rainforest. There were exotic fish and replicas of jungle animals so lifelike that several times, she had to remind herself they weren't real. An elephant close to their table seemed ready to charge, and Amber wanted to run for fear of being trampled. But best of all, a simulated thunderstorm occurred every quarter-hour, or so.

Afterwards, while the delicious taste of the sirloin steak dinner still lingered on Amber's tongue, they strolled the boardwalk. Not many people did that this time of year. Except for patrons scurrying to one casino or another, they were alone.

They stopped by the railing to look out at the waves crashing against the shore, and enjoyed it together in silence. A chilly wind flipped Amber's hair off her shoulders, but it wasn't frigid. Evan wrapped his arm around her, pulling her close, which warmed her. A delightful shiver ran through her body.

"Are you cold?"

"Not really."

"Here." She didn't think it was possible, but he pulled her closer still, rubbing his hand up and down her arm.

"Mmm." The sound accidentally escaped her lips. Her feelings had a will of their own, forever betraying her mind.

Evan had been kind and caring all evening. Just like he'd always been up until the big argument they'd had on the day she left. But because some of the things he'd said seared her heart, she acted on impulse. And that stupid decision had taken her to this point, feeling caught in a quagmire of her own making. Putting her faith on the line, violating her marriage vows, risking everything dear to her.

She'd agreed to go on this date mostly to determine whether she should go through with the divorce. The answer to that depended on Evan's reaction when she told him about the kiss she shared with Dr. Hines. If she could find the right words, she would tell him tonight.

And if she needed them, the divorce papers were tucked inside her purse.

CHAPTER 19

Amber was killing him. Evan could detect her desire for his nearness, his touch, but a part of her seemed unreceptive. He knew she held something back. Had she developed genuine feelings for Hines? Couldn't be. Not after what he'd done to Ashley.

They continued to stand quietly by the railing, looking out at the deserted beach. He turned and studied her profile in the darkness. Something did bother her and he ached to comfort her, massage away those crinkles between her brows, tell her everything would be all right. Kiss away her fears just like he used to. But she didn't believe in him anymore. Not since she'd changed her mind about having children, and he hadn't.

Evan wanted to repair that broken confidence, but he needed time. Something he didn't have a whole lot of. He vowed to do it though, no matter what. And he'd begin tonight. One thing he hadn't done, so far, was apologize to Amber for the things he'd said to her the day they split. "Amber—"

"Evan—" Their words overlapped. They both laughed nervously, then he indicated that Amber should go first.

She hesitated, then took a deep breath. "Evan, I need to apologize."

"For what?"

The crease between her brows deepened, and her obvious pain gripped his heart.

Amber chewed on the nail of her thumb for a second. "I . . . did something . . ."

"O-kaaaay." He drew out his voice "What did you do?"

Tears pooled in her eyes, and she turned away, shaking her head. "This is so hard to explain." She sniffed.

"Just say it, Sweetheart. This is me, remember? I don't bite."

She nodded, straightened her shoulders, and looked him in the eye. "At the end of our date the other night, Dr. Hines kissed me—"

"What!" Evan saw red. "Did he try anything else?"

"No, but—"

"I knew it would happen sooner or later. And don't think he'll be satisfied with just a kiss for long." He paced in an imaginary four foot square, feeling hot. He tore off his coat and threw it on the ground. His hands. He needed to do something with his hands before he punched something. Or someone. Anyone. The first person that walked by.

Amber gathered up his coat. "Evan, please, calm down."

He wouldn't be soothed. "You have to quit, Amber. I don't want you to go back there. We're done. We have enough information."

"Evan, you didn't let me finish. Please stay still."

He forced himself to stop moving. Breathing heavily, he faced her. "Okay. Hit me."

And that she did.

"It isn't just that he kissed *me*." She poked her thumb against her chest. "I kissed him back."

* * *

Evan stumbled back a few steps, hand over his heart. He reminded Amber of Redd Foxx in an old rerun of *Sanford & Son*, when the comedian experienced "the big one." Only this wasn't a sitcom, and no one was laughing.

She waited for his outburst, but it didn't come. Instead, he stared at her, silent.

"Evan?"

His shoulders slumped.

"I'm sorry. I don't know what else to say." She could tell him that in spite of what things looked like, she still loved him; or that she'd spend the rest of her life making it up to him. But her mouth wouldn't utter a single thing.

"How could you, Amber?"

"I didn't plan it. It just . . . happened."

"Just happened? Rain just happens, Amber!" His arms flailed. "The sniffles just happen! But a kiss?" He shook his head. "Must've been something special for you to return it."

"No, it wasn't special, really. I guess I just got caught up in the moment."

He turned away from her and faced the beach. "Is that supposed to make me feel better?"

"No," she whispered, feeling as bad as he looked like he felt. She didn't expect this defeated attitude. It tore at her heart more than his trademark tantrums ever had. How would she make things right between them?

Amber touched Evan's arm, and he shook it off. *No!* She couldn't handle his rejection. Couldn't take it if he stopped loving her. And couldn't stand losing his trust. Yes, she had left him, but she never gave up on him. Now, after spending such a pleasurable evening with Evan, Amber's heart rebelled against serving him those divorce papers.

"Evan?"

He didn't face her but continued to stare out to sea. She looked at the ocean, too. The waves crashing against the shore matched the tumult inside her.

"I can't look at you, right now, Amber."

A gasp escaped her, and she took a step back. She never expected such a harsh reaction. "But . . ."

"Go somewhere else. I want to be by myself, right now. I'll meet you at the car in a little while."

She stood staring at his taut back for a few moments, willing him to change his mind.

He didn't.

* * *

Amber huddled against the passenger door of the car, shivering. Forty-five minutes had passed since Evan ordered her to leave his presence. In an effort to pass time, she had meandered back to the parking garage, stopping to peer into a shop window, here and there, not really seeing the displays inside. After twenty minutes, she'd reached the car, figuring Evan would soon follow.

She checked her watch again. Almost an hour, and still no sign of him. Maybe she should seek refuge from this frigid night air in a restaurant or casino. But as angry as Evan was, he might leave without her. Although he'd never been so callous before, with his current state of mind, she couldn't risk it.

A few minutes later, Amber spotted Evan loping toward her. When he got close enough, he took one look at her and dashed to the trunk of his vintage Mustang.

"Amber, I'm sorry, I didn't think!" He pulled a blanket out and wrapped it around her shoulders. "Here." He unlocked the door and guided her inside.

Amber continued to shiver and couldn't say a word. Evan turned on the heat, blasting from both the dashboard and floor vents.

"Feel better?"

"Y-yes, th-thank you." She didn't realize how numb her lips were until she needed to talk.

They drove in silence for a short time, before Evan spoke. "I probably shouldn't have reacted the way I did, but you know me, the drama king."

She looked over at him, waiting. Was he going to say he forgave her? That is wasn't such a big deal?

Evan sighed. "I have to admit that even though you didn't sleep with the guy, the thought of you kissing that creep really hurts."

"I know. There's no excuse." No sense in trying to justify it. She'd feel the same way if the situation were reversed. "Can you forgive me?"

Another sigh and a pause. "I do forgive you, but it's going to take some time to get over it." He glanced at her, then turned his attention back to the road ahead. "You know, in all the time we've been apart, I never once sought the company of another woman, let alone kiss one. There's never been anyone else but you, Amber. There never will be."

Now why'd he go and say something like that, making her guilt feelings triple? "You have to believe me, Evan. It's the same for me."

His shoulder went up in a half hearted shrug. How should she take that? Maybe he didn't believe her.

Or maybe he didn't care anymore.

CHAPTER 20

After Melly woke from her nap on Sunday afternoon, Amber planned to take her to the park. Though still chilly, the temperature remained above average for the season. March had not come in like a lion, but she hoped it would still go out like a lamb.

As she waited for nap time to end, Amber puttered around, packing things into a tote bag for their outing: a ball, Melly's Clifford the Big Red Dog Pull Along toy, a small container of dry, o-shaped oat cereal, and juice boxes. The simple chore allowed her addled brain to revisit what had transpired last night between her and Evan. She'd hurt him by kissing the doctor. She'd hurt him when she left, too. Would she ever stop hurting him? But then things didn't look much better from her end. Okay, he'd made it clear before they married that he never wanted to be a father. However, if he really loved her, wouldn't he have done it, at least once, for her? A wistful sigh pushed itself past her lips.

While she rummaged in the refrigerator for fruit, the doorbell rang. Amber tsked and went to answer, hoping she and Melly wouldn't be detained. Since she wasn't tall enough to reach the peephole, Amber shouted as quietly as she could, "Who is it?" through the door.

"It's me."

Amber's breath caught. What was Dr. Hines doing here? He hadn't even called.

She kept the chain lock on and opened the door as far as it would go. "Al. I didn't expect you," she said through the crack.

"I know. A spur-of-the-moment decision. I was able to wrangle some free time this afternoon and thought we could do something."

The audacity. She glanced over her shoulder, as if Melly might be standing there. "Uh, I can't. We—I have plans."

His face fell in obvious disappointment. "Okay. Then can I come in for just a few minutes?"

Her palm felt clammy on the doorknob. "No. I'm sorry. I'm

getting ready to leave now." She couldn't help sounding short. If Melly woke up and came into the living room that would be the end of it. Thinking she heard the bed creak, she discreetly cocked her ear toward her daughter's room.

"I see. I'll try to give you more notice next time, then." His words were stiff, his eyes stormy.

She threw him a shaky smile. "That would be good."

He stood rooted to the spot. "Okay, then. I'll see you at work tomorrow—"

"Yes," she shot back. She heard Melly's bedroom door squeaking open and wanted him gone, pronto. "'Bye." She waved through the opening, which was more like a shooing action.

She closed the door, just in time.

"Mommy?"

Amber found Melly rubbing her eyes with her little fists. "Hello, sleepy-head. Are you ready to go to the park?"

"Yeth."

"Okay, let's get your shoes on and skedaddle." They walked toward the sofa.

Melly laughed heartily. "Ske-dad."

"No, *skedaddle*," Amber said, slipping Melly's sneaker onto her foot. She smiled as Melly again said the word incorrectly.

Amber helped Melly off the sofa and grabbed their jackets from the closet. Ready to head out, a sudden thought struck her. What if Dr. Hines was outside waiting for her to leave? Or watching from someplace, ready to follow her? She shook her head. No. Preposterous. Al was too self-important to become a stalker. But maybe that was the trouble—thinking he had a right to control people.

She rushed to the living room window and carefully lifted a slat in the blinds the tiniest fraction. She sucked in a sharp breath. There he was, standing against the side of his pristine Lexus. No way could she take Melly out now. But then if she didn't go somewhere, he'd think she lied. Plus, she'd promised her little girl the park, and would not disappoint her.

Her main concern, though, was how strangely Dr. Hines had acted. Almost . . . dangerous. Chills ran up her arms. As kind as he could be, it seemed he refused to let anything stand in the way of what he wanted. Even if it was the very *thing* he wanted. Well, she couldn't risk Melly's safety and would make doubly sure Dr. Hines never found out about her. She'd never thought this assignment would intrude into her child's happy, carefree life. She would see that it did not go a step further.

Amber concentrated on finding a solution to the problem at hand and one came to her almost immediately.

She shouldered the tote bag and took Melly's hand. "C'mon, sweetie." She moved with purpose.

Out in the hall, she knocked on the apartment door next to hers. When the door opened, Amber dispensed with the usual amenities and got straight to the point. "Nora, I desperately need a favor, if you have some time to spare."

"Sure, what is it, honey?" The petite, pretty, middle-aged woman stepped aside so Amber and Melly could enter.

"Could you watch Melly for me for about twenty minutes or so? I've got something I need to do. Then I'll be right back."

"Of course. Is there anything else you need?"

"You're so sweet, Nora. But this is all I need, thanks." She placed the tote bag on the floor, and laid their jackets on top of them. "Mommy has to do one thing, then I'll be right back so we can go to the park." She kissed Melly's cheek.

Her child's face crinkled up with disappointment. "No, Mommy."

She pushed some stray tendrils of soft, dark hair out of Melly's eyes. "I promise, Sweetie, I won't be long."

"No . . ." Melly caught and clung to Amber's sleeve.

She couldn't waste time pacifying her daughter. She had to get rid of Dr. Hines first. "I'll be back as soon as I can," she said to Nora.

"Take all the time you need, Amber." The older woman tousled Melly's hair. "I'll be here all day."

Amber thanked God for this wonderful woman who had been there for her ever since she moved in. Of course, it helped immensely that Nora fell completely in love with Melly.

Amber grabbed her jacket and opened the door to leave.

"Mommy?" She could hear the tears in her baby's voice.

"I'll be right back, Sweet Pea."

Before walking out, she saw Nora take Melly's hand. "Guess what we're going to do until Mommy gets back? We're making cookies. Would you like to do that?"

Melly slowly turned her face away from Amber and nodded solemnly in answer to the woman's question.

Amber closed the door before she could change her mind and join her neighbor and her daughter in baking cookies.

Out in the hall, she took a moment to collect herself.

Placing a finger at the inner corner of each eye, she dabbed away the tears that threatened to seep out. Disappointing Melly tore her heart to pieces, but she'd be a complete basket case should any harm come to her little girl. This way was best.

Amber took a deep, cleansing breath, then headed outside.

* * *

Car keys in hand, Amber stepped out of the building and descended the steps. Dr. Hines still leaned against the side of his car, arms crossed over his chest, looking cocky. Oh, she would love to tell him off. But that would ruin everything. All the work she and Evan had done, so far would be for nothing. As would the hardship she'd endured in this so-called relationship with the good doctor.

Trying to look surprised, she said, "Al! You're still here."

He pushed away from the Lexus and stood straight. "By the time I got out here, I realized you seemed to be in a big hurry to get rid of me. I stood here imagining all sorts of reasons, but one stuck in my mind." He paused for a moment, his intense gaze impaling. "Amber, are you seeing anyone else besides me?"

An ironic laugh escaped her lips before she could stop it. Strange he should ask that now, while thoughts of last night remained fresh in her mind. Could he sense a difference in her? She hoped her answer would satisfy him.

"My situation is pretty much the same as when we first met. I told you I had been through some things recently and wasn't ready to get serious. I certainly wouldn't complicate matters with multiple relationships."

He didn't react with relief as she expected. Instead, he stared down at her, his expression closed, his thoughts undetectable.

At times, she felt completely at ease with Dr. Hines. But this wasn't one of those times. With a simple look, he could melt her confidence down as quickly as the sun can melt an ice cube.

She needed to get rid of him.

"Well, I, uh, have to leave." She gestured toward her minivan. "I'll see you at work tomorrow."

He gave a curt nod. "Okay. I'll walk you over to your car."

A master manipulator, he ensured she'd have to leave first. Amber knew he would follow her.

Lord, what do I do, now?

She'd drive over to her parents'.

The Odyssey wasn't far away, and it seemed ridiculous he should walk her there. As they approached, he took the keys from her and clicked the remote. She heard the locks pop open. Silently, Dr. Hines opened the driver-side door. Staring into her eyes, he lifted her onto the seat, each movement surreal. But his gaze didn't communicate tenderness. More like a warning, which sent a chill through her bones. He placed the keys in her hand, and roughly brushed a kiss against her lips. No smile. Nothing.

She got the point.

"I'll see you tomorrow," he said, his voice turning gruff.

With relief, Amber thanked God that Dr. Hines was so bent on his subtle control of her, he hadn't seen far enough into the Odyssey to notice Melly's car seat in the back.

Dr. Hines moved away from the minivan a few steps, nodded, and gave a brief wave. But he stood there, waiting, watching. She had no choice but to leave the parking lot. As she turned the key, Amber pasted a smile on her face. Waving, she slowly pulled out of the parking spot.

Before she could shift into drive, Dr. Hines headed to his car. She couldn't just sit there waiting for him to leave first, so she drove out of the lot. Maybe if she hurried, she could get well ahead of him and lose him in traffic. Her foot pressed harder on the gas pedal.

Keeping careful watch on the rearview mirror, Amber noticed the Lexus fall into the line of cars behind her. Shaking her head, she frowned. She'd have to drive to her parents' house after all. If they weren't home, she would let herself in with her key, and Adolf Hitler Hines could think what he wanted.

* * *

Amber pulled her minivan into her parents' extra long, extra wide driveway behind their twin Toyota Camrys. She exited her vehicle, resisting the urge to look around. The need to focus on staying calm and move at a slow pace took priority. Since Ma and Dad were at home, she only needed to pull open the screen door and push through the shiny, carved oak door.

"Ma? Dad?" she called, and they soon emerged from various directions.

"Amber, honey!" Ma stooped to kiss her cheek. "I didn't know you were coming today."

"Neither did I. Hi, Dad."

Her father also kissed her cheek. "Where's that granddaughter of mine?"

Amber decided to leave her jacket on and moved into the

cheerful, sunlit living room. "I had to leave her with Nora." She pushed herself onto the sofa under the huge picture window and peered through the open slats of the blinds without touching them. If Dr. Hines watched the house, he wouldn't be able to see her looking out.

"What? Why?" Ma asked, following her.

"What's going on, Amber?" Dad's voice had that protective, authoritative tone she always loved. It told her she needn't worry about a thing, and he'd always fix what needed fixing. Except now she was an adult entangled in a mess of her own making.

"After Melly's nap, we were supposed to go to the park. Dr. Hines showed up at my door, thinking we could do something spur-of the-moment. I was so afraid he'd see Melly, and didn't let him in. I told him I had plans and got rid of him. He must have sensed my skittishness, because when I looked out the window before we left the apartment, he was still out there."

Ma's face turned angry. "What nerve!"

Dad, the practical one, said, "So you took Melly to Nora's." He paused, then added, "He followed you here."

Amber nodded as she saw his black car slowly cruising past. Watched it come to a stop with Dr. Hines's face turned toward the driveway. A sudden weakness overtook her body. "There he is." She leaned against the sofa cushions, still watching the street through the window. Ma and Dad came over and stood against the couch, bending to see out. All three of them continued watching as, seemingly satisfied, Dr. Hines moved on.

Amber turned away from the window. "When I went outside, he asked me if I was seeing someone else."

Dad stood before her, hands in his pockets and rocking on his feet. "And how did you get out of that one? You *are* seeing Evan."

She couldn't believe her father thought along those lines at a time like this. She frowned and said, "I told him things were the same as they were on the day we met."

"That's still a lie, Amber." Ma crossed her arms over her chest. "You're seeing Evan."

"We went out once, Ma. Besides, he's my husband. One doesn't 'see' their husband."

"If you still think of him as your husband, then act like it."

"But Ma—"

"Forget that now." Dad glared from one to the other.

"This guy's getting suspicious. Amber, you've got to end this thing before it becomes dangerous."

"I told her doing this undercover stuff would get her in trouble some day. Practicing deceit always brings about consequences."

"Darla, please, let's stick to the immediate situation." Dad turned to Amber. "What are you going to do if he's still out there watching?"

She turned to the window again, knowing that just because she couldn't see him, didn't mean he wasn't still out there waiting somewhere. "I don't know, Dad. I had hoped if he saw me leave the apartment building, he'd be satisfied I was telling the truth."

He stood for a moment, looking thoughtful. "I have an idea. You and your mother go out to the car. If he sees you with an older woman, he'll naturally assume she's your mother and figure you couldn't be meeting another man."

In spite of the seriousness of the situation, Amber couldn't help smiling at the look Ma shot Dad when he referred to her as an "older woman."

"Drive over to the strip mall like you're spending the day shopping together. Go into that lingerie store—what's it called?—Bare Essentials. Believe me, he won't follow you in there."

Amber climbed off the sofa. "I don't think Ma should get involved."

"Of course I'll go, dear. Just let me get my purse." Ma glared at Dad in mock anger as she passed him. "And see if I don't come back with something that shatters your image of me as an 'older woman.'"

Dad smiled and shook his head.

As they left the house with Dad waving from the porch, Amber glanced up and down the street hoping she didn't look obvious.

"What's his car look like?" Ma asked as Amber backed out of the driveway.

"It's a black Lexus."

Ma pulled down the sun visor and peered into the mirror. "I hope you understand that I'm not trying to control you when I warn you about the dangers of taking on these covert investigations. It's just that I worry about you."

Amber glanced at the rearview mirror. "I know, Ma. But it's not like I don't know the hazards of the job." She reached over and patted her mother's hand. "Please don't worry. I'll be fine."

Sometimes, she wasn't so sure she believed that herself. Not that she feared the threat of danger, or even death, but the outcome of an investigation could affect more than the journalist. Now, with Melly to consider, perhaps this would be the last time Amber participated in such an operation.

A thought came to mind. She pulled the phone from her jacket pocket and handed it to her mother. "Could you find Nora's number in the directory and call her? When she answers I'll talk to her."

Ma initiated the call and handed the phone to Amber, who told her neighbor she'd be a bit longer than she first thought. As she spoke to the woman, Amber's eyes wandered to the rearview mirror again. This time she saw Dr. Hines's Lexus moving into line two cars behind hers. She ended the call and flipped closed the phone. "There he is."

"Where?" Ma's eyes shifted to the visor mirror.

"Two cars back."

"We'll see if your dad is right and he leaves once he sees where we're going."

Amber turned the minivan into the parking lot of the Towne Center and cruised by a half dozen stores before finding a spot close to the lingerie store. At this time on a Sunday afternoon, people swarmed the walkway of the large strip mall.

They exited the car and went into Bare Essentials. Amber had no need for, nor interest in any of the merchandise displayed. If she and Evan were still together, maybe . . .

While Amber kept watch on the storefront window, Ma perused the items arrayed on tables and hanging on racks. She pulled down a lacey set consisting of a soft pink bra and thong underwear. Holding it up for Amber to view, she said, "I bet this would make your dad reconsider his thinking of me as an 'older' lady."

Amber was taken aback. "Ma-a!" Her mother was a petite, attractive, middle-aged woman. Never before had Amber realized that the prospect of aging bothered her. Must be something new.

Even with all of the movement outside in the lot, Amber caught sight of Dr. Hines's car rolling slowly past the store. She could see his face turn briefly toward the window, but he did not stop. After he drove by, Amber stepped closer to the window, her eyes zoning in on the Lexus and its progress. She watched as it slightly sped up and exited the parking lot. Heaving a sigh of relief that had been stuck in her chest, she assumed he was satisfied.

Amber turned to tell her mother they could leave, but Ma stood in line at the cash register, holding a number of gauzy, soft-colored items in her arms.

Despite the gravity of her own situation, Amber couldn't resist a grin. She shook her head, and hoped she still had a mind to entice her husband at that stage of her life.

That thought stole her humor. After what transpired between her and Evan last night, would he still be her husband in twenty years?

CHAPTER 21

"Someone call 9-1-1!" Dr. Hines's voice rang throughout the clinic.

Amber froze. The box in her hand fell to the floor. She and Doug looked at each other for a split second before simultaneously racing for the wall phone. Having the advantage of longer legs, Doug got there first and punched in the emergency number.

Amber ran into the hall. Maggie rushed by, concern coloring her features. "What's going on?" Amber asked.

Already halfway up the hall, Maggie turned to answer. Her brows furrowed and her eyes held a panicked look. "Death during procedure." She turned into Dr. Hines office.

Amber followed and found Maggie standing at the desk with the phone receiver to her ear, punching in numbers. "Doug's already called."

Maggie took a deep breath. "Oh." She let the phone slide from her ear and placed it back on the hook. Sinking into Dr. Hines's chair, she leaned her head into her hands.

Amber went to stand beside Maggie, placing a hand on her shoulder. "What happened?"

"The patient most likely had an adverse reaction to the anesthesia."

They stayed there for a few moments without speaking, Amber unconsciously rubbing Maggie's arm in an effort to comfort her. The wail of a distant ambulance broke the silence, and crescendoed within a minute. The thud of large vehicle doors slamming shut and others being opened echoed in the tense silence. Amber heard the rattle and bounce of metal, like a cage, and her heartbeat soared. Ever since Ashley's death, the sound of stretcher legs unfolding and hitting the ground did that to her. Feet pounded in the reception area, then along the hall.

She couldn't help herself. Like the pull of metal to a magnet, she left the office and floated down the hall to the room the paramedics had just entered. A strong chemical odor she could not identify burned her nostrils. At the doorway, she stopped and watched. Dr. Hines and Rita stood off to the side, as the two attendants hovered over the patient, blocking Amber's view.

"She's gone," the female one said.

When the emergency service workers moved apart, Amber's breath caught in her throat at the sight of the woman on the table. The one whose signature she'd acquired for donating the fetus to research not more than forty minutes ago. Long locks of soft, wavy blond hair had escaped the surgical cap. Hair that looked exactly like Ashley's.

For one, long, tormenting moment, the woman on the table became her sister.

"No!" Amber's voice reverberated throughout the room, and surprised her as much as it must have the others. Four faces turned and stared down at her—the two paramedics, Rita, and Dr. Hines.

"What's the matter, Amber?" Dr. Hines's eyes showed concern.

"I—um, no—nothing." She backed out of the doorway. "Excuse me," she mumbled and raced down the hall.

In her office, Amber closed the door and climbed into the chair behind her desk. She plucked a tissue from the box sitting on its surface and dabbed moisture from her forehead, neck and above her lip. What happened back there? She must be losing her mind, thinking she saw Ashley on that table. This place was starting to get to her.

Dr. Hines burst through the office door without knocking and Amber nearly shot out of her chair like a human cannonball. Seriously, she had to pull herself together.

"Amber, are you okay? What's wrong?" He lowered his lengthy frame into one of the black fabric chairs by her desk.

After the incident with Dr. Hines on Sunday, Amber had managed to avoid him so far today. But because she'd created this situation out of her own weakness, here he sat, not three feet away, acting all concerned. She nodded and tried to smile, but failed. "I'm fine, Al."

"But why that little outburst?" His eyes were earnest, not filled with suspicion.

"I—I can't explain it. Seeing that woman lying there just brought me back to . . . well, it reminded me of someone whose death I witnessed some years ago. Someone I was very close to."

Dr. Hines stared at her for a moment. "You've never gotten over it." He paused, then, "Do you want to talk about it?"

Amber shook her head. "No. It's one thing to be reminded, but quite another to rehash it."

He stood up. "Okay, then." Tenderly caressing her cheek, he said, "Whenever you want to talk, I'm here."

Moments like this could almost make her forget the side of him she'd seen on Sunday when he'd become her predator.

Almost.

* * *

Later that day, Rita marched into Amber's office.

She stood over Amber's desk scowling, arms crossed over her chest. "What are you trying to do?"

Amber wanted to tell the nurse she shouldn't go barging into people's offices, but instead she said, "What do you mean?"

"You know perfectly well what I mean. You're trying every trick in the book to steal him away from me."

Poor Rita. Amber wished the woman *did* have Dr. Hines. "What trick? What are you talking about?"

Rita batted her eyelashes and turned her voice exaggeratingly sweet. "The 'I'm-so-fragile-please-take-care-of-me' routine. You know he has a soft heart, and you take advantage of it every chance you get."

Amber fought to control her temper and took a deep, calming breath. "Listen, Rita, I'm not trying to steal Dr. Hines. We're just friends, right now."

"Oh, come on, Missy! I wasn't born yesterday." Rita's eyes flickered over Amber from top to bottom. "I'm going to keep an eye on you. When I have enough of even the tiniest things that can be used against you, I'm going to Dr. Hines. I want you out of my way for good." She turned and strode out of the office.

Amber stared at the open doorway where Rita had just exited. The woman sure had it bad for the doctor. To see what women like Rita found so attractive in men like Dr. Hines, Amber only had to look to herself. When she was with him, he made her feel like no other woman existed. His charm mesmerized, and though his possessiveness bordered on stalking, oddly enough, he also made her feel wanted and secure.

And then he held that quality of danger that so many women find appealing . . .

CHAPTER 22

On Friday evening, Amber pulled out the black dress she'd declined to wear for her first date with Dr. Hines because of the low neckline. It really wasn't that bad, or she'd never have gotten it. Dr. Hines had asked her to accompany him to a charity event hosted by his sister, Jasmine, and for some reason the attire was to be only black and/or white.

As she stepped into the dress and shimmied it up over her shoulders, she thought that although tonight she'd be in the company of Philly's elite, she'd much rather be with Evan. If it hadn't been for their argument last week in Atlantic City.

God, please bring us together.

* * *

As Amber entered the ballroom of the Royal Hotel with Dr. Hines, all heads seemed to turn their way. While she had become used to stares because of her dwarfism, she suspected these people stared because she happened to be a dwarf on the arm of an average-sized man. A very tall average-sized man. Lifting her chin and straightening her spine, she ignored the boldness of the other guests and took in the sparkling atmosphere. Tables lined each side of the room, leaving an ample dance floor. Specks of light from the dimmed crystal chandelier that hung overhead dappled the glossy floor. Amber imagined that, when lit full force, the humongous thing cast a blinding light over the guests.

Jasmine Tate disengaged from a small group standing off to the side and, smiling, approached Amber and Dr. Hines. Her black sequined gown fit snug against her slender form and her light brown hair, which matched her brother's, was pulled back into a simple bun. On Jasmine, it looked to be the most elaborate of hairstyles.

"Hello, Albert." She hugged Dr. Hines and kissed his cheek.

"Jas, you remember Amber?"

She took Amber's hand in a stiff, cold handshake. "Of

course. Welcome to the Fifth Annual Charity Ball for Duchenne dystrophy." Her tone of voice matched her grip.

"It's a pleasure to be here."

Jasmine turned her attention to her brother. In an obvious snub, she took his arm and guided him toward a table at the front of the room, leaving Amber to trail along behind. Amber wondered what she ever did to Jasmine to deserve such treatment.

"Albert, how much longer will it be before you have enough specimens for me? My client is champing at the bit and threatening to go elsewhere."

What's this? Specimens? Is the doc's sis in on the business, too?

"Shouldn't be long, now, Jas. Another few weeks, at the most."

Jasmine seated them at her own table, then excused herself. "It's important to mingle and keep the colleagues and clients happy."

Dr. Hines made a dismissive gesture with his hand. "Sure. We'll talk later."

Amber watched Jasmine float away. The brother and sister looked so much alike, they could have been twins, but Amber knew Jasmine was a couple years older. "Your sister doesn't like me."

Dr. Hines showed no surprise by her statement. "It's not that. She's very protective of me. She'll tell me I need to get out more, or that I need companionship, but then when I introduce her to someone new, she acts standoffish toward that person. I think she just wants to make sure I'll be treated right."

"That's understandable, considering how close the two of you seem."

He nodded and fiddled with the silverware laid out in front of him.

She wanted to find out about the specimens Jasmine mentioned, but he might think she eavesdropped on their conversation. *So what.* "I couldn't help overhearing Jasmine talk to you about specimens. Is she somehow involved in medical research?"

He stared off, as if watching a scene from another time and place. "When my son died, I was devastated and became depressed. Jas ached for me. In order to give me purpose and get me out of my funk, she started these fundraisers. But first, she made me see how I could keep my son's memory alive through supporting the research."

He had successfully dodged her question. "Well, I think that's wonderful."

The music began to play, and the lights dimmed. Dr. Hines looked at Amber. "Why don't we dance?"

Amber glanced at the couples drifting onto the dance floor. They curled their arms around one another and swayed to the slow, whining music. She liked to dance, but not with such a tall partner. "No, thank you. We'd look ridiculous out there."

He looked over at the dancers, then shifted his eyes to hers. "You're right. How about if we try a fast number when the band plays one?"

She grinned. "You're on."

With each new song, the band picked up the tempo, and at the fourth one, Amber and Dr. Hines took to the floor. Although the guests dressed elegantly, all refinement was forgotten as they abandoned themselves to the funky beat of the seventies disco hit, *Get Down Tonight.* Dr. Hines hammed it up with a few exaggerated John Travolta moves from the movie, *Saturday Night Fever.* But when he got down to some serious dancing, she was not surprised that, with his long and lean frame, the doctor could move so gracefully. Although she could hold her own, Amber didn't think she looked as good as he did. As more and more people crowded onto the floor with each new song, Amber became overheated. Her tongue felt glued to the roof of her mouth. She stopped dancing. "Al, can we get something to drink?" She yelled.

The music vibrated so loudly, that Dr. Hines gestured that he couldn't hear her, so she mimed holding a drink and guzzling it down.

He nodded, took her hand, and led her out of the multitude.

For dinner, they had prime rib, which tasted okay, but didn't compare with the succulent Primal Steak and coconut shrimp she'd had at The Rainforest Café with Evan. Perhaps being with the one she loved rendered all aspects of that evening unforgettable.

Oh, why didn't she think of that before she kissed Dr. Hines?

* * *

Dr. Hines parked the car in front of Amber's apartment building and she knew he expected to be invited up. As he reached for the door handle, she laid a hand on his arm. "Don't

123

bother getting out, Al. I can see myself up."

He stared at her. "Will I ever get to spend the night?"

Amber met his eyes with a steady gaze. "Never. That's just not my way."

One corner of his mouth lifted into a half-smile. "Requires the old wedding band on the finger, first, eh?"

She pulled on the door handle. "That's right. And we're far from thinking along those terms, right now." She stepped out of the car.

Before she could push it closed, Dr. Hines called out her name. She peered back into the darkness of the vehicle. His expression serious, he said, "Don't be too sure."

Her mouth went dry. She had no immediate answer. "Good night, Al." She closed the door and hurried up to her apartment.

Once she'd changed into her nightclothes, Amber had an undeniable urge to talk to Evan. They hadn't had one of their late-night conversations in a long time, and she'd always enjoyed hearing his voice before drifting off to sleep. When they were still together, they'd get into bed at the end of a hard day and turn out the lights. Talking and laughing together in the dark helped to release the tensions of all that went on throughout the day. A soothing calmness would come over her that not even a sleeping pill could provide.

She cracked open the window and stood before it, taking in the cold night air. The heater was working overtime again. She'd ask maintenance to check it tomorrow. She climbed into bed, turned off the lamp, and plucked the phone from its base. As she pushed the number for Evan, she realized this was the latest she'd ever called. After the messy ending to their date last week, she didn't know if he'd even welcome her call.

But her desire to speak with him overwhelmed her.

"'Lo." His voice sounded heavy with sleep, and she imagined him lying there in the dark with his eyes closed and holding the receiver to his ear.

"Evan, I'm sorry to wake you."

"Amber?" He sounded more alert, now. "Is everything okay?"

"Yes. I just . . . I just . . ." What could she say? *I just wanted to hear your sweet voice?*

"Are you sure you're all right?" He sounded alarmed. "What do you need? I'll be right there."

She could hear fabric rustling, as if he were disentangling

himself from the bedclothes.

"No! Oh, Evan, I'm sorry. I didn't mean to make you think this was an emergency. I know it's late."

"Oh. What is it, then?" He sounded more relaxed, and she could see him lying back down and rearranging the covers. He must have gotten over their argument on Saturday night.

Ah, she'd just thought of an excuse for her call. "I just returned from the charity ball with Dr. Hines and wanted to talk about it. If it's not too late for you," she added.

"It's never too late. Call me anytime."

How would she ever bring herself to serve him those divorce papers when he treated her with such care? She rearranged her pillows to lie flat. "Thank you." She needed to get on with this before she started bawling. "The event took place at the Royal Hotel in Philly. Dr. Hines's sister, Jasmine, sponsored it for research on a cure for Duchenne dystrophy."

"Hold it. What's her last name?"

"Tate. Why?"

"Remember when I went to Philly to meet with one of the gifting companies? The owner of that company was Jasmine Tate, if I remember correctly. I don't know why, but it just came to me."

"Hmm. I should have noticed the name when I read your notes. Anyway, I overheard her mention something about specimens to him and a client who is waiting for them. I asked him about it."

"What'd he say?"

"He avoided giving me a direct answer. He just said she raised money to donate to the research for a cure for Duchenne dystrophy in honor of his son."

She heard his frustrated breath blow through the phone. "Seems you haven't yet earned his trust."

She understood how he felt. The longer it took her to get Dr. Hines to open up to her, the longer this investigation would take. They both wanted it to be over so they could get back to normalcy.

"I know. I didn't tell you about the day he dropped by my apartment unannounced. I had plans and wouldn't invite him in. He obviously didn't believe me, and I found him waiting outside when I left."

Evan tsked. "That was bold of him. What did you say to him?"

There was so much she had to leave out of the

explanation: that her plans were with Melly; how Dr. Hines lifted her into the car and kissed her. She hoped Evan didn't see the holes. "I asked why he was still here. You won't believe this, but he said I seemed in a hurry to get rid of him. He asked if I was seeing someone else."

"Whoa. The guy's perceptive. What'd you tell him?"

Amber yawned. "That things were pretty much the same as when I met him."

She heard squeaking, as if Evan shifted on his bed. "Did that satisfy him?"

"No." Well, here goes. She switched the phone to her other ear. "He followed me to my parents' house."

His sharp intake of breath sliced through the receiver. "Amber, I don't like it. He sounds wacko."

"I know, but everything's fine, now. It's like it never happened."

"Just be careful, Sweetheart."

Shivers ran up her arms at the endearment. "Don't worry, I will."

A short pause, then, "So, are you busy tomorrow?"

There were a million things she should do tomorrow. "Actually, no. Why?" As if she didn't know.

"Want to do something?"

Sure, she did. "I don't know, after what happened the last time . . . ."

"Come on. I thought we'd go bowling. I remember you used to love it."

She did, but she hadn't been bowling in years. Why not? Maybe then she would muster up the courage to hand him those divorce papers that she *didn't* want him to sign. "Okay, but I'm a little rusty."

"No problem, so am I. I'll pick you up at one."

"Why don't you let me pick *you* up, this time?" She could drop Melly at her parents' house first, and not have to worry that Evan might show up at her apartment early, finding Melly still there. Plus, her parents wouldn't have to do the running around.

"O-kay." He dragged the word out, as if unsure what to think. "I'll see you here at one, then."

"Great." She paused. "And I'm sorry that I woke you."

His voice deepened a notch. "Baby, you can wake me anytime."

After hanging up, Amber smiled into the darkness as she watched the shadows of tree branches dance on her ceiling in the reflection of a nearby street light.

CHAPTER 23

"I thought you said you were rusty," Evan said to Amber after her fourth strike.

She smiled at him. "I am. Normally, I would have double the amount of strikes, by now, and you know it." Having this casual fun felt good, for a change, and relaxed her. The Ball and Pins Bowling Lanes smelled of stale coffee, burgers, hotdogs and fries, but the place resembled heaven to Amber. Sure, those papers sat in her handbag, waiting to be given to Evan. Until then, she'd enjoy this time they had together, because it would end sooner or later.

Evan chuckled. "You're right. Whenever we bowled together, you beat me 99.9 percent of the time." He walked over to the rack and picked up his dark blue marbleized ball. Taking the bowler's stance, he pointed the ball, took several quick paces and released it into the lane. The ball rolled swiftly and knocked down nine pins.

Amber raised her arms straight up. "Woo-hoo!"

Evan walked over to the return and waited for his ball to appear on the rack. "What are you cheering for? I only knocked down nine pins."

"Nine's good." They'd always done that. Even though they played against one another, they'd cheer each other on. That was love, pure and simple. Right now, her love for Evan overflowed, like it used to when they were still together.

Oh, why hadn't she told Evan she was pregnant when they'd separated? And why didn't he change his mind about not having children in the first place? Feeling as she did about him now, how would she ever bring herself to serve him those papers? Maybe she *should* have let the lawyer take care of that through normal channels. But no. She thought if she did it herself, she could make sure the time was right; that Evan was in a good mood. She wanted to hand them to him at a time when he'd be more accepting. But who was she kidding? There would be no such time.

Deep down inside, Amber depended on the right time

never arriving. It provided an excuse for her to put off passing those papers to Evan. Her life hung in limbo. The kiss was obviously no longer an issue, but Melly's existence would be.

What a mess she'd made of everything. She sighed. Maybe she should wait awhile, see how things progressed with Evan. His feelings could change about having kids. Yes, that's what she would do.

"Your turn, Amber." Evan's voice seemed far away.

"Oh." She looked down the end of the alley, but new pins were already set up. Lost in her thoughts, she'd missed whether Evan had knocked down that last one. "I'm sorry, I got distracted. What happened?"

Evan shook his head. "What do you think happened? I got the last one, as usual." He motioned toward the lane. "Go take your turn."

Amber picked up her ball and brought it up close to her face, lining up the pins in her sights. She lowered her arm, ready to swing back, and—

"Amber, would it be okay if I went to church with you tomorrow?" Evan said from his seat behind her.

Caught off guard, the ball slipped from her fingers, landed on the hard wooden floor with a thunderous boom, and rolled backward. She chased after it to where it stopped at Evan's feet.

"Whoa! What gives?" He picked up the ball and handed it to her.

"Sorry. Got away from me," she said taking it from him.

What should she say? If he came to church with her, people would ask questions

Most of the people from church knew she'd been separated from Evan, but they'd never seen him. They'd wonder who this guy was, introduce themselves, chat with him. Her greatest concern, though, was Melly. Sure, she took her daughter to the nursery, but her church family knew Melly and loved her. They'd be certain to ask about or mention her in front of Evan.

Evan's voice pulled her out of cogitation. "You didn't answer my question."

Clawing the ball through the finger-holes in one hand, she rubbed the sweaty palm of the other against her slacks. "Um, I don't know. Don't you still go to Calvary?"

His expression turned sheepish and he lowered his head. "No. I stopped going after you left." He mumbled.

"Why?"

He started to speak, but an announcement that a set of

car keys were found crackled over the loudspeaker. Immediately after, he looked eagerly up at her. "So, can I?"

Evan looked like a puppy with those big, sad, dark eyes. Lord, help her, but she caved in. She puffed out a breath. "Okay. I guess it will be okay." Again, she'd have to pawn Melly off on her parents. It almost seemed as though she didn't have a child, lately.

Her deception was turning her into a bad mother.

After four games, they called it quits, and grabbed a bite for dinner right there at the bowling alley. On the way back to Evan's house, they chatted and laughed about anything and everything.

Amber pulled the minivan into the driveway to let Evan out.

"Good night, Amber. See you tomorrow morning."

What a let-down. She felt sure he'd ask her in, and she'd been prepared with an answer. She would have gone. She wanted to. "What?" she said, half-jokingly, "You're not going to ask me in?"

Evan turned in the seat, fully facing her. He gently tucked a lock of her hair behind her ear. "No." His beautiful, dark eyes held hers in a serious gaze. "The way I'm feeling, I'd probably take advantage of you, and I know you're dead-set against that."

He was wrong about that; the way she felt about him right now, she would have let him.

* * *

On the way home, Amber called her parents. There was a law in Jersey that said you couldn't use a cell phone while driving, unless you had the hands-free type. She had one, but by the time she plugged it in, her call could be over. She'd be quick.

"Ma, hi, it's me. How's Melly."

"Oh, you know Melly. She's so pleasant. We all had a wonderful time together."

"Terrific. Listen, can Melly stay the night and go to church with you and Dad tomorrow?"

"Sure, but what's up?"

Amber blew a frustrated breath into the phone. "I didn't know what to do. Evan asked if he could go to church with me. I said 'yes.'"

"Amber." Her mother spoke in that authoritative tone, after which she knew there'd be some sort of berating. "You've got to tell Evan about Melly so you can start spending more time with her, like a mother's supposed to."

That cut right to the core. She really had been neglecting her daughter.

She and Evan were getting along so well, though. They had taken their relationship to a new level, but it was bound to end soon. Whether she gave him the divorce papers or told him about Melly. She didn't want to speed up its progress.

* * *

Evan stepped out of the Mustang and straightened his suit jacket. He lifted his face toward the sky and took in a long, cleansing breath, savoring the mid-morning sun's warmth on his skin. He looked forward to attending this service with Amber.

"Thanks for letting me come with you," he said when she alighted from the passenger side. "As I said yesterday, I haven't been to church since we split, so I feel more comfortable having you with me my first time back."

She looked at him with wide eyes. "Why haven't you been to church all this time?" When she'd asked him at the bowling alley yesterday, an announcement over the PA system had interrupted them.

They reached the big double doors and he pulled one open, holding it for her. "I couldn't face people, knowing they would ask questions I didn't want to answer. Plus, I wasn't feeling much love toward a God that allowed our marriage to fall to pieces."

She didn't ask any more questions. He knew she understood and probably wanted to blame both God and Evan too. But he also knew that she understood they'd made their own choices along the way without consulting the Lord. They had created this mess themselves.

"Amber!" He heard a sweet female voice and turned to see an older woman rushing toward them, arms wide. "It's good to see you. How are you?" she said, bending to hug Amber.

"I'm doing well, Mrs. Gardner. And yourself?"

Mrs. Gardner waved a dismissive hand. "You know me, can't complain." She seemed to just notice Evan standing next to Amber, and smiled. "Oh. And who might this handsome young man be?"

Amber inclined her head in Evan's direction. "Mrs. Gardner, this is my . . . husband, Evan."

The woman stared at Evan in silence for a moment before a look of recognition flashed in her eyes. "Oh!" she burst out. "Well, hello. I'm so glad to meet you." She grinned as she pumped Evan's hand and shot Amber a knowing look. He guessed Amber must have confided in some of the people here about their marital situation.

Mrs. Gardner's gaze swept the floor. "Where's—"

Amber cut her off. "We have to go in, now, Mrs. Gardner. Will you excuse us?" Amber didn't wait for an answer, just pulled Evan by the hand into the sanctuary. He'd never seen her act so rude. What was up with her?

"Amber." He tugged back and she stopped walking. "That was a pretty blatant brush-off back there. That's not you. What's going on?"

Her eyes turned scared-rabbit. "Nothing's going on. Why would you ask?"

"Like I said, this isn't you."

She tugged at his sleeve. "C'mon, let's find a seat."

He hung back. "Wait a minute. You didn't answer my question."

Shifting her weight from one foot to the other, and wringing her hands, she said, "Yes, I did. Now let's find a seat before—"

"Amber, honey!" An attractive couple about the same age as he and Amber approached. The woman had red hair, and the man had blond. They held hands like high school sweethearts.

"Hi, Gail." Amber said. They hugged and kissed each other on the cheek. "I'm sorry I haven't called you, lately. Things have been crazy."

Gail rolled her eyes. "Believe me, I understand crazy."

"Gail and Brad, I'd like you to meet my husband, Evan."

Expressions of recognition and meaningful wide-eyed gazes were shot at Amber, again. Handshakes all around. Amber and Gail whispered quietly among themselves, while Brad made small-talk with Evan. He'd sure like to know what the women were saying, though. Suddenly, he felt as if all eyes in the place were glued to him, watching his every move. This would take some getting used to.

After a few more such introductions, they finally sat down. The pastor was a merry gentleman with a pleasant voice. His sermon immediately drew Evan in. After being away from the church for so long, Evan absorbed every word like rice absorbs water. Remembering how his and Amber's spiritual lives used to intertwine, his heart swelled with an indescribable joy. Slowly reaching over, he took Amber's hand, linking his fingers with hers. She glanced at him, smiling. By the left corner of her mouth was that dimple that used to appear only for him.

All was right with his world.

* * *

After a quick lunch at Taco Bell, Evan and Amber spent the remainder of the afternoon at a small local art gallery. At five-fifteen they arrived back at Amber's apartment. Although she wanted him to stay for a long while, Amber offered Evan only a quick cup of coffee. She needed to pick up Melly at her parents' house in a bit.

Evan followed Amber to the kitchen. She scooped grounds into the filter, added water to the machine and turned it on. Before she had a chance to move away from the counter, Evan stepped up and embraced her from behind.

"Evan—"

"Sshh. I just want to hold you for a moment. That's all, I promise."

While the dark, aromatic liquid sputtered and poured into the carafe, they stood silently. Amber curled her arm back around Evan's neck and nuzzled her face against him. Breathing deeply, her senses filled up with the scent of that *Attraction* cologne he always wore.

Remembering that this was how she caved in and ended up kissing Dr. Hines, shame and self-disgust took hold of her. Evan deserved better. She pulled free from his arms. "Um, the coffee's done."

Without a word, Evan sat down at the table while Amber filled their mugs. His gaze held a question which Amber was relieved he didn't ask.

After he finished drinking, Evan stood. "I'd better go." He seemed reluctant. "Thanks for letting me come along with you today."

Amber stood, too. "I'm glad you did." He came up close and tenderly cupped her chin. She desperately wanted to tilt her face up for the anticipated kiss. He stared into her eyes for a moment, then placed a light kiss on her forehead.

"I'll get my jacket," he said.

With mixed emotions, she almost wished he'd ignored her signals and *really* kissed her. "Okay. I'll be right out."

Evan headed into the living room and she carried the cups to the sink. Glancing at the dish drainer, she gasped at the sight of Melly's pink toddler cup she'd washed that morning.

If he'd noticed he would have said something. Wouldn't he?

* * *

Evan approached the sofa. Amber was holding something back from him, he could feel it. As he pulled his jacket out from under the pile, Amber's open handbag slipped to the floor, spilling its contents. Shaking his head, Evan laid his jacket down and bent to gather them up. Some papers that seemed to have been folded together had separated. He picked them up, spotted his name and examined them closer.

What he read there slammed his chest like a wrecking ball.

Amber had filed for divorce.

* * *

When Amber entered the living room and found Evan hunched over what appeared to be items from her purse, she knew something was wrong. "Evan?"

He looked up at her, and she saw what he held in his hands. *Oh, no.*

His eyes narrowed. "With the way things have been between us, I assumed you'd changed your mind about this."

She moved closer. "I did," she said, then closed her eyes and shook her head. "I mean, I'm not sure."

"I don't understand."

"After that kiss with Dr. Hines, I hated myself. Even though we're separated, I felt I had cheated on you. I wanted to make things right. To free you to move on, I filed for the divorce."

Evan stood and stuffed the papers into the pocket of his jacket. His wounded eyes searched hers. "What makes you think I want to be free to move on?"

He might want his freedom after he finds out he's a father and she never bothered to tell him. "I just thought it best."

"Without my having a say in it?"

What a stupid move. Why did she always try to take control of every situation, and never consult God? Disgusted with herself, she averted her eyes. "I'm sorry, Evan."

A huge sigh. "The hurt just keeps on coming with you, Amber."

He picked up his jacket and walked out of the apartment without a backward glance.

CHAPTER 24

Amber trudged out to the reception area to call the next patient. She'd cried all night, and on this crisp and sunny Monday morning, she felt like crap. At least there were no clouds or precipitation to make her feel worse.

"Kathy—"

The front door crashed open, and a tall, husky, youngish man bounded into the waiting room. "Nobody move!"

Amber froze. The man held a gun.

Everyone stopped what they were doing and a few seconds of pure silence reigned. Then gasps exploded and one woman screamed.

The man swung his gun in that general direction. "Shut up!"

This couldn't be happening. Heart pounding and knees shaking, her eyes panned the reception area to assess the situation. Present in the room were Carol, three women waiting for various procedures, the burly gunman, and herself. Doug, Rita, Dr. Hines, and a patient occupied several rooms at the back of the building. She hoped at least one of them heard the disturbance and would call the police.

Not knowing what would happen, Amber knew someone had to keep the situation from getting out of hand. Saying a quick, silent prayer, she took one wobbly step toward the man. "What can we do for you, sir?"

"I said don't move!" His features twisted in anguish. With both hands wrapped tightly around the weapon, he aimed the gun straight at her, breathing heavily.

Amber stepped back. "I'm sorry. I just thought I could help you in some way." She would have to be careful. This was no cool, calculated move on his part. She eyed the guy's shaky finger poised on the trigger. That gun could go off without his even meaning it to.

Beads of moisture dappled his forehead. "Where's my girlfriend? Tell me where she is and nobody gets hurt."

"Are you sure she's here?" She tried to appear calm, but

failed to keep the tremor out of her voice.

He slowly nodded. "Oh, yeah, I'm sure. I just want to get her out of here before it's too late."

Amber wished he'd chosen a better way to do it. "What's her name?"

"Maureen. Maureen Lawrence."

Great. Maureen Lawrence *was* here, and had already gone back to have her procedure. "I'll go and see if she's here." She turned to leave the room, hoping to get to the phone in her office and call the police.

"Hold it!"

She stopped and looked back at him. He now held the gun in one hand and swiped a finger across his nose with the other.

He looked indignant. "You must think I'm stupid."

Shaking her head, she said, "No, not at all."

"You think I'm gonna let you go back there, so you can call the cops?"

If keeping that woman from having the abortion would save everyone, she needed to get back there now. "What's your name?"

"That's none of your business, lady!" He waved the gun around.

"Look, I think Maureen is here. If you want to stop her from having the abortion, let me get her before the doctor begins."

He raised his eyebrows. She could see he realized she was right. "Yeah." He looked around. "Uh . . . wow."

A peace came over her, and her confidence grew. Like an inchworm, but still growing. "I know what you're thinking. If you let me go back, I could make that call to the police. If you come with me, someone up here could do it. But we've got to act fast."

As he thought about it, Dr. Hines walked into the reception area.

"What's going on out here?"

Scott shifted the gun in the doctor's direction. "Stop!"

Dr. Hines pulled up short and raised his hands in surrender. He didn't look surprised to see the gun, so Amber knew he'd heard at least some of what had already transpired.

Dr. Hines's expression softened. "What can I do for you?"

The gunman's eyes scanned the doctor who was clad in a green gown and cap. "You the doctor?"

"Yes, I am."

"Where's Maureen?"

"You mean Maureen Lawrence?"

"Yeah, that's her. That's my girlfriend."

Dr. Hines pointed behind him with a thumb. "She's back there in a room. I've just administered anesthesia."

The gunman started to walk toward the back. "I'm going to take her home."

Hines blocked his path. "Whoa, hold on. You can't go back there."

"This gun says I can." He waved it in Dr. Hines's face.

"Look, son—"

"I'm not your son! My father would never stoop to do what you're doing."

Placing a hand lightly on the man's shoulder, Dr. Hines advanced a few steps. It seemed as though he tried to guide the young man back toward the door. "I'm sorry. What can I call you, then?"

His eyes narrowed. "Nothing." He shrugged the doctor's hand away. "You're not fit to say my name."

Dr. Hines flinched at that but recovered nicely. "All right, then, *sir*, I'm sure you understand that I can't release the patient to you."

"It doesn't matter what you say. I've got the upper hand, don't you think?"

Dr. Hines looked very calm as he took in the weapon aimed at his chest. "Yes, that's true. But that's not the point. I have a duty to protect my patients. I don't know what your relationship is to Ms. Lawrence, nor do I know if she'd even want to go anywhere with you. Something else you need to consider is that you could be charged with kidnapping if you took her out of here while she's under anesthesia, which was administered with her consent."

The young man seemed to consider this.

Dr. Hines went on. "Why don't you go home? We won't complete the procedure, and we'll have her call you when she awakens."

He frowned at the doctor. "As if I'd believe that. I have a better idea. We'll all wait right here until she wakes up. Then she's leaving with me."

"All right. Then you won't mind if I have a seat while we wait." Dr. Hines sat down in one of the chairs. "It could be awhile."

"Wait. You got anybody else in the back? I mean, you got to have a nurse, or somebody helping you." He rolled his eyes, as if realizing he should have thought of this before.

Dr. Hines did not answer immediately. Amber could tell he considered whether to tell the truth. "I do have a nurse back there."

"Then holler back to her to let us know when Maureen wakes up. But tell her not to do anything stupid, like call the cops while we wait."

Dr. Hines stood up. "I can buzz her from the desk, here." He walked over to Carol's desk. Carol handed him the receiver to her phone, then pressed a button. "Rita, please let us know when Ms. Lawrence comes off the anesthesia."

"Don't forget to tell her not to call the cops while she's back there, or someone gets hurt."

The doctor nodded, then spoke into the phone. "Don't call the police, or he'll hurt someone." A pause. "Yes, I know. Thank you." He hung up the phone.

Amber knew Rita had told the doctor she or Doug had already made the call. "Okay, now we wait." The gunman waved the weapon at a chair. "Sit down." He turned to Amber. "You, too."

Before either of them could move, the phone at Carol's desk rang. Amber jumped at the loud jangle. Some other people did, too, while others gasped. Carol looked at the man. "Don't answer it," he said to her. "You got voicemail?"

"Yes," she said.

"Good. It should stop after several rings."

Carol nodded, her eyes huge and solemn.

He quietly waited it out. The ringing stopped. And started again, almost immediately. He patiently stared at the phone. It stopped.

"Okay—"

The ringing started again.

"Aarrgh! What's going on here?"

"This is a place of business," Dr. Hines said. "We get calls all day."

The gunman twisted his face into a mixed expression of irony and annoyance. "I know that."

Again, the phone rang several times, then stopped.

There was a pattern here, Amber noticed. It seemed that as soon as voicemail picked up, whoever called would hang up and redial. Dare she hope that someone knew their situation and they would be rescued soon?

"That thing is driving me nuts." The man strode over to the desk. "Move," he commanded Carol, who sprang from the chair and scooted out of his way. He reached behind the phone, grasped the wire, and yanked. "There. That's better."

This was not better. Amber felt more isolated, now. Like the world outside these walls didn't exist.

Another phone in the office rang. Then another and another. Soon every phone in the center trilled at different levels, creating a cacophony of notes that sliced through the brain. Most everyone had their hands up to their ears. But the man couldn't do that. If he did, he wouldn't be able to keep his gun trained on everyone.

"All right, I can't stand it anymore!" The gunman turned to Amber. "You. Put that wire back in and answer it. Just take a message. No funny stuff."

She went over to the desk on shaky legs, did as he told her, then picked up. "Cedarview Women's Center."

"This is Corporal Rob Stanton of the Cedarview Special Response Team," the voice on the phone said. A sigh of relief escaped her lips. "We've been told you have a hostage situation going on. Can you tell us if there have been any casualties?

She tried to keep her voice low. "No. No casualties."

"So everyone is safe, so far."

"Yes."

"Good. Do you know his name?"

"No."

"All right, let me talk to him."

Surprised that they'd want the man to know they were already involved, Amber held the phone out to the gunman. "It's the police. They want to talk to you."

He threw her an incredulous look. "What? I don't want to talk to no cops. And why are they calling? Who told them I was here?"

She didn't know what to do. If he told her to hang up, they'd lose contact with their only hope. "I don't know any of that. All I know is he asked to talk to you, so he can find out what you want."

"Just tell them no one will get hurt if I can only get my girl out of here where we can talk," he ordered. "I gotta keep an eye on things here."

Amber complied, happy to keep them on the line.

"Has he said if there's anything else he wants?"

"That's it, so far," she murmured into the mouthpiece.

"Nothing else?" He sounded surprised.

"He hasn't mentioned anything else." These questions annoyed her. Why didn't they just burst in here and be done with it?

The young man glanced her way. "Don't be having no conversation with them," he called. "Hang up, now."

And lose our only hope of being rescued? No way. "They want to know if there's anything else you want, besides your girlfriend."

He glanced at her again, looking irritated. "All I want is Maureen. Now hang up, lady."

"You'd better go so you don't make him angry," Corporal Stanton said.

What? That's it? "Aren't you going to do something?" she whispered.

He expelled a deep breath into the phone. "Just stay calm. We're doing everything we can. We have several squad cars at the site, now."

"Lady, I mean it. If you don't hang up now, I'm gonna come over there and make you," the gunman yelled. He started toward her.

"Look, we're not breaking communication. We're staying on the line. Even if you hang up, we'll still be here. Try to keep the phone off the hook so we can hear what's going on. If it gets—"

"I've got to go," she said quickly.

The man ripped the phone from her ear and slammed it on the hook. "I told you to hang up!"

Panic coursed through her for a few seconds. Would he shoot her now? Oh, God, no. What would happen to Melly? She remembered Stanton said they'd keep the connection. Amber placed her hand on the desk, very close to the phone, to push herself off the chair. As she did so, she pretended to accidentally bump the receiver off the hook. She walked away hoping Carol wouldn't go back to sit there and hang it up.

* * *

Nick Russo poked his head into Evan's office. "Thought you might like to know there's a hostage situation at the women's center."

Evan sprang from his chair. "What! Are you sure?"

Nick clipped his press card to his jacket. "Yep, just got the tip a few minutes ago. I'm headed there, now. Want a lift?"

He was already at the door. "Yeah." He'd never be able to drive himself.

God, keep Amber safe.

CHAPTER 25

Amber watched as Rita entered the reception area and whispered into Dr. Hines's ear.

"What's going on?" the gunman said.

Dr. Hines turned to look at him. "Maureen's come to."

"About time. Where is she?"

"She doesn't want to see you," Dr. Hines told him.

"Why not?"

"She's afraid of you."

An expression of complete surprise came over him. "Why is she afraid? I've never done anything to hurt her."

Dr. Hines crossed his arms. "Son, with all due respect, you *are* standing here with a gun aimed at all these innocent people."

The man looked stumped. "Uh, um." He looked around, as if trying to figure out what to do. Trembling, he waved the gun around. "I guess I'll just have to go back there and talk to her, and you're all coming with me."

Dr. Hines looked at him in astonishment. "That's ludicrous." He swept his arm toward the entire waiting area. "Look, you haven't hurt anyone, yet, and you don't want to. Let these people go and everything will be all right. You don't want an audience listening in when you talk to your girl. You want to speak to Maureen in private."

The gunman seemed to be considering this when a female voice called out from another room, "Don't be putting words in my mouth, Doctor. I'm not going to talk to him!"

Dr. Hines made a face, as if to say "How stupid can she be?"

The man frowned. "Maureen! Come on out here so we can talk. I won't hurt you. I won't hurt anybody."

Silence.

"Maureen! I love you, baby. There's no reason to be afraid."

In any other situation, Amber would have been touched by his declaration.

"If I come out, you'll keep me from having this abortion," Maureen yelled.

"Why don't we just talk about it?"

"We already tried that, Scott. You have a one-track mind."

Now Amber and the rest of them knew his name.

Scott fisted his free hand and tapped his forehead. "Maureen, this is your last chance. You better come out here, now!"

"Or what?" came her defiant voice.

Scott looked around the room until his eyes rested on Amber. She watched, rooted to the spot, as he strode toward her, determination stamped on his face. He wrapped an arm around her midsection and swept her up. "I got a hostage, Maureen. I have my pistol pointed at this little lady's head, right now."

The metal from the gun he pressed against her temple felt like ice.

* * *

Evan and Nick stood outside The Cedarview Women's Center among other reporters who looked eager for a story. Some worked for newspapers; some had shown up with camera crews. As for Evan, he just wanted to see that his wife was safe. When they'd arrived, they found no evidence of negotiations taking place. No flashing lights, no one speaking through a bullhorn, offering the perpetrator a deal. The police simply milled around, as if waiting. But for what? Why weren't they doing anything? If someone didn't tell him what was going on Evan would storm the place himself.

He stared hard at the large windows, hoping to get a glimpse of Amber inside. But the partially opened blinds showed nothing through the minimal spaces between their slats. He couldn't bear it if he lost her this way. If only he hadn't walked out on her the other day. Sure, he'd been hurt that Amber had filed for divorce after that kiss with Hines, but she did say she was trying to make things right. A twisted solution to the problem, in his eyes, but he could see where she came from. The guilt had undoubtedly gotten her to the point that she beat herself up over it, again and again.

As soon as she got out of there, he'd tell her that none of that mattered. He'd hold her and never let her go. He'd—

He'd call his friend, Uriah Washington, at the police station, that's what he'd do. He took out his cell phone and dialed.

"Detective Washington, here."

"Uriah? Evan. What's going on with The Women's Center? You guys working on it?"

"There's not a whole lot we can do, right now, Ev. The guy just wants to talk his girlfriend out of an abortion and take her out of there. We're waiting it out, for now."

"What if he starts shooting?" He tried not to picture this scenario.

"Then the tactics change."

Evan rubbed the back of his neck. "Why can't you change the tactics now?" Without waiting for Uriah to answer, he lowered his voice. "Uriah, my wife is in there."

"What's she doing up in there, man?" His voice became screechy.

"What do you think?" Evan snapped. "She's a reporter."

Washington sighed. "Ev, I really wish I could help, but I can't discuss this with you any further. I've got to go. I'll keep you posted." He hung up.

Evan flipped the phone closed.

Nick turned to him. "Anything?"

"They can't do anything because all the guy wants is to stop his girlfriend from having an abortion."

Nick shook his head. "Doesn't that beat all?"

Evan eyed the building again. "Yeah." Maybe there was something he could do himself.

* * *

"Come out here, now, Maureen, or I'll start shooting! Starting with this little lady I got right here. I'm sure you wouldn't want anyone killed because of you."

Amber's heart pounded, and her ribs hurt where Scott's arm squeezed them. All she could think about was Melly. If something happened to her, her little girl would grow up without a mother. *And* a father. Evan wouldn't want Melly. He'd told her as much on their date in Atlantic City. Of course, he didn't know they were talking about Melly, specifically. And although her parents would gladly raise their granddaughter, it wouldn't be the same.

Amber knew she needed to do something. But what? Talk to this angry, scared and frustrated guy? Not a good recipe for a discussion, but she could think of nothing better. She closed her eyes and breathed a quick, silent prayer.

He held her against him so that she faced out. Turning her head, she spoke over her shoulder. "Scott, I know you didn't mean for things to go this far."

"Yeah, well, now I've got to deal with it." His breath seared her cheek and its sour odor gagged her.

"Do you really think this is the best way?"

He wiped his nose on his shirt sleeve, the gun barely missing her head. "Of course not! But it's the only way available to me, right now."

"No. You're a smart man. I'm sure you can come up with a better way."

"Shut up! I can't think with you yammering at me."

Dr. Hines stepped forward. "Look, let this woman go. Take me instead."

Amber snapped her head up and stared at Dr. Hines. He had offered to lay down his life for her. She was touched, but couldn't let him do such a thing. "Don't, Al—"

"Step back, doctor." Scott aimed the gun directly at Dr. Hines's forehead.

The doctor glared at Scott, but didn't move.

"Al, please do as he says." She surprised herself with the whimper.

"Quiet, Amber." Dr. Hines's look said he expected her obedience.

She felt Scott brace himself. "Don't think I won't shoot you."

He cocked the gun.

CHAPTER 26

Amber had never seen Dr. Hines so flustered.

"Don't do this. You're making a big mistake. Let her go." Dr. Hines's stance indicated he'd pounce in a millisecond, if need be.

"Seems this little lady's mighty important to you." Scott's voice taunted. Amber began to slip from his grasp, and he hitched her up, so that his arm held her across the pelvis. The shift caused difficulty in balancing her upper body. After a minute or two, her back muscles weakened so that she had to sag over Scott's arm, feeling like an unused coat.

Scott tightened his hold. "Oomph." What did he think she was, a rag doll? She grabbed the bottom of Scott's jacket for extra support, and lifted her head to look at Dr. Hines. A ghostly pallor covered his face. His eyes, as they met hers, pleaded with her to hang on. She had no intention of letting go. Physically or figuratively.

The doctor raked a hand through his hair. "Look, if you let her go, I'll cooperate with you. Do whatever you want." He stretched his arm out and pointed toward the rooms down the hall. "Matter of fact, I'll persuade Maureen to come out here, right now."

"You would do that, doctor?" Scott said. He paused for a moment. "Tell you what. You go and bring Maureen out here and this one's all yours."

Dr. Hines gave one quick nod and disappeared from Amber's view. In a moment, loud voices could be heard. It didn't sound good.

Amber tried to lift her head and look up at Scott. "Scott, try to be gentle with Maureen. You need her to trust you."

He moved Amber back to an upright position, like one holds a baby on the hip.

"Oh, thank God," she moaned.

"You're lucky I don't do worse. None of you people here deserve to live."

"I understand how you feel, but you can't go around

taking matters into your own hands."

"I have a right to my own child. And how can you say you understand how I feel when you work in a place like this?" He shook his head. "I oughtta blow this place up."

"That wouldn't solve a thing. There are clinics like this all over the country."

"Yeah, well—"

Before he could finish his sentence, Dr. Hines returned to the reception area, dragging Maureen by the arm. She wore a paper exam gown held closed with a matching belt.

"You're hurting me! Let go!" Maureen pulled herself free from Dr. Hines's grasp and rubbed the bruised area. She looked at Scott. "Are you crazy? What are you trying to do?"

"Didn't you think I was serious when I said I didn't believe in abortion?"

"Of course I did, but this is *my* body. Nobody has a right to tell me what I can or can't do with it."

"We're not talking about just you anymore, Maureen. That's my child you're carrying."

Dr. Hines cleared his throat. "Excuse me, Scott, but you promised to let Ms. Blake go if I got Maureen out here."

Scott looked at the doctor with disdain. "I lied." He waved the gun in the direction of the chairs lining the wall. "Now sit yourself down over there, *Doctor*, and I'll release her when I'm ready."

Dr. Hines frowned. "You lied already. How do I know you're not lying again?"

He pointed the weapon at Dr. Hines. "You don't, but I'm the one with the gun."

Dr. Hines pressed his lips into a thin line.

Amber could see he hated having to acquiesce, always wanting to be the one in control. *Please keep him from being so stubborn, this time*, she prayed.

Finally, Dr. Hines sat down.

Maureen looked at Amber, held by Scott and hanging there between them. "Put this woman down, Scott. Then we can talk."

"I can't. I may still need her. Let's just get talkin'."

She crossed her arms. "What is it you have to say that you haven't already?"

Amber felt his body shudder with intensity. His sigh seemed to rise from deep within. "Baby, please, don't kill our child. I love it without having even seen it yet. That's because it's a part of you. It's part of both of us."

Amber saw tears spring to Maureen's eyes. Heck, her own eyes had filled up. She felt like an eavesdropper on a very intimate conversation.

Maureen sniffed and swiped at her nose. "I'm not ready to be a mother. I want to finish college first, start my career."

"You can still do that. I'm not going anywhere. I'm right here. I'll help all I can." A smile lit up his face. "We can get married. Be a real family."

Maureen hung her head, lifted an end of her belt, and wiped the wetness from her cheeks. "Oh, Scott, that's sweet, but I don't want to get married yet." Lifting her head, she looked into his eyes. "Please understand."

"All right, then, we don't have to." Amber could hear the disappointment in his voice. "But we can still raise it together."

So touching. She couldn't understand how Maureen could keep from giving in. How many men were willing to take responsibility for their illegitimate child?

She cringed. Here she was rooting for the bad guy. He'd broken the law, and for that he'd probably pay. But she could say he'd done it for all the right reasons. She looked around at the others in the room. No one seemed afraid anymore. They were on the edge of their seats, engrossed, as if this were a live soap opera playing out before them. The quietness seemed to suspend them all in time.

"I don't want a child, right now," Maureen said.

"I know, but I'll take care of him or her. You won't have to do a thing, if you don't want to."

Maureen sighed and put a hand up to her forehead. She moved to one of the chairs and lowered herself into it. Shaking her head, she said, "I don't know, Scott. That would be kind of weird. It would have to live with you, and when I'm over there"— she looked up at him—"what? I ignore it? And what if things don't work out between us? What happens then?"

He was silent for a moment. "You could grant me full legal custody. If we break up, I'll raise the kid myself."

Maureen shook her head. "What if you go to jail after this stunt?"

Amber slipped again and he hitched her back up. He had to be tired of holding her. "We'll work something out. My mom will help in all this. I know she will."

Maureen nodded, as if she knew that was true, too. "Okay. You win. I just hope I'm not making a mistake." She looked down at the weapon he still held. "Now will you put that thing down and let this poor woman go?"

He looked at the object in his hand as if he'd forgotten it was there. "Oh. Yeah." He loped over to Carol's desk and laid the gun down. Finally, he set Amber down on shaky legs and she almost fell. Scott looked at Maureen. "Will you go outside with me?"

Maureen nodded, tears running a trail down her cheeks.

Dr. Hines sprang up. "Wait. Rita, will you go get this young lady's things?" The nurse hurried down the hall and returned with some clothing and a handbag. Dr. Hines went to the door and carefully opened it. A collective "click" of triggers being cocked rang out from the guns of the waiting policemen. Amber remembered Officer Stanton saying they were there, watching and waiting.

"Please, don't shoot! They're coming out," Dr. Hines shouted from the doorway. He turned and nodded to Scott, who had his arm around Maureen.

Together, the couple solemnly went through the door. Dr. Hines closed it against the chaos that suddenly broke loose.

Dr. Hines swiftly moved toward Amber, scooped her up into his arms, and buried his face in her hair. Astonished, she didn't know what to do. Over the doctor's shoulder, she could see the shock on Rita's face, just as it must have been on her own, as he carried her directly to his office. The door slammed shut behind him, and he sat in the chair behind his desk, cradling her, not saying a word.

Amber realized now that she'd been trembling. "Doc? You okay?"

He pulled away and looked at her. "Me? You're worried about me?" He pulled her back against him. "Oh, little one, you amaze me. When that guy grabbed you, I thought I'd lose it." Again, he pulled away to look at her. "But you . . . you held yourself together through the whole thing." He hugged her again. "I was afraid I'd lose you," he whispered.

This unexpected reaction took her aback, and left her at a loss for words. She squirmed free of his grasp and stood. The arms she longed to have holding her at this moment were Evan's and she felt guilty that she couldn't be more receptive to Dr. Hines's declarations.

She wondered if Evan knew what went on. After the way he had left her apartment yesterday, did he even care? She wanted to leave this place and run to him.

But would he welcome her?

* * *

The crowd had dispersed, and Evan stood staring at the red brick building. Nick found out that Amber had been held at gunpoint. The thought of how close he came to losing her for good made him ill. Throughout the ordeal, he had itched to burst in, rescue her, and carry her out like a knight in shining armor. But he couldn't, of course. And he couldn't even go in to comfort her now.

He knew there were no casualties. The guy hadn't even fired the gun. But Amber had to have been scared, and he couldn't do a thing about it. The fault for this whole thing fell on him. If he hadn't asked her to team up with him, she would never have been caught in the middle of such a dangerous incident.

"You ready, Evan?" Nick called from beside his car.

He turned and started walking. "Yeah, I'm ready."

He stared at the center as they drove off. Nick had gotten some pretty good interviews. He talked to a couple of Dr. Hines's patients, a staff member, and Maureen Lawrence, the gunman's girlfriend. Seemed the whole situation had a happy ending, of sorts. But neither Nick nor Evan had gotten a glimpse of Amber or the doctor.

He didn't know what to make of that.

CHAPTER 27

The entrances to her folks' home were rarely locked during the day. Amber trudged up the front steps and pushed through the door. The warmth distinctive to this house immediately wrapped itself around her, and she could feel some of her tension ebb away.

She hung her purse and jacket on the closet doorknob as she passed and entered the living room.

"Ben?" her mother called from some other room.

Amber climbed onto the sofa and curled herself into a corner. "No, Ma, it's me."

"Amber? Oh, I'm so glad you're here." Ma appeared in the living room, wiping her hands on a dish towel. She pressed a hand to her chest, as she perched on the arm of a chair. "We heard about what happened on the news and were so worried. Are you okay?"

"I'm fine, but Dr. Hines decided to close early so we could all recuperate. He said we could even take tomorrow off, if we need to. I just might do that." She didn't mention that he'd told her especially to stay home tomorrow, as she wasn't sure Ma and Dad knew she had been as involved as she was. If they didn't know, she wasn't telling them. Why give them more reason to worry?

"Where's Dad and Melly?"

"Oh, they went for a walk. Your dad said being out in the brisk air would help calm him after what happened." She paused. "Amber, when is this going to be over? Things seem to be getting more and more dangerous."

"Soon, I hope, Ma."

Ma threw the dish towel onto the couch. "That's no answer."

"I know. I'm sorry, but I've got to see it through." Amber looked point-blank into her mother's eyes. "If you'd made such a commitment, you'd follow through, wouldn't you?"

Ma looked away. Her eyes swung back to Amber's. "I wouldn't have made such a commitment knowing I had a child to consider."

Amber blew out a frustrated sigh. "Okay, I made a mistake, but now I have to live with it. I'm hoping it won't take much longer." She adjusted herself on the cushions. "Do you mind if I just rest here until Dad and Melly get back?"

"Sure, you go ahead."

She closed her eyes and smiled when she felt Ma kiss her forehead and cover her with a throw blanket from a basket next to the sofa.

* * *

Evan could wait no longer. He figured he'd give Amber some time to deal with fallout over what happened earlier that day, but an hour was as far as he could go. He wanted to talk to her no matter what had happened between them on Sunday. He wanted to talk to her *now*.

He pushed the speed dial for Amber's cell phone.

"Hello?" She sounded worn out.

"Hey, kiddo. How're you doing?"

"Evan?" Her voice perked up and she sounded surprised.

"Yeah, who'd you think?"

A pause. "I . . . didn't think you'd want to talk to me."

He grabbed the remote in front of him on the desk and hit the mute button. "Of course I want to talk to you."

"I guess you heard what happened."

"Yeah. I was there for part of it."

"Really? You were there?"

Didn't she know him anymore? Did she think he was some callous jerk? "Really. I wanted to go in there myself and rescue you."

"How sweet." Her voice had changed, sounding more intimate.

"So are you okay? Want me to come keep you company for awhile?"

"I'm at my parents' house. Just taking a nap, but I'm staying the night."

"A nap? I'm sorry, did I wake you?"

"Don't worry about it. You know, I'd like it if we could meet for breakfast tomorrow."

"Breakfast? Won't you be going to the center?"

"Dr. Hines gave me the day off. So how about it?"

Rubbing his finger behind his ear, he thought about it. He wanted to do more than that. "How about I *cook* you breakfast? Your favorite, Belgian waffles?"

"Mmm. I remember when I'd wake up on my birthday each year to the smell of those things floating upstairs to our bedroom. Then you'd put them on a tray with strawberries and whipped cream and serve me in bed."

He pulled in a slow, deep breath. "Yeah, I remember, too." He hoped she couldn't tell how that particular memory got to him. She couldn't know that on her last two birthdays, he'd made those waffles, wishing she were there to eat them. He'd ended up throwing them down the garbage disposal. But he'd made them.

"Evan?"

The sound of her lovely voice shook him out of the past. "Yeah?"

"I'd love to come have Belgian waffles. Even if it isn't my birthday."

"Terrific. See you at eight."

Now if only he could serve them to her in bed.

* * *

Amber sat at the table in Evan's kitchen and swallowed the last bite of waffle. "That was delicious, Evan. Thank you so much for doing this. It's been—"

"Two years, nine months, one week, five days."

She stared at him, impressed. "Well, I see you've done the math, but I was only going to say it's been a long time since I've had your Belgian waffles."

He covered her hand with his and looked deeply into her eyes. "Your birthday comes up again in a couple months. I'd love it if I could also make them for you then."

Her heart melted at his sweetness. "I'd love that, too."

His gaze resembled that of a little boy's. "Then do you think there's a chance we'll be together by then?"

How could she answer that? She'd love to tell him she hoped and prayed for that, but things between them were still precarious. She could tell him right now about Melly, if she wanted to, but she feared losing what little headway they'd made. She'd thought about this a lot, lately. The best thing to do would be to take things slow, wait until after this business with Dr. Hines ended, then sit down together and have a long talk. Hopefully, by then, they would have torn down some of the other obstacles they'd been dealing with.

"Evan, I think that, at least until we're finished with this story, we should just take one day at a time. Don't you agree?"

He picked up his fork and poked at miniscule pieces of

waffle in his dish. "I'm not sure if it's right, but if that's what you want, then that's what we'll do."

She flashed him a smile. "Thank you."

* * *

That night, after Melly had gone to sleep, Amber lay soaking in a bubble bath. One last delicious chance to unwind before returning to the center tomorrow.

She and Evan had enjoyed a wonderful morning together over the delectable breakfast he'd made, talking and laughing without the burden of "the story" looming over them. That proverb in the Bible turned out to be true: A merry heart really *did* do good like medicine. Afterward, she'd spent a much longed for and needed afternoon with Melly.

The phone rang. Evan? She hoped so.

Amber reached up to wipe her hand on a towel hanging on a bar above her head, then grabbed the phone off the edge of the tub. She checked the caller ID. A number hadn't registered.

"Hello?"

Silence.

"Hello? Anybody there?"

Still silence, but she could hear slight breathing.

She frowned.

"Evan is that you pulling one of your crazy stunts?"

Still no answer. She shrugged and pushed the off button. Probably some kid making random crank calls.

Time to get out of the tub and turn in for a good night's rest. She wanted to be totally refreshed for her work at the clinic tomorrow. She dried off, donned a robe, let the water out of the tub and went to her bedroom.

The phone rang again. This time the caller ID showed Dr. Hines's number. Could he have been the one who called before?

"Hi, Al."

"How are you feeling?"

She quickly threw a nightshirt over her head. "I'm doing okay. I was just ready to turn in so I'll be well rested for work tomorrow."

"Are you certain you can make it.? If you need another day, Rita can cover for you."

She didn't want to slow down the progress of this story one more day than was necessary. "Nope, I'm good."

"That's the spirit. Oh, and on Saturday, I'd like us to spend a quiet evening at my place. We need to talk, and I don't want any distractions. That okay with you?"

She hesitated. Just what did they need to talk about? "Sure."

"Good. See you tomorrow."

"Okay." A brief thought flickered in her mind. "Oh, Al?"

"Yes?"

"Did you try to call me a few minutes ago?"

"No, why?"

She started on her way back to the bathroom. "The phone rang, but I couldn't hear anything on the other end." She climbed onto a step stool and pulled her toothbrush from the holder mounted above the sink.

"Wasn't me."

Holding the phone between her ear and shoulder, she reached into the medicine cabinet for the toothpaste. "Okay. I just thought it could have been one of those calls where the caller can hear you, but you can't hear them, and then you have to re-do the whole thing."

"Nope. Still wasn't me."

"Okay. See you in the morning."

Amber pushed the disconnect, put the phone down, and began brushing her teeth. Now what was so serious that he needed to speak to her alone on Saturday? She stopped brushing.

At his place.

Alone.

Oy.

CHAPTER 28

Amber turned the minivan onto Park Drive, the street where Dr. Hines's home was located. According to his directions, she needed to go another two blocks before looking for his house.

Her cell phone rang. She dug into her purse for it and tried glancing at the screen to see who it might be. The number wasn't available. Using the hands-free adaptor, she picked up. "Hello?"

Nothing.

"Hello, who's there?"

Silence, just like the other night.

"Hello, hello."

A loud click, as if the caller had slammed his or her phone down in anger.

Well, that was sweet.

Amber pulled the minivan into the driveway at the address Dr. Hines had given her. A large house for a single man. Two-story. Looked like there could be at least four bedrooms. Two-car garage.

When she rang the doorbell, ferocious barking startled her out of her skin. More than one huge dog, by the sound of it. Yikes! Guard dogs and little people didn't mix well.

"Hold on, I'll be right there!" Dr. Hines shouted through the door. She could hear some scuffling sounds, a distant whistle, the tap-tap of animal claws on bare tile.

The door finally flew open, and Dr. Hines stood there smiling. "Sorry, I wanted to get rid of the dogs, first. Dobermans can be intimidating to anyone, but for someone of your stature . . ." He shrugged.

"Thanks, I appreciate that." And she meant it. There were some ways about him that she couldn't abide. Yet, there were times, like now, when his thoughtfulness touched her. Such a Jekyll and Hyde personality.

He moved aside. "Come on in."

She stepped into the art-deco entryway with black and

white tiled floor and watched as he closed the door, then punched in a code on a finger pad by the door.

"An alarm system, guard dogs—why all the security? You have a fortune stashed here?" She meant it in a joking manner, but he wasn't smiling.

He reached his hands out, indicating she give him her coat. "Because of what I do, there has been some vandalism, death threats, that sort of thing. Makes you paranoid. The police suggested one or the other, but I'm not one to do things halfway, so I got both."

She shrugged her jacket off and handed it to him. "That's understandable."

After hanging the jacket in a nearby closet he said, "C'mon, let's get comfortable." He led the way down a short hallway toward the back of the house to a large kitchen. Her breath caught in her throat. Industrial type stainless steel appliances, aqua-colored, glass mosaic tile countertops, grey ceramic tile floor. She'd kill for a kitchen like this. Amber wondered of what use it all was to Dr. Hines.

"How about some coffee?" he asked.

He had invited her to dinner, but she had already promised her parents. She'd stuffed herself to capacity with her mother's cooking. But the aroma of an exotic brew kindled a craving for a cup of the rich, dark liquid. "I'd love some." She sniffed the air. Fruity and wild-flowery. "What flavor is that?"

"It's Ethiopian Moka Harrar. I think you'll like it." He poured two cups and set them on a tray, where he'd already placed sugar and cream. Next, he went to the refrigerator and removed a plate of chocolate éclairs. As he'd told her a few minutes ago, he was not one to do things halfway.

He picked up the tray and headed out of the kitchen. "Let's go in here."

Amber followed Dr. Hines into what might be called a family room. Although it wasn't very cold outside, a fire blazed in a fireplace that took up an entire wall. The plush, violet carpet accented the olive green, overstuffed, sectional sofa with chaise. Dim lighting set off the whole effect of a cozy, inviting atmosphere.

He put the tray down on the coffee table and motioned for her to sit next to him on the couch. As they sipped from their cups, they talked about several insignificant things: the weather, hockey, the theater.

She could take the suspense no longer. "Al, what

specifically did you want to talk to me about?

He shifted his position and cleared his throat. "I wanted to talk to you about this 'thing' we have going on." He gestured with his hand, moving it to and fro in the space between them.

She didn't say anything, knowing he'd eventually expect her to say *something.*

Again, he cleared his throat. "This is difficult for me. It's been such a long time since I . . ."

She had a feeling about what he struggled to tell her and wanted to stop him. But then again, if she let him say it, there might be some way to deflect the situation and put an end to it. "Yes?"

Dr. Hines took a deep breath. "I have feelings for you. I'm not sure what they are, yet, but they run deep. I'd like to explore the possibilities with you. I want us to be together." He let out a breath, as if relieved he'd finally said it. "Especially after what happened the other day. The thought of losing you overwhelmed me, Amber."

Even though she'd expected this, it still stunned her. She'd already planned what to say, but wasn't sure it would be adequate. The intensity with which he spoke almost brought tears to her eyes; almost melted her heart. And she didn't want to break his. Even though he caused her sister's death.

She started to speak, but he stopped her with a raised hand. "Don't say anything, yet. I want you to think about this for a while. I know I normally come on like gangbusters, but that's when I really don't care about a person. It started out that way with you, but as we spent more time together, my feelings grew into something I haven't experienced in a long, long time." He looked at her, now, expectant.

Words would not come. Though he didn't want an answer this instant, she knew he wanted to hear that her feelings were strong enough to consider it. She certainly did need to think, but not about whether to explore a serious relationship with him. She needed to examine her own heart. Probe those dark, ugly corners. He'd stolen a very special part of her the day Ashley died, and Amber had wanted revenge. That was a no-no, but if she were honest with herself, that's exactly what it came down to. She'd used the excuse that he needed to be exposed for the fetal harvesting. But now he had become a very real person to her. No longer the beast she'd imagined all these years. Her hunger for vengeance had weakened. And yet, that stalking incident had left her feeling disturbed.

His eyes searched her face. She had to say something.

"Al, have you considered what you'd be in for by getting seriously involved with a little person? There would be a whole gamut of new things to deal with."

He nodded. "I realize that, though I don't pretend to know to what extent. That's why we—or rather, I—should slow down and get to know about all of those things. Not because any of them would change my mind, but just so I could understand it all. Figure out how to prepare for it." He sighed and shook his head. "I'm saying this all wrong."

Amber reached over and placed her coffee mug on the table. "No, you're not. There's never a wrong way to say it. This is just the way things are. You have to go into it with both eyes open."

He nodded. "I agree."

Head tilted, she studied him for a moment. "Can I ask you something?"

"Sure, anything."

"What is it about me that attracts you? I mean, I would think a man of your stature would be more interested in a tall woman."

"Normally, I would be. But, Amber, you are the most refreshing woman I've ever met. Your courage, your spunk, sense of humor . . ." He shook his head and raised his shoulders. "I'm just amazed. Plus, you *are* kind of cute, too." He winked.

Too much praise made her feel uncomfortable, so she just thanked him quietly.

He took her hand, stared at his own hands caressing it. "There's something else I need to tell you." His eyes met hers, now. "A confession."

This was something new. She never figured him for the type of guy to "confess" anything to anyone. Amber thought she might not want to hear this confession, but she said nothing.

"Remember that day I dropped by, but you had other plans?"

Somehow, he said this in a way that still accused. She nodded in answer to his question.

"You as much as told me I was the only one you're seeing. I didn't believe you, so I followed you. To that house, and then to the strip mall." He at least had the decency to look sheepish.

But this unexpected side of him threw Amber off-balance.

He hadn't been caught, so no reason to come clean. Then again, because of the feelings he'd professed to her, she supposed he wanted to start fresh. Well, she wouldn't let him off the hook so easily.

Feigning surprise, she said, "Why would you do such a thing, Al? Have I ever given you reason to doubt me?"

Dr. Hines dropped her hand and gathered the mugs, pastry, and utensils onto the tray and lifted it. "No, you haven't, but I can feel that you're not putting your whole self into this relationship." He headed for the kitchen.

Amber did not want to follow Dr. Hines. She wanted to run, leave this house with the huge dogs and the huge fireplace with flames from hell that seemed to reach their scorching fingers out to her, because hell is where she belonged. But he needed to be reminded of what she'd told him in the very beginning.

She walked into the kitchen. "Al, I *did* tell you early on that I wasn't ready for a serious relationship. Do you remember?"

At first, he didn't answer, but pulled open the refrigerator door and placed the cream inside. It swung shut and he turned to her. "I remember. But like I said, after what happened the other day, I don't know what I'd do if I lost you."

Yes, he *had* said that, but she had been too overwrought to think about what it might mean. She did not want to be his obsession. Nor his possession.

"Okay, if you have those feelings for me, I can't stop you. Maybe we should call it quits. I won't be forced into something I'm not ready for." What was she saying? How would she get him to tell her things relative to the story without spending time with him?

He'd been rinsing the mugs in the sink and whipped around with such force that water from his hand splattered large spots across that beautifully tiled floor. "No!" He grabbed a towel from the counter and wiped his hands. He stepped toward her. "No. We'll continue to see each other and I promise not to push you."

Still the dictator. At least she could still get close to him in a noncommittal way. She didn't answer immediately, wanting to give the impression she was considering his command. "Okay, but, as you said, let's slow it down, and not let things get too intense. We were headed that way, and I was starting to feel uncomfortable."

He nodded, but his expression showed that he did so

reluctantly.

"One more thing." She might as well go all the way. "No more kissing. It clouds my judgment. That's where we made our mistake before."

He gave that cocky half-smile. "I don't see it as a mistake, but I'll let you have your way."

Somehow, the way he said it made her feel she wasn't getting her way at all.

* * *

Early Monday morning, Amber ran into Maggie in the center's parking lot. "Hey, Mags, good weekend?"

Maggie tipped her hand back and forth. "So-so. You?"

She stepped through the door after Maggie. "Pretty good. Nothing very exciting."

Maggie laughed and nudged Amber. "We're a pair, aren't we?"

They walked down the hall and parted ways. "See you later," Amber called. Maggie waved.

She went to her office, deposited her handbag in the desk drawer, hung her jacket on the coat tree, and headed for the coffee room. Approaching Dr. Hines's office on the way, she rapped sharply on the closed door. Without waiting for a reply, she pushed open the door. "Morning, Doc."

He whirled around to face her, as if he'd been caught performing some forbidden act. "Oh, it's you. Good morning, Miss Amber." Recovering, he turned back to the door he'd just closed, inserted a key in the knob and turned it.

"That's a very unflattering way to be greeted."

Pocketing the key, he said, "Sorry. I didn't mean that the way it sounded. You know I'm always happy to see you." He sat down at his desk.

That declaration emboldened her, so she forged ahead. "What are you hiding in the closet there, Doc?" She grinned to give the impression of a half-joke.

He didn't answer immediately, just searched her eyes. "A legitimate question." He indicated the locked door with a tilt of his head. "Someday I'll show you what's in there. But not today."

"I look forward to it. Well, I'd better get to work." She started to go, then turned back. "After I have my caffeine fix, that is."

"While you're at it, I could use a cup myself."

"Sure thing." She sauntered off toward the coffee room, passing Rita, who gave her a dirty look. She couldn't worry about the nurse, right now. What Dr. Hines kept in that closet occupied her thoughts. Could she hang in there until he felt ready to trust her with his secret, or would she need to find out on her own?

* * *

Amber felt light and free now. As she drove the Odyssey toward Evan's place after work on Monday (which she sincerely hoped would soon be her place again, too), she anticipated what his reaction would be when she told him how she managed to change the rules of her relationship with Dr. Hines. At one time, the good doctor had the advantage. But no more.

She pulled into the driveway and exited the minivan, practically flew up the front steps and jammed her finger against the doorbell button. When Evan didn't answer immediately, she rang it again. The door swung open and she almost fell into the house.

"Amber! What are you doing here?"

She drank in the sight of him. He wore black sweats, and his hair was slightly tousled, as it might have gotten from changing clothes recently. The urge to throw herself into his arms almost overpowered her sense of dignity, but she held back.

"I'm feeling sort of celebratory, so I came straight over. I hope you don't mind. I won't stay long."

He hesitated a moment, then said, "No, come on in and tell me what this is all about."

He stood aside and she stepped in, heading to the family room off the foyer. As she entered, she noticed Evan's coat lying over the back of the sofa, together with some sort of wide, green, satin sash. "I'm sorry, were you going somewhere? I shouldn't have barged in."

"No, really, it's no problem. But you know what?" He pulled the sleeve of his shirt up over his watch and checked the time. "Just let me make a quick call."

What an idiot she was flying straight over here without even considering he might have plans. "No, don't change anything for me. I should have called first. I'm sorry. I'll go and we'll talk later." She turned to leave, but he caught her by the arm.

"Please. I'd much rather you stayed."

His eyes had that puppy-dog look she couldn't resist. "Well, if you really want me to."

"I do. Now just wait here for a second." Evan went over to the sofa and dug into the pocket of his coat, pulling out his cell phone. He flipped it open, hit a single number, then waited. She listened as he spoke to someone he called *Sifu*. A little confused, she hoped this person wasn't some other woman he might be seeing. After all, she technically dated Dr. Hines. What prevented him from seeing someone else? He had been served the divorce papers, in a manner of speaking, so nothing stood in his way. But that's crazy. All along he'd been professing his love for her, asking her to come back to him. Of course, she'd been stubborn, resisting her own desires. Now she regretted her actions and attitude. Maybe he'd changed his mind about getting back together. She may have pushed him too far, waited too long.

Evan ended the call and laid the phone on an end table. "Now, what's on your mind?"

What she wanted to tell him suddenly seemed stupid. "I thought I'd tell you I set down some rules for Dr. Hines and the dating."

He walked around the sofa and sat down. "Really? What are they?"

Amber took a seat on the couch, also. "At first, I suggested we quit seeing each other."

"How did he respond to that?"

"He didn't like it at all, so he agreed that if we continue as we are, he won't push for a commitment."

Evan frowned. "Hmm. I would have preferred no dating at all."

"So would I, but I do need to stay close to him if I want to find out what his big secret is. I think it has to do with something in a locked closet in his office. I asked him point-blank what he's hiding in there, and he said he'd show me someday."

"Couldn't you just go snooping when he isn't around?"

"I could, but he keeps the key on him. I could try picking the lock, but, as you know, I've never been able to make it work."

Evan shot her a wry look as he nodded.

"Anyway, getting back to 'the rules,' I did add one more thing. I told him no more kissing."

He puffed out a sigh. "What a relief. How did he take it.?"

She stood up and started straightening the magazines on the cocktail table. Evan was never one to keep order to such small things. "Not bad, really. But his reply sort of unsettled me. He said he'd let me have my way, only he gave me a look that meant just the opposite."

"Did you expect anything different from the Master of

Manipulation?"

She thought about this for a moment. Honestly, she did after his declaration the other night. She couldn't explain that to Evan, though. Not because she wanted to keep secrets from him, but why get him all worked up over nothing? She may have been confused early on, but the feelings she had now certainly weren't mutual.

She simply shrugged in reply to Evan's query, then noted the time on a wall clock. "I'd better get going, and I'm sure you've got things to do."

Evan stood. "Yeah, I've got to practice my Kung Fu, now that you've kept me from a lesson." He smiled as he said this.

"You're taking lessons? That's terrific! Is it hard?"

"Nah." He executed a few jabs and pulls of the arms, then a jump and swift kick to the air, with a Bruce Lee-ish, high-pitched yell. "I'll earn my black belt in about twenty years."

She snickered. "I would love to stay and watch you practice, but I've got things to do, myself."

She walked to her car still smiling. Kung Fu. Imagine.

CHAPTER 29

On Tuesday, Amber planned to ask Rita to go out to lunch with her. Just the two of them. Her heart had been heavy, lately, over the hurt she'd caused the woman because of her relationship with Dr. Hines.

Upon arriving at the center that morning, Amber strode down the hall to her office and caught sight of Rita preparing one of the procedure rooms. She stepped inside.

"Good morning, Rita."

Rita looked up from the tray where she was placing various surgical instruments. She greeted Amber with a glare.

"Would you like to have lunch together today?"

Her flinty eyes widened. "What makes you think I'd agree to eat lunch with *you*?"

Amber's jaw dropped. She never expected such direct hostility. "I'd like us to be friends."

"Friends! Ha!" Rita held a sharp instrument and pointed it at Amber, shaking it. "I'll never be friends with you. Not after what you've done to me."

Amber swallowed and walked further into the room. "What have I done to you personally, Rita? I just want us to get along, or to at least tolerate each other. Wouldn't that be easier than all this avoiding you do?"

Rita dropped the instrument onto the stainless steel tray with a clatter and placed her hands on her hips. "I'll tell you what would be easier, Missy! If you would just leave here. We all got along perfectly fine before you came. Now please go so I can finish my work." She turned her back to Amber.

"Please reconsider, R—"

"GO," she said, still facing the other way.

Amber hesitated, trying to think of something else she could say that would change Rita's mind. Nothing presented itself. Slowly, head down, she ambled from the room.

Lord, please help Rita.

* * *

"Are you coming, Amber?" Doug asked, as he shrugged

into his parka.

She placed some absorbent wadding in a box for cushioning. "In a bit, Doug. I just want to finish this last one."

He leaned against the wall by the door. "Okay, make it quick."

She looked up at him. "Why don't you go? I'll make sure everything's cleaned up, turn off the lights . . ."

"You sure?"

"Positive. Go on, I'll be fine."

He straightened up. "Okay. Good night, then."

"Night."

Good. He's gone. Amber hurried to finish packing the box, because she had decided to take Evan's suggestion and check out Dr. Hines's office. Even though she had seen him pocket the key to the locked closet that one time, it didn't mean he didn't keep a spare. If she found the key, she could see what he kept behind that door. She'd surprise Evan with the results and get this thing over with. Then they could concentrate on healing their marriage that much sooner.

After cleaning up the area, Amber quickly scanned the room. Everything seemed to be in order, so she flipped off the light switch and went to her office. She dug in her purse for the car keys and gathered her coat and other belongings. On the pretext of saying "good night" to the doctor, she would check to see if he was still in there. If so, she'd just try again tomorrow, and every day after until the opportunity presented itself.

The door to his office stood ajar, as usual. Trying to be noiseless, she tiptoed close, and pressed herself against the cold wall. Darn! She heard voices. Rita and Dr. Hines.

"Why don't you come by tonight, Albert?" she heard Rita say. "I'll fix a nice dinner and afterwards . . ."

"No, Rita. We can't go back to that. We tried it before and it didn't work. Remember?"

What? Rita and Dr. Hines were together before?

"What I remember are the good times. What we had between us." Rita sounded wistful.

"We had nothing but sex between us, pure and simple." Dr. Hines's voice sounded full of disgust.

"Well"—Rita's voice became low and flirty—"I wouldn't exactly call it pure *or* simple."

Amber's jaw dropped. Was this the same Rita she'd come to think of as prim and proper? Goes to show, people weren't always what they seemed.

"Call it what you want, but that's all it was to me."

"Maybe someday it could turn into more." Rita's voice cracked.

"'Fraid not."

Callous jerk!

"What is it with Amber, then? You can't possibly have feelings for that . . . that midget!"

Amber flinched. She could hear the anger and disdain in Rita's voice. That, along with the insult itself, cut deeply.

"I'll not discuss our relationship with you."

"Oh, it's a relationship, is it? How quaint. But I don't think she's your type. Look, Albert, let's get back together. I'll do whatever you want. It'll be better this time. I promise."

Oh, Rita, Amber thought, *don't be so pathetic. That's the last thing a man like him wants in a woman.*

"No, Rita," Dr. Hines said. "You have to stop this. I knew this would happen. If you can't act professionally while working here, then . . ."

"What?" Rita's voice shrieked. "You'll fire me?"

Silence.

"You wouldn't dare! I'll tell everyone what you've been doing with the chambers."

Another silence, then:

"I think maybe we can come up with some kind of a compromise." Dr. Hines's voice dripped with sexual innuendo.

Footsteps moved toward the door and Amber back-stepped, but no one came out. The door closed with a loud click, like the closing of a chapter in a book.

Shoot! She moved close to the door again and listened. All she could hear were muffled voices. But they weren't arguing. Did that mean they were patching things up? The Dr. Hines *she* knew would never be pushed into an unwanted attachment.

That thought stayed with her, as she unzipped her purse to retrieve her car keys. They weren't in there. Oh, that's right, she'd already removed them, and must have left them on her desk.

On her way back out, she ran into Rita leaving Dr. Hines's office. She flashed Amber a bright smile that did not reach her eyes. "Good night, Amber."

The smile and the acknowledgement stunned her. This was a new Rita. The woman glowed.

And yet, something felt very wrong.

CHAPTER 30

Wednesday morning brought gray clouds and the threat of possible steady April showers. The kind of day Amber would have loved to stay curled up in bed for some hours watching the morning news shows.

Melly must have felt the same. "No," she said when Amber woke her, and the usually brightly colored room lay cloaked in shadows.

"Come on, sweetie. Mommy needs to get going."

"No. Seep."

"I know, Mommy wants to sleep, too, but we have to get up anyway." Amber sat on the edge of the tiny bed and stroked Melly's hair. She gently pulled Melly up onto her lap. Melly squeezed her eyes shut and crawled back onto the bed.

Amber huffed out a breath. "I'm sorry, love," she said, trying to control her frustration. "We have to go." She lifted a struggling Melly off the bed and began dressing her. "You can sleep late on Saturday, and then we'll spend some time together."

Even to her own ears, the words sounded like an empty promise.

Amber yawned as she led Melly to the kitchen. She shouldn't have stayed up so late last night. After getting Melly settled into bed, she'd called Evan to discuss the conversation she'd heard between Rita and Dr. Hines.

But the call had turned into more than that. She smiled at the thought. They had spent a long time talking about all kinds of things: what kind of day each of them had had, Evan's martial arts lessons, the Lord, politics. You name it. It almost felt like when they were together and snuggled in the dark, whispering and laughing. The room had grown too warm, as it often did. She'd excused herself to crack open the window. Evan joked that if he'd been there with her, she would need to throw the sash wide open.

Amber looked over at Melly, who sat at the kitchen table in a booster seat playing with her oatmeal. "C'mon, Peaches, we have to get going to Grandma and Grandpa's."

Melly frowned and folded her arms across her chest. "No."

Amber went to the table. "C'mon, Sweetkins, don't do this." She lifted Melly out of her seat. "Mommy has to get to work. Mom-mom can give you something to eat when you get there."

Melly shrieked and squirmed. Amber wrestled her into the living room, and set her on her feet, holding her in place. She snatched Melly's jacket off the sofa and deftly slipped it on before the child knew what was happening. When she turned to put on her own coat, Melly climbed onto the sofa and buried her face in a big, soft pillow. Amber went and bent over her. Smoothing the soft tendrils of Melly's hair, she said, "Come on, my love." She pulled Melly up into her arms. "In a few weeks, this will all be over, and then we can spend all the time in the world together." She kissed Melly's forehead. "I promise."

Hollow words again. She was glad her baby understood none of it.

Melly struggled in her arms. Whew! Her daughter was getting too big for her to manage in this way. Having Melly's father around to help would be nice. She smiled again, as she picked up her purse, keys, and Melly's bag.

One step at a time, though.

* * *

Amber trudged into the office after her tussle with Melly. As she passed the reception desk, Carol said, "Light day for all of us. Dr. Hines took the day off and had me reschedule all of his appointments."

Fine with Amber, considering how fatigued she felt. But if she had known, she *would* have stayed home with Melly. Well, no use in wishing for what could have been. She was here, now, and might as well make the best of it. Sometimes, women or young girls came in just to get advice about their pregnancy. Amber would feel more comfortable giving them alternatives to abortion without Dr. Hines around.

A few hours later, Maggie popped her head into Amber's office. "Got a minute?"

Amber shot her a you've-got-to-be-kidding look. "What's on your mind?"

"Just chit-chat." She moved into the room and took a seat across the desk from Amber.

When the cat's away, and all that, Amber thought.

"Something fishy's going on," Maggie said, running her

fingers through her short, brown hair.

"How so?"

"Rita's scheduled to be in today, and she hasn't shown up." She fixed Amber with a pointed look.

"What makes that fishy?" As soon as the words were out, the thought hit her. She remembered the conversation she'd overheard last night. "You mean because both Rita and Dr. Hines are out at the same time?"

"Well, there's that, but then there's the fact that no one's heard from Rita. Carol tried calling her house and there's no answer."

Amber's phone rang. She indicated to Maggie she'd only be a second and answered. Carol had a patient waiting to speak to her. "Okay, I'll be right out." She hung up and looked at Maggie.

"As much as the woman gets on my nerves," Maggie continued, "I can truthfully say she's very dedicated. This is so unlike her."

Amber got down from her chair. She had that impression of Rita herself. "Why doesn't somebody call Dr. Hines? Maybe he knows something. At the very least, he'll know what to do."

Maggie stood. "Yeah, Carol or I can do that."

They both moved toward the door.

"You know," said Amber, "Rita could just have decided to take the day off to do something special and forgot to call. Of course there'd be no answer at her house if she's out."

"True, but something just doesn't feel right."

Maggie veered off into the beige office she shared with Rita, and Amber continued out to the reception area. She agreed with Maggie that something didn't feel right, but she'd bet that Dr. Hines would offer no answer about Rita.

Amber again recalled what she'd heard between Rita and Dr. Hines last night. The doctor had only decided on "a compromise," as he'd put it, after Rita threatened to tell something about him. Whatever Rita knew must be what Maggie alluded to when she first came to Evan and Amber about the story.

* * *

On Thursday, the sun shone brightly and the dewy morning predicted a lovely spring day ahead.

Melly had again given Amber trouble getting up and ready, so she didn't arrive at the center as early as usual.

"Has Rita shown up today?" she asked Carol, as she

passed the receptionist's desk.

"Nope."

"How about Dr. Hines?"

"Yes, he's here."

Amber continued down the hall and stopped at Dr. Hines's office. The door stood wide open and she saw that he sat staring down at his desk. "Hey, Doc. Glad to have you back. How are you feeling?"

He looked up at her. "Hello, Amber."

"Were you sick? Are you feeling better, now?"

His expression conveyed puzzlement. "Oh! You mean because I was out yesterday. Had some personal business that couldn't wait. That happens from time to time."

"Right." She turned to leave. "I'd better get to work."

Amber heard the tap-tap of Dr. Hines's foot on the large, plastic chair mat under his desk. "How did things go in my absence?"

As she looked at him sitting there, something in his appearance seemed out of place. And was he trying too hard to act natural? "Things were quiet, as you would expect."

He nodded, adjusted his tie. That action directed her attention to what had been bothering her about him: there was a small brown stain on Dr. Hines's tie. This didn't fit with his image of perfectionist and stickler for order.

"Oh, and we all wondered about Rita," she said, vaguely, her mind still on the tie.

A slight change in his gaze that she couldn't pinpoint. "Rita? What about Rita?" The foot tapped again.

"She never showed up. No one heard from her, and Carol tried contacting her with no luck."

He looked away. "Hmm. I'll have to check into it. Very unlike her." He waved a dismissive hand. "Well, as you've said, better get to work."

As she ambled down to her office, the image of that stain festered in her mind like a canker sore.

* * *

That night, Amber mentioned Rita's strange disappearance to Evan. He'd said, "Give it one more day. Then we'll decide what, if anything, needs to be done."

On Friday, again, Rita did not show up.

"I wish we knew what's going on with that woman. I'm getting tired of subbing for her without a day off," Maggie said to Amber.

"I'm sure we'll hear something soon," Amber said, not too convinced herself. "Why don't we go to her place at lunchtime, see if she'll answer the door?"

Maggie frowned. "All right, but I hate wasting my lunch hour on that witch."

Amber just smiled to herself. She knew Maggie did not hate Rita as much as she pretended to. She could see the faint worry lines between Maggie's brows.

* * *

"Her car is here, so she's home," Amber said to Maggie, as she pulled the Odyssey in front of Rita's house.

"Well, she'd better have a good reason for being here, after all this."

"Relax, Mags, I'm sure there's a perfectly reasonable explanation. As everyone says, she's dedicated."

Amber reached up and rang the doorbell. As they waited in silence after the loud buzz, Amber took in the house's facade. It seemed a sad little bungalow. Tiny, with only one bedroom, most likely. Gray shingles, peeling paint.

After about two minutes, they still heard no movement from inside and threw each other a worried glance. Then Maggie jabbed the bell, as if pushing harder would make it ring louder, thus bringing Rita to the door.

Still nothing.

Amber rapped several times on the storm door, and they waited an appropriate amount of time. Maggie pounded.

No Rita.

"I can't believe this," Maggie said, and descended the steps. She walked over to the picture window at the front of the house and craned her neck, trying to peer in. "I can't see anything. She's not here, Amber, let's go." She trudged toward the minivan.

Amber followed Rita and climbed into the Odyssey. They sat quietly for a moment, each lost in their own thoughts.

"So now what?" Maggie asked Amber.

Amber shrugged. "I guess the next step would be to call the police. But we should ask Dr. Hines to do it. It would be best coming from him, since he's her employer."

"Gladly," Maggie said, as Amber pulled away from the curb.

When they arrived back at the center, Maggie and Amber knocked on Dr. Hines's partially open door.

"Enter."

The two of them went into his office and sat down across from him.

Leaning back in his chair, Dr. Hines linked his hands behind his head "To what do I owe the pleasure of a visit from the two prettiest ladies at this clinic?"

Amber jumped in. "We've been to Rita's house."

He shot forward and leaned on the desk, listening.

Amber continued. "Her car's there, but she doesn't answer the door."

The doctor still remained silent.

Maggie let out what sounded like an impatient sigh. "Could you just call the police and have them check it out. We thought it best that you did it, as her employer."

He thought for a moment. "All right, I'll call them today."

"Let us know what they say," Maggie said.

"I'll do that." He began reading some papers that were on the desk in front of him, and they knew he'd subtly dismissed them.

They stood and left his office. Out in the hall, Maggie whispered, "Now we're getting somewhere. All this waiting was getting on my nerves."

Amber nodded her head, but she didn't tell Maggie that the whole thing left her unsettled. A feeling deep down in the pit of her stomach. A gut reaction? She'd read somewhere that the gut is like another brain and we should listen to it.

Since the day Dr. Hines followed her and her mother to the lingerie store, a strange feeling had crept inside her and took hold.

Now, with this Rita thing, that feeling had shackled itself to her rib cage.

* * *

As Amber drove home from the center that day, Evan called on her cell phone. Rather than taking the time to hook up the hands-free adapter, she pulled over on the shoulder of the road to answer.

He jumped right in without preamble. "You know what I'd like to do this weekend?"

"What?"

"I'd like to visit your parents. I miss them."

Watching the cars speed by, she struggled for something to say. If she and Evan were at her parents, who would stay with Melly? Nora? Yeah, good. She'd ask Nora.

"I know they'd love to see you. Let me check to make

sure they don't have plans." They *would* have plans, too, if Nora were unavailable to babysit Melly.

"Sure. Any news about Rita?"

"No, but Maggie and I spoke to Dr. Hines and he said he'd call the police."

"Hmm. I wouldn't think he'd give in so easily.

"What do you mean?"

He cleared his throat. "Nothing. Just thinking out loud. Okay, Sweetheart, talk to you later." He hung up before she could question him further.

But he'd called her Sweetheart again. Every time he did, a delicious warmth ran through her.

When Amber arrived at her parents' house, her mother came out of the kitchen holding Melly's hand. Her baby looked like she had gone to heaven, as she munched on a sugar cookie. Crumbs framed Melly's mouth and lined her little fingers. Amber frowned.

Ma apparently saw Amber's look. "Before you say anything about the cookie, I only gave her one after feeding her dinner."

Amber perked up at that. "She's already eaten?" At least that would be one less thing she needed to worry about when she got home. She kissed Melly, and when her daughter kissed her back, crumbs stuck to Amber's cheek.

"I knew that would please you," Ma said with a knowing grin.

"Thanks, Ma. Where's Dad?"

"He's having dinner with one of his friends." She brushed the crumbs from Melly's mouth and hands, not seeming to care that they landed on the immaculate hall carpet.

"Well, then I'll just ask you. Are you and Dad busy on Saturday?"

"No, not really. Why?"

"Evan said he misses you and Dad and would love to visit."

"Amber, that's wonderful!" She bent to hug her daughter. "We'd love to see him, too. Does this mean the two of you have patched things up?"

"We're working on it, Ma."

"Oh." Ma's voice went flat. "You haven't told him about Melly, yet, have you?"

Her hand clenched on the strap of her handbag at Ma's tone. "I can't just yet, but soon. I want to make sure things between us are solid before springing that on him. I don't think what we have, right now, can take the blow."

"But that means we'll have to hide any evidence of Melly's existence, like *you've* been. You're asking us to lie, too. I don't like doing that." Ma looked down at Melly and wistfully ruffled her hair.

"If you don't say anything at all about Melly, then there's no lying involved, right?"

She was served with a stern silence, and a look that told her she'd just said something she knew was entirely untrue. "It's called a sin of omission, Amber."

Ma certainly knew how to lay the guilt on. Still, it was one of those "rock-and-a-hard-place" situations. But she desperately wanted things to work out with Evan, this time. "Please? Just this once? When I tell him about Melly, I don't want any distractions. Very soon we'll be finished with this story, and we can concentrate on us."

Ma blew out a frustrated breath. "I'm not happy about it, but I'll do as you ask."

Relief rushed through her. "Thanks, Ma, you're the best!"

"Yes, well, let's just hope I can convince your father."

As Ma helped her pack up Melly's things, Amber could hardly bear the heaviness in her heart. Sins of omission, Ma had said. She was guilty of both those, and sins of *commission*. Not only had she been deceiving Evan, but Melly, too, by failing to have her see her dad face-to-face. Now she had also brought her parents into her web of lies by asking them to lie, too.

A sudden thought crashed through Amber's mind: was she any better than Dr. Hines? She was just as willing to do wrong to get what she wanted. He would do anything to gain some twisted recompense for his son's death; she would do anything to get Evan back.

CHAPTER 31

At two-forty-five on Saturday afternoon, Amber made one last check of her parents' home to make sure there were no traces of Melly's existence. Evan said he'd arrive at three, but she knew he'd be a few minutes early, as always. She walked into the living room where Dad sat on the couch, looking calm and comfortable. Unlike his daughter, who felt rattled and uneasy. Her eyes scanned the room again.

"This is ridiculous, Amber. I don't like having to hide the truth from Evan," Dad said.

She walked over and climbed up beside him. "Oh, Dad, I'm so sorry to have to involve you and Ma in this mess. I just want to make sure it's the right time before I tell him."

He took her hand, held it between his own. "Amber, is there ever a right time for something so delicate?"

The sound of a car engine brought both Amber and Dad to the window for a peek. Evan had just turned into the driveway.

Her insides quaked.

A car door shut. Footfalls on the front steps. The doorbell. Here goes.

Amber went to the door and pulled it open. He looked good in his jeans and heather gray mock turtleneck under a navy blue sport coat. She smiled. "Hi."

"Hi, yourself."

She moved aside for him to enter. He stepped inside, accidentally brushing against her arm, and electrifying her already taut nerve endings. He looked around, heaving a great sigh as if he'd finally arrived home after a hard day at work.

"Shall I take your jacket?"

"No, I'm good."

Dad came out of the living room. "Evan, my boy!" He held out a hand. "So good to see you."

Evan took Dad's hand for a shake, but Dad bent down and the two men embraced.

"It's great to see you, too, Ben."

"Evan!" Ma's voice preceded her presence. She

appeared with her arms spread wide, her hands covered with oven mitts. "We've missed you fiercely." She hugged Evan so hard, his feet nearly left the floor.

"I've missed both you and Ben, too, Darla."

Ma straightened and placed her hands on her hips. "Now, you know what you're supposed to call us, Evan. None of this Ben and Darla stuff."

His mouth spread into a sheepish grin. "I know . . . Mom, but I wasn't sure after all this time."

"Oh, Honey." A tear glistened in Ma's eye, as she patted his shoulder.

Evan's eyes again scanned his surroundings, and he took another deep breath, as if hungrily absorbing what he saw. "It's good to see nothing here has changed."

Ma glanced at Amber a little longer than necessary. "No, we haven't changed much since we last saw you, except . . ."

Amber stared at her mother with wide, pleading eyes. She wouldn't. Would she? Her heart picked up its pace.

". . . we moved things around some in Amber's old room."

Amber let out the breath she'd been holding and shook her head at her mother.

Dad shot a frustrated glance at first his wife and then his daughter. "Let's go into the family room and get comfortable, shall we?" Good old Dad, always ready to defuse the tension.

They all filed down the hall. Ma stopped in the kitchen to deposit her mitts, then joined the rest of them.

Evan sniffed the air. "Mmm. That's a familiar smell."

"Roasted lamb," Ma said. "Your favorite."

He seemed humbled. "Thank you, Mom."

They chatted for a while about old times and caught up on new news. Ma served hors d'oeuvres and ginger ale.

Dad rested back in his favorite chair, his gaze including both Evan and Amber, together on the couch. "I know you don't like to talk about the stories you're working on until they're out, but how's this most recent one coming? Any light at the end of the tunnel?"

Evan and Amber glanced at each other, then Amber said, "Yeah, we think it will be over soon."

"There's just one key element Amber needs to find, then she's outta there," Evan added.

"Oh, good," Ma said. She fixed a pointed glare on Amber. "Then the two of you can get on with your lives."

If her mother didn't stop giving her those looks, she was

going to scream. But then Evan took her hand, as he spoke to her parents, and held it between his own like a prize he'd won. The heat that small gesture generated oozed through her veins like warm maple syrup, lulling her into a dream-like state. She hadn't felt so content in a long time.

Later, the four of them sitting at the dinner table, talking and laughing just like they used to, felt so comfortable and right.

Evan stuffed the last forkful of Ma's homemade cheesecake into his mouth. "Mom, that was the best meal I've ever had." He rubbed his stomach.

Ma blushed and waved a dismissive hand. "Oh, Evan, you've said that every time you've eaten here."

The whole scene seemed to Amber like a Norman Rockwell painting. And then she caught a glimpse of the collage of family photos on the dining room wall over the buffet and realized Melly's picture was missing. She suddenly filled up with tears and fought to hold them back. Melly should be here, too, sharing this special moment with her dad. Sharing in the love. Loving in return. But because of Amber's stubbornness, her baby girl had missed out. The tears threatened to spill out again, and she fought them until her eyes burned.

When it was time for Evan to leave, they all walked him to the door. He kissed Ma, shook Dad's hand, then looked at Amber with such a tender gaze, she thought she'd melt into a puddle right there where she stood. He placed a soft, sweet kiss on her forehead and caressed her cheek. Her breath caught in her throat at the gentle warmth of his hand. "See you, Sweetheart," he said.

Then he was gone.

Ma had tears in her eyes. "Oh, I never realized how much I missed that boy."

For a few seconds, Amber had forgotten her folks were there.

"There, there, Darla." Dad placed his arm around Ma. "I have a feeling we're going to be seeing more of him from now on."

The whole day had taken an emotional toll on Amber. She could hold back no longer. "Um, excuse me," she mumbled, and headed for the bathroom. After locking the door, she leaned against it, tears trickling down her cheeks.

Unbelievable, she thought. She had fallen in love with Evan all over again. More deeply than ever before.

And it hurt like mad.

CHAPTER 32

Amber awoke thirty minutes early on Monday morning. The sun's rays reached through her window like magic fingers to brighten the darkest corners of her room. Taking a deep breath, she stretched before climbing out of bed.

Because she had extra time before showering, she felt moved to spend time in prayer and devotion. Something she'd been neglecting lately. For too long, she had been doing things in her own strength, forgetting her Lord was sovereign. That had always been her problem; why she sometimes made stupid choices. But He always worked things out for her good, no matter how dire the circumstances.

Feeling refreshed and strengthened, she got up off her knees and headed for the shower. Things were going to change. She could feel it. One way or another, Dr. Hines would soon be exposed, and then she and Evan could concentrate on healing their marriage.

Two hours later, Amber pulled the minivan into the parking lot of the Cedarview Women's Center. Strangely, the sun had gone in, and the area seemed shrouded in a cloak of doom. When she stepped inside the clinic, she knew immediately something was wrong.

Everyone huddled around Carol's desk, and Amber joined them.

"Hi guys, what's up?"

Maggie and Carol turned tearful eyes on her, while Dr. Hines and Doug looked at her solemnly. No one answered her.

Amber's gaze took in each of them in turn. "What?"

Dr. Hines let out a shaky breath. "I heard from the police. They found Rita's body in her home over the weekend."

She felt like the air had been sucked out of her. "Her body? Does that mean . . . ?"

"Yes," Dr. Hines said.

Oh, Lord. All sense of balance drained from her body, as she stumbled toward a chair and perched on its edge. She looked up at Dr. Hines. "How? What happened?"

Coming toward her, he said, "They're not sure, yet, but it seems to be of natural causes."

"Natural causes? What natural causes?" She could hear the anxiety creeping into her own high-pitched voice. "She seemed to be a healthy woman."

Dr. Hines sat on the chair next to her and took her hand. "Amber, I only know what they've told me. There will be an autopsy. We'll know more then."

Amber nodded and looked down at the floor. What insanity. The last time she saw Rita had been almost a week ago. Ironic laughter almost erupted, but she squelched it. Shortly before she . . . died, the spunky nurse had chewed her out for stealing Dr. Hines from her. There had certainly been no indication of failing health.

Rising, Dr. Hines said, "Well, I can't focus on any work today. I'm closing the center in observance of Rita's death. Let's all go home."

The rest of them moved toward the back offices like zombies, except for Carol. She went to her desk and picked up the phone. Of course, all of that day's appointments would need to be canceled before leaving. Amber hadn't even put her things away, yet, so she turned around and walked back out the door.

As she started the Odyssey's engine, she thought again to that last day she'd seen Rita and the conversation she'd heard between Rita and Dr. Hines. What had transpired in the time between their argument and the nurse's death?

* * *

Amber stood at Evan's office door and rapped twice. Without waiting for a response, she pushed it open and stepped through. One of the staff reporters was seated across from Evan, and seeing she had interrupted them, Amber immediately spun on her heel to leave.

"Whoa, hold on!"

Evan's voice stopped her, but she felt foolish now for barging in unannounced. She turned away from the door. "I'm so sorry. I should have called, first."

"No problem. We're just finishing up. You remember Nick Russo?"

Amber inclined her head toward the man. "Hi, Nick."

Nick's face broke into a huge, bright smile, as he stood. "Hello, Amber. You're looking well."

Amber knew that, at the moment, she didn't look her best, but she accepted the compliment, anyway. "Thanks." She remembered Nick was one of nine siblings. "How's the family?"

"As boisterous as ever. You know how we Italians are."

"Yes, but I also know you all love each other fiercely."

Evan cleared his throat. "Nick, show me what you have when you're finished."

Nick took the hint, said goodbye, and left.

She now had Evan's full attention, He stood up and his gaze turned tender, understanding. Thank God he knew her so well. With a great sigh, she fell into his ready arms.

He stroked her hair. "Hey, what's the matter?" he asked softly.

Breathing deeply of his scent, she snuggled against him. "Just hold me for a moment?"

"Sure." And they stood there, molded together for too brief a time. Evan slowly pulled away and said, "Now, what's this all about?"

She removed her jacket and placed it with her purse on the chair Nick had vacated minutes before. "The police found Rita's body in her home over the weekend."

He tilted his head and looked toward the floor. "Wow." Taking a deep breath, he looked up at Amber again. "What happened?"

"They don't know much, yet. They'll do an autopsy, but it looks like she died of natural causes."

Evan looked pensive as he walked back around to his chair. He climbed into it, picked up a pencil, and began tapping it on the desk. "Amber, do you think it's possible that Dr. Hines is somehow responsible?"

"What, use some drug to cause heart failure? The thought briefly occurred to me." Weariness set in and she took the seat behind her desk. "I immediately dismissed it, because it doesn't seem to fit who he is."

He frowned. "Amber, we already know that doesn't have to be the case with murderers. They are sometimes perceived as churchgoing, upstanding citizens. And you've seen firsthand some of the unconscionable things he does."

She had to agree, but because there were many good qualities to the doctor's character, she had never felt physically threatened. The day of the hostage situation flashed through her mind, and how Dr. Hines tried to save her, offering to take her place. She could never forget that. And she recalled the sadness in his eyes when he'd told her about his son's death and his anguish over being helpless to prevent it. These were things

Evan had never seen.

"I know you're right, Evan, but in this case . . ." She shook her head, torn. "Maybe Rita did it herself. Committed suicide because of Dr. Hines's rejection. She's a nurse. She'd have access to all the same drugs as Dr. Hines"

His face took on the look of a gathering storm. "Why do you insist on defending him at every turn?"

"I'm not defending him. I'm trying to be objective. Have you forgotten I've spent lots of time getting to know this man?" As soon as the words were out, she regretted them. Closing her eyes against Evan's angry expression, she waited for the floor to open and swallow her up. Dear God, she was allowing her emotions to affect this investigation.

"How could I forget," he said quietly, "that my wife has been spending so much time with another man?"

Her eyes flew open. The anger remained on his face, but it had been joined by hurt. "Oh, Evan, I'm sorry. I didn't mean . . ." She got off the chair and went to him. Her hands automatically cupped his face, and she studied it for a long moment. "I love you, Evan Blake. I've never loved anyone else, and I never will."

His arms enveloped her, drawing her closer. "It's so good to finally hear you say that, Amber. Sometimes, I wondered."

"Well, wonder no more." She kissed him

Evan stood up and kissed her back. Her arms curled around his neck. His fingers roamed through her hair. They stayed there for some time, kissing like a young couple just fallen in love.

A sharp rap on the door startled them into parting.

Nick Russo stood in the open doorway looking embarrassed. "I'll, uh, come back later." Before either of them could respond, he was gone.

Immediately, Amber realized how she must look. Her hands flew up to smooth her hair. "I'm so embarrassed. I probably look a mess."

Evan's eyes twinkled. "You look beautiful."

"Oh, stop it. You'd say that if I looked like the Wicked Witch of the West."

He pulled her close again. "You're right, but you don't." He gave her another soft kiss.

Amber needed to get to her parents' house and pick up Melly. If she stayed here any longer, she'd never leave. "I've got to go."

He nodded. "I know. If you stay, I'll never get any work

done, and we'll end up having to lock the door."

She giggled like a teenager, and swatted his arm. "As if!" Smiling, she gathered her jacket and purse. "See you later."

Evan grabbed her arm, his eyes penetrating. "We need to talk, Amber. Seriously. Without any distractions."

"I know."

As she left the building, Amber thought about the imminent "talk" Evan spoke of. After what just happened in his office, she knew he'd ask her to move back home. She wanted that so badly, but there was still the issue of Melly. She didn't want to tell him about her, just yet, because the resulting upset would hinder their concentration on the investigation. At the same time, the investigation would hinder their focus on reconciling. She knew these were poor excuses. Maybe she just wanted to avoid the impending firestorm telling Evan about Melly would ignite.

But the thought that Evan could be right about Dr. Hines nagged at her. Though she didn't want to believe the doctor could have in some way caused Rita's heart attack, it wouldn't be wise to put anything past him.

CHAPTER 33

The next day at the center, Amber sat at her desk writing notes in a patient's file. She threw down her pen, as her thoughts turned to Dr. Hines. He had been preoccupied, lately, and seemed to be having a hard time accepting Rita's death. If he cared for the nurse, then why had he treated her so badly?

Amber hoped this preoccupation would keep him from wanting to take her out. Now that she and Evan had moved toward restoring their marriage, she knew seeing Dr. Hines was blatantly wrong. And, though she found it hard to believe, if she kept in mind Evan's speculation that Dr. Hines might be responsible for Rita's death, she could almost go back to hating him.

A knock on the door interrupted her thoughts.

Dr. Hines poked his head in. "I need to talk to you."

She swallowed. "Sure."

He entered and sat down across from her. "Doesn't seem we're getting as many donated fetuses lately."

Thanks to her efforts. She had been able to help a few of the women make a more informed choice. She made sure not to preach, but she asked enough probing questions to help them realize there was more to the process than they knew.

She said nothing and clasped her hands on the desk in front of her.

His piercing eyes captured hers. "I know it's because of you, Amber."

She did a double-take. Okay, he wasn't a stupid man. She'd always figured he would notice, one day and even take her to task on it. But in light of Rita's recent death, she never expected him to confront her about it so soon. Maybe the poor woman's death wasn't what had been bothering him, after all. "What do you mean, Doc?"

He held up a hand in resignation. "Don't worry, I'm not going to fire you over it. Actually, it's okay. Better than having suits filed against me because a woman says she didn't know all the facts before submitting to a procedure."

A sigh of relief slipped out. "I'm glad you feel that way."

"I should probably be thanking you for it."

Never in a million years did she expect gratefulness. And just minutes ago, she'd been telling herself she could hate him.

But she knew every coin had two sides.

She closed the file in front of her. "No need to thank me. I only try to help these women be sure that this is the way they want to go."

"As it should be, and I'd like you to continue doing that." He looked at her with a strange gleam in his eyes that sent creepy vibes radiating across the space between them.

No matter. The next time he left the clinic at a decent hour, she would check his office for the keys to that locked closet. When she discovered what he kept in there, this whole mess would be over and she'd never be subjected to his subtle intimidation again.

* * *

Evan paced the living room floor. He'd left the office early, because Amber promised to stop by after work for their "talk." He gave an ironic laugh that echoed through the room. Work. What a joke. You might think her position at the clinic was a real job. But how else to refer to it? He shook his head. None of it mattered. Soon he and Amber would be together again. That was all he cared about.

A deep breath relaxed him a little. He heard the front door open and Amber's voice in the entryway. "Evan?"

"In here."

Two seconds later, she appeared and her smile calmed any jitters he may have been feeling.

"Hey," he said.

"Hey." She came over to him and placed a light kiss on his lips.

He accepted it gladly, hungrily. "Let's sit down," he said.

They made themselves comfortable on the couch. Amber's familiar vanilla scent lingered in the air around them. She looked at him expectantly, as if to say, "So, talk."

The words didn't come easily. "Sweetheart, I think you know what I'm going to say, so I'll get right to the point." He cleared his throat. "I feel it's time for you to come home. I want you to move back in."

For a moment, she said nothing, but her eyes softened as she looked at him. "Oh, Evan, I would love that."

He let out a sigh of relief.

"But don't you think it would be better to wait until we're finished with this story?"

He could feel his brows crease, as anger rose up inside him like hot lava. "What for? This is your home. It's where you belong. With me."

Amber shifted her weight on the couch. The set to her mouth spoke volumes. He'd better tread carefully.

Then the look left her face as she took a deep breath. "I feel the same way, but hear me out." She looked down, for a moment, as if trying to figure out her next words. "First of all, although he's been preoccupied, lately, Dr. Hines could ask me to go out with him again. He'd probably want to pick me up. Then what? Have him come here?"

Okay. In his haste, he hadn't thought of that. When she told him she loved him the other day, everything else in his brain fell by the wayside. "There's no way you could stall him? Tell him you'll meet him there instead?"

She shook her head. "If only I could. But I've told you how manipulative and demanding he can be. And if he wanted to go someplace special, we'd have to go together. He'd have to pick me up."

Evan twisted his mouth into a frown, stared down at the sofa cushion, and allowed himself a moment to brood.

"You don't want to jeopardize all our work, do you?"

"Definitely not. But I think if we really tried, we could come up with a way around it." He narrowed his eyes at her. "I think you're making up excuses."

She shot him an indignant glare. "That couldn't be further from the truth."

"Then prove it." He moved closer, embracing her. "Stay with me tonight."

When she pulled away and stood up, his blood boiled, and he wanted to throw something.

Looking down at the floor, she said in a small voice, "Evan, I know you're not going to understand this. And please don't be mad, but I'd like us to wait until we're *really* back together."

"What?" He stood, too, and tried to quell his frustration, but it wasn't working. "We *are* really back together. We still love each other, we're ready. We agreed. What's not real about that?"

"What I mean is, until I've actually moved back in, and everything's back to normal. I want everything to be perfect. Like a celebration of our reunion. I don't want anything to ruin the moment, like knowing I have to go in to the center the next day."

Women. No wonder it had been said they're from Venus. They were always thinking, coming up with trivialities that drove men crazy. He let out a frustrated sigh. "Okay, I won't try to force you."

"Thank you, Evan," she said softly. "I appreciate it."

"Yeah, yeah," he growled, waving a dismissive hand.

Amber kissed him lightly. "I love you, Evan." Then she was gone.

* * *

The silence unnerved her. Amber climbed off her chair and walked around the desk. She grabbed her blazer and purse and exited her office. The opportunity she'd been waiting for finally presented itself. Dr. Hines left early today, and she would take full advantage of the time alone here. She hoped no one planned to return.

As she moved down the hall, the thud of each footstep reminded her of a tribal drumbeat just before some sacrificial jungle ritual. She rubbed her nose. That ever-present chemical odor that permeated the clinic never ceased to annoy her.

Stopping at Dr. Hines's office door, she hesitated and listened for any sounds of movement within. None. She grasped the knob and turned.

Inside, she closed the door quietly and perused the room. Taking a deep breath, she noticed stale remnants of Dr. Hines's cologne. Not as pleasing as Evan's scent. She walked over to the closet door and tried to open it. Locked, as usual.

Turning to the desk, she pushed aside the cushiony swivel chair and pulled out the top center drawer. Not much resided here. Some pens, a stapler with an extra supply of staples, a few notepads. She slid her hand back as far as it could reach and hit nothing but bare wood. Now the side drawers. In the top one, she found a hand-held mirror, an electric razor, and a bottle of aftershave.

At the back of the drawer, her fingers grazed a cluster of metal objects. Keys! Looping the ring over her finger and letting them dangle, she examined them. Not one resembled a door key. These looked like office furniture keys. Heaving a sigh of frustration, she placed the keys back where she'd gotten them.

Pulling the handle of the large bottom drawer produced no results, so she returned to the previous drawer for the keys she'd found a moment ago.

The keys all looked alike, and none were marked, so it

took longer than she expected to find one that fit. Visions of Dr. Hines bursting in on her while she crouched there, pretty as you please, and handling all his business stuff marched through her mind. With shaky fingers, she chose a key and inserted it into the lock. "*Aha!*" Dr. Hines would say, pointing a finger at her. A trembling began at the pit of her stomach and spread to her limbs. Feeling as if she'd donned a pair of rubber gloves, she fumbled the keys.

Finally, one key turned in the lock, and the drawer opened. Although it was designed to hold file folders, instead, she found a ledger. That meant money. Something she thought the doctor didn't care about.

Straightening up, she placed the book on the desk and leafed through the pages. Her saliva turned acidic, as her tongue began to feel heavy as wet wool. Entries in the columns of these pages ranged from tens of thousands to hundreds of thousands. Though these numbers obviously represented dollar amounts, nothing here indicated where these huge amounts of money came from, nor where the payable amounts went.

With a sense of urgency, she went to the copy machine room and made copies of several pages in the ledger. She hurried back to the office and returned everything to order. To be sure she left nothing out of place, her eyes scanned the room once more.

In that moment of complete silence, a slight thumping sound could be heard. Amber looked around, wondering where it could be coming from. She took a few steps to the left, and the sound seemed to fade away. Going toward the right, it returned, and even seemed to come from behind her.

The closet.

She pressed her ear to the door and listened, afraid the pounding of her heart would drown out the slight noise she sought to hear. It didn't. The thumping came from whatever Dr. Hines kept behind this door.

What does he have hidden in there?

That familiar squeak from the door out front alerted her. Someone had returned to the clinic! She'd already put everything back in place, so all she need do was collect her things and go. Shaking, she snatched up her jacket and purse and left the room, shutting the door behind her as quietly as possible.

She started down the hall as Dr. Hines rounded the corner from the reception area. He seemed intent on reading some messages he held in his hand. That extra few seconds it took him to pick them up from Carol's desk had provided Amber with the precious time she needed to scoot from his office.

Thank you, Lord.

Dr. Hines looked up and stopped mid-stride, as if startled. "Amber! What are you still doing here?"

Moisture broke out on her palms, and the hairs on the nape of her neck prickled. "I had a few things I wanted to catch up on." She wondered at the damage these frequent half-truths must be doing to her relationship with God. Both her personal and professional lives were a mess. If she came through these recent developments of both unscathed, she vowed to deal only in total truth for the remainder of her days.

"I see."

His expression told her he really didn't see, and she knew the wheels of his mind were beginning to turn with suspicion and unasked questions. Lately, he didn't seem to trust anyone.

She needed to get out of there.

"Well, see you tomorrow, Doc."

He didn't answer immediately, or move, so she passed around him and headed toward the door.

"Good night, Amber."

A simple farewell. But his tone belied what must really be going through his mind.

As she climbed into her minivan, Amber hoped she'd returned everything in his office to its proper place. Glancing back at the building, she knew he was in there, right now, checking to make sure nothing had been touched.

CHAPTER 34

When Amber arrived at the center on Thursday morning, Dr. Hines had called a meeting in the conference room. He watched solemnly, as everyone took their seats at the small, round table. The scent of yesterday's coffee still lingered in the air, and the stale smell made Amber nauseated.

Dr. Hines cleared his throat. "I'll make this brief. The police have informed me that the medical examiner has confirmed Rita's cause of death as a heart attack."

Everyone remained silent. Doug lowered his head, shaking it. Maggie looked off to the side. Carol dabbed her moist eyes with a tissue.

The doctor stood with hands clasped behind his back, his expression stoic. "That's all." He turned to leave the room.

That's it? Amber thought. That's all there was to it? It just didn't sound right. There had to be more. "Wait!" Her plea stopped Dr. Hines at the door. "Didn't they say what caused the heart attack? Did she have a history of heart disease? She seemed pretty fit."

His eyes flickered. "That's all they told me." His gaze scanned the small group of workers. "I know nothing of Rita's health history."

Amber couldn't let it go. A woman lives a lifetime, then one day she doesn't show up for work. Her whole existence is snuffed out in the time it takes for her heart to stop beating. And this is how it's summed up?

Amber looked up at Dr. Hines. "What about a funeral?" A service would at least give some sort of tribute.

His eyes flickered again, and she wished she could interpret its meaning. Perhaps speaking of Rita's death was too painful. He hadn't been himself since the news hit. Maybe he cared for Rita more than any of them knew. "They can't release the body until all efforts are exhausted to find the next of kin. That could take months. I'm sorry." He nodded once and walked out.

On the way back to her office, Amber's mind swirled with

thoughts of Rita's death, and she intended to press Dr. Hines further. She noticed his door was open about five inches, as if he'd entered and swung it behind him, but not hard enough for it to catch. That small space provided a marginal view of the doctor sitting at his desk.

But the way he sat there—elbows on the desk, head bent, and his hands collaring the back of his neck—made her think better of barging in on this private moment. Perhaps she should offer some consolation. But what could she say? Thinking back to that night she'd overheard Dr. Hines and Rita speaking in this very office, what she remembered most was his indifference, his harshness toward her. Could he feel remorse for how unkindly he'd treated Rita on the last night he'd seen her alive?

Another glance through the door, and she saw that rare moment had ended. He seemed to be concentrating on paperwork, his facial expression the same as usual.

No need to comfort him, at all.

* * *

On the drive home, Amber decided to swing by Evan's office. She should have gone straight to her folks' to pick up Melly, but she couldn't resist having just a few minutes alone with her husband.

Oh, she wished this investigation would hurry up and be over.

A few minutes later, she rapped lightly on Evan's door and entered. "Hi."

His face lit up when he saw her. "Hi," he said, as he got to his feet. He came around the desk and gave her a light kiss. "How was your day?"

She let out a shaky sigh and stared down at the phone on the corner of his desk. "Dr. Hines told us today the M.E. has ruled that Rita's death was caused by a heart attack."

Evan nodded, but looked skeptical.

"What?" she asked.

"It just seems too pat. Don't you think?"

Eyeing the coffeemaker, she went over to it. "It's in the autopsy report." She poured herself a mug of the lukewarm liquid and carried it to her desk.

He shifted his gaze toward the window and repeatedly clicked the button at the top of his pen.

Amber sipped the coffee and made a face at the bitter taste. "I know what you're thinking," she said. "I guess it's possible, but I doubt it. We don't know what really happened, or if Rita had some undiagnosed heart problem. Besides, Dr. Hines seems upset by her death."

Crossing his arms over his chest, he fixed her with a glare. She could almost see the steam puffing off the top of his head. "Why do you continually want to exonerate the guy? Need I remind you his carelessness caused your sister's death?"

His point hit home and she felt chided like a wayward child. She couldn't bear to meet his eyes. "I don't know. At first, I did want him to pay for that, but now that I've seen a little of what he's really like, I guess I feel there's some good in him."

Evan's glare increased. "You've got to be kidding." He dragged out the words, as if she were a foreigner who needed time to understand the language.

Again, she had to glance away. The first thought that came to mind was how Dr. Hines had offered his own life for hers during the hostage situation. For some reason, she couldn't bring herself to tell Evan about that. Maybe because revealing how much the doctor cared for her would send him over the edge. He'd find some excuse to take her off the story and away from the clinic.

"Look," she finally said. "I know what he does goes entirely against what we believe. I admit he can be cold and ruthless and I sometimes feel uncomfortable around him. But knowing how deeply his son's death has impacted him and how he somehow believes what he's doing is helping some small part of humanity"—she shook her head—"It just doesn't fit."

He sprang off the chair and the action forced a lock of his hair to fall onto his forehead. "How can you think that?"

"Okay, calm down." She got to her feet, too. "I didn't come here to argue."

As she stepped toward him, he said, "What *did* you come here for, then." A twinkle flashed in his eye. How quickly his anger dissipated these days.

"This." She curled her arms around his neck and met his lips with hers.

"Mmm. You came to the right place."

"I'm no dummy."

He indulged her with a second helping of kisses.

And she stayed as long as she could, wanting to quench her thirst for him but never quite reaching her fill.

CHAPTER 35

On Friday evening, Amber deliberately took her time preparing to leave the center at the end of the day. She'd been doing that a lot in the past weeks, hoping that Dr. Hines would leave before her. Each time, she figured there would always be another opportunity to search his office for the keys to his mysterious closet.

She hadn't heard him leave yet. Too much time had passed to wait any longer, and Dr. Hines might get suspicious. She wanted to get home to Melly.

Going down the hall toward his office, she heard the soft thud of a door closing and the familiar jingle of keys. She stopped at his door. "Good night, doc."

He turned from the closet and sat down at his desk. "Good night, Miss Amber."

Miss Amber. He must be in better spirits. Her eyes slid to the closet. Should she just flat out ask him? He did, at one time, say he'd someday show her what he kept in there.

"Something on your mind?"

"Huh?" She met his gaze.

He smiled and inclined his head in the direction she had been staring. "You seem to have great interest in that door."

Caught off guard by his directness, she scrounged for an answer while he studied her.

"Would you like to see what's in there?"

His offer both stunned and relieved her. If he wanted to show her, there couldn't be anything so bad in there. Nothing to fear. "Yes, I would very much like to see."

He stood and removed the keys from his pocket. "I think it's time." Pushing the key into the lock, he added, "Now that Rita's gone, I need someone to assist me." He opened the door and stepped through.

Amber stood rooted to the spot. This was it. As soon as she walked in there, she'd know his big secret. She'd find out why he kept the door locked, what Rita had threatened to tell, what made the thumping sound. But for some reason, she couldn't make herself move.

Dr. Hines poked his head out. "Amber?"

Her heart skittered. "Yeah, doc. Coming." She forced her leaden feet to cross the threshold. The thumping grew louder and clearer, and she realized it was the sound of a machine-generated heartbeat. She swallowed hard and looked to her left where the sound came from.

At first, Amber wasn't sure what she was looking at. Lined up against the wall were glass containers with metal tops that resembled fish tanks. She blinked. Unable to believe what she was seeing in these tanks, she moved closer. *Babies!* Six of them, each perfectly formed. All hooked up to umbilical cord-like tubes, which led to what looked like small oxygen tanks that stood beside each container.

Heart slamming against her chest, Amber turned to Dr. Hines. "I don't understand. What's—?"

"These don't go out with the specimens Doug ships," Dr. Hines said, gazing at the array of tanks as though they were prized possessions. "I save these for Jasmine. She has a client who specifically researches Duchenne dystrophy and prefers them live. I've created a simulated mother's womb to keep them that way. It's just a pity they can't take all of them, and the extra ones born alive have to be destroyed."

Movement from one of the tanks drew her attention. The baby in that one was sucking its thumb. She stared. He was a little boy, and she could see the motion of his jaw and cheeks as he sucked. He had hair, too! Beautiful dark hair. Another one kicked her little foot out several times. A third, another boy, turned over as though he sought a more comfortable position.

Her limbs went weak and her breath threatened to choke her. She thought she would die on the spot. Each of these babies belonged to some woman who didn't even know it was alive!

Amber felt sick to her stomach.

She couldn't trust herself to say another thing. Her tongue seemed paralyzed and she feared what she would blurt out. Besides, no words existed for such a time as this.

"So what do you think? Will you take over for Rita?" He looked at her, expectant.

Her heart doubled its beat and her breath couldn't keep up. She would hyperventilate at any moment. She wanted out of there. "I'm sorry, Doc. This is too much to take in, right now. I have to go. We'll talk about it on Monday."

Though she couldn't feel her legs carrying her, somehow she made it down the hall and out the door. Before she knew it, she was in her car driving away.

Pictures of what she had seen flashed through her mind. Babies. Tiny, *live* babies, lying in those . . . tanks. And the baby boy sucking his thumb!

Her cell phone rang. She pulled it from her handbag to read the caller ID screen. Dr. Hines. Her stomach lurched, and she broke out in a sweat.

Should she answer? If she didn't he'd probably drive over to her apartment. She'd better answer it.

"Hello?" She couldn't control the quiver in her voice.

"Amber, are you okay?"

"Y-yes. I'm sorry, Doc, I just wasn't prepared for that. I've never seen anything like it."

"I understand. I know how sensitive you are. I probably shouldn't have sprung it on you that way."

She agreed but didn't say so.

"I can trust you, right, Amber?"

It took a few moments for the lie to roll off her tongue. "Of course." Did he notice her hesitation?

"See you Monday, then?"

She would rather never go back there again. Just knowing those babies were in that room while she went about her business . . .

"S-sure."

"Good. Talk to you then."

* * *

Amber pulled into Evan's driveway. She'd made it. Even though she had to drive while slumped over the steering wheel, clutching it like a lifeline. She got out of the minivan and trudged up to the door. The cool evening air against her clammy face sent shivers spiraling through her body. She hadn't even bothered calling to see if Evan had come home. Turning the knob, she pushed open the door.

"Evan?" Her voice sounded shaky.

"Amber? Is that you?" She could hear him from upstairs. "I'll be right down."

She stood waiting at the bottom of the steps, teeth chattering, until he appeared.

"I'm sorry I didn't call first."

"No problem. I just got home and was changing out of my suit." Half-way down the stairs, he stopped and studied her.

"What's wrong? You look like you've seen death."

He seemed to take forever to reach her. When he finally did, she fell into his arms.

"Hey, what's the matter?" He rubbed and patted her back, comforting her. "You're trembling. C'mon, sit down in here." Turning her around, he led her to the living room and helped her onto the couch. As he took a seat next to her, she grabbed a throw pillow and clutched it to her chest.

Everything spilled out in a rush. A raging river through a broken dam. "Oh, Evan, Dr. Hines showed me what he kept in that closet, which really isn't a closet, but a small room, and there was thumping and fish tanks and babies, with one sucking its thumb, a little boy, and—"

"Hold it, hold it." He said this softly. "Now, take a deep breath and start from the beginning, slowly."

She nodded and tried again. "On my way out, I stopped by Dr. Hines's office to say goodnight. He was just locking his secret closet, and when he caught me looking at it, he asked if I wanted to see inside." She paused for a breath.

"He actually asked if you wanted to see? Unbelievable." He shook his head.

She nodded. The shaking hadn't stopped. "I said okay, so he unlocked the door, saying it was time he showed me, and then suggested I help him now that Rita was gone." Her lips twisted and her brow wrinkled.

"Well, what did Rita do for him?"

She shrugged. "I don't know. I did hear her say something once, like she'd taken care of 'the chambers.' She must have been talking about those fish tank things."

Evan held up a hand. "Wait. Back up. So you went inside and you saw these fish tanks?"

"Right." Her voice became shaky, again. "Only they didn't hold fish. There—" She could feel the tears welling up and covered her face with a hand.

Evan reached over and touched her shoulder. "Take your time."

"There were babies." Her voice came out in a whisper. The tears spilled over, rolling down her cheeks. She swiped at them. The memory of those little ones would be branded in her mind forever.

"Wait." Evan got up and left the room. He returned in a moment, holding a hand towel. "Here. Let me." He gently dabbed at the wet streaks on her cheeks. Drawing back, he studied her.

"Can you go on?"

She nodded. "I think so." She took a quivery breath. "Anyway, these looked like babies that were late-term abortions. Ones that survived, maybe, or that he'd purposely kept alive. I don't know." Covering her face with her hands, she sobbed softly.

Evan sucked in a breath. "*Live babies?* He's keeping live babies?"

She nodded.

"But what on earth is he doing with them? How's he keeping them alive?"

Shaking her head, she probed her brain. "He said he created a simulated mother's womb, and I saw tubes attached to small oxygen tanks."

"Are you sure they're alive, Amber?" His eyes searched hers.

She looked straight at him. "Positive." The image of that little baby boy flashed through her mind. Her stomach clenched. "That *one*. The boy. He was sucking his thumb. I could see"—her body shook with silent weeping—"his jaw and cheeks working."

Evan moved closer and put an arm around her. "Poor Sweetheart."

Amber laid her head on his shoulder. "Oh, Evan, I'll never forget what I saw." Lifting her head to look into his eyes, she asked, "What should we do about them?"

"I'll tell you what *I'm* going to do." He took his arm from around her and scooted off the couch. "I'm calling the police. Matter of fact, I'll call Uriah."

He stood and reached into his pocket, then tsked. "My cell phone's upstairs." Heading out of the room, he said, "I'll be right back."

She could hear his voice from the kitchen, where he must have decided to use the land line. The conversation was short. A tiny space of silence, then she heard his voice again.

Her cell phone ringing sent a jolt through her body. It was Ma calling to find out why she was so late picking up Melly. "I'm with Evan discussing the story, but I'll be leaving in a bit," she whispered quickly.

"Oh, I see," her mother said in a tone that implied she'd read more into it than there was. "Melly's ready to nod off, but take your time. I can even put her to bed here."

"No, really, Ma, I'll be there soon."

Evan returned just as she hung up. "Uriah gave me an

after-hours phone number for the FBI. He said they'd probably act on Monday, since no one was in imminent danger. I left a message with the information. The situation is in their hands now."

She nodded. "I guess my work at the clinic is done, then." She was relieved. She certainly didn't want to be there when the FBI found those babies, though. She could just imagine Dr. Hines's cold, accusing stare.

They sat there quietly for a time, snuggled against one another, each lost in their own thoughts.

Evan's voice jolted Amber out of her daze. "Who was on the phone?"

"Huh?"

"The phone. Who were you talking to when I came back from my call to Uriah?"

She cleared her throat and sat up straight. "Oh. That was just Ma."

"Oh? Does she need something?"

"No. I was supposed to stop over there after work." She looked at her watch. "I've got to go. We'll talk tomorrow, okay?" She pushed off the couch.

"Are you sure you're all right?" He followed her to the door. "If you're not up to driving, or being alone you could . . . stay here tonight."

Amber stopped abruptly and gulped. If only she could. Spending the night wrapped in Evan's reassuring arms would do her a world of good. She turned around and smiled. "That's sweet of you. I'm rattled, but I'll be fine."

He looked disappointed, but he nodded. "Call me if you need me. For anything at all. You never know what Hines will do now that you know his secret."

She *was* a little spooked by that thought. After what she'd seen tonight, Dr. Hines was probably capable of anything.

CHAPTER 36

On Monday morning, Amber came awake slowly. She did not want to get out of bed today and face the inevitable. She and Evan had decided to take a much needed reprieve over the weekend and spend a little time together. The larger amount of time she spent with Melly. It felt good to act like a regular mom again. Later today they would meet to finish the story and it would break tomorrow.

She reached for the phone on the nightstand. She would call in sick to make things look as normal as possible. Actually, not showing up after running out on Dr. Hines Friday night was not normal. He'd definitely assume she was avoiding him because he'd shown her those babies. Let him think what he wanted. Once the FBI found those born-alive fetuses and whatever other evidence he had hidden around the clinic, he would probably be arrested and she'd never have to deal with him again.

After leaving a quick message about not feeling well, she prayed the FBI would show up quickly.

Amber had promised Evan she'd arrive at the house close to twelve o'clock, so they could work on the story. She would take Melly to her parents' house after eleven. As she was helping Melly into her jacket, the phone rang. Glancing at the caller ID screen, she stiffened.

Dr. Hines.

Moving into the short hallway as far as she could and still keeping Melly in sight, she answered.

"Hi, Doc."

"Are you avoiding me?" he asked without preamble.

Of course I am. "No, why?"

"Come on, Amber, I wasn't born yesterday. Calling in sick right after I show you my special project? That's too much of a coincidence."

She sighed into the phone, as she watched Melly pick up a baby doll from the couch and kiss it. "Okay, Doc. You got me. I'm not really sick. I have something important I need to do today. I didn't think you'd mind so much." That's it. Turn the tables and lay the guilt trip back on him.

"Why didn't you mention this on Friday?"

"It just came up over the weekend." Melly was singing to the doll and walking toward her. She needed to hang up before Dr. Hines heard.

"It doesn't matter, now. Go do your 'important' thing." He hung up.

Amber stared at the phone. He sounded perturbed and unconvinced. And she was doubly glad she wouldn't be there today when he was finally found out.

* * *

"I'm not sure any of this will be such a big deal to a lot of people." Amber sat at the computer, while Evan did his usual pacing. They'd been working for two hours.

"It doesn't matter," Evan said. "Our job is to get the story out. The rest is in God's hands."

"I know you're right, but—" Her cell phone ringing cut her off. It was Maggie. "Hi Mags, what's up?"

"How did you get the FBI to come here?" she whispered.

"They're there now?"

"Yes, he took them to his office. Why didn't you tell me they'd be coming?"

"We wanted to keep it real by having you be as surprised as the rest of the staff."

"Well, it worked. What happened to make this all come about?"

"It's a long story and I'll tell you the details later. Let's just say you were right about more going on than what you told us in the beginning. Dr. Hines showed me something"—she paused as a shiver ran down her spine—"horrible on Friday night. I told Evan about it, he called the FBI. They spoke with him this morning then quickly got their search warrant, I guess."

"Well, don't keep me waiting too long for those details, lady. You know I—wait they're coming out. I'll call you back."

Amber flipped her phone closed and glanced at Evan, who was looking at her expectantly. "The FBI was in Hines's office and came out again while I was talking to Maggie. She's going to call back." She thought for a brief moment. "Doesn't seem like they were in there very long."

Evan shrugged. "All they really needed to arrest him was to see he had those babies."

They tried going back to work while they waited, but

Amber's taut nerves made it impossible for her to concentrate. When Maggie still hadn't called back after twenty minutes, Amber swiveled the chair around to face Evan. "Can we take a break? I don't think I can get anything done until I know what happened."

"Sure. Why don't we have some coffee?"

She hopped off the chair. "I'll go make a pot."

They sat quietly at the kitchen table, sipping their coffee, each lost in their own thoughts. Amber kept the phone by her cup. When it rang, she jumped. Finally!

"Mags, what's going on?"

"I don't know. They left."

"What? They didn't arrest him?"

"No. He showed them around the clinic, then walked them out, smiling. Told them to let him know if he can do anything else for them. Then he walked back to his office with a grim look on his face."

Amber was floored. What could have happened?

"Listen, Mags, I'll have to get back to you."

As she hung up the phone, Evan's phone rang. Shooting her a puzzled look, he reached into his pants pocket. "Evan Blake here." He paused and listened to the caller. "You're sure?" Another pause. "What are you going to do?" Nodding, he said, "Okay, thanks." Looking perturbed, he closed the phone and laid it on the table.

"What?" Amber asked.

Emitting a troubled sigh, he looked at her. "There were no babies. They couldn't arrest him."

"What!" She jumped out of her chair. "No babies? How can that be?"

"Easy, Amber. They figure he got suspicious after showing them to you and moved them."

"What about other evidence? Receipts for the equipment he uses? Anything?"

Evan shook his head. "Nothing."

Feeling defeated, she climbed back onto her chair. "What do we do now?"

"We finish the story. Let things take a natural course. Wait for word from the feds."

He was right. That's all they had, for now.

* * *

Amber kneaded the crook of her neck, as she clicked the "Save" option on the computer program. After completing the story and implementing multiple revisions, they were finally finished. The clock at the bottom right corner of the monitor showed eight-fifteen.

She swirled the chair around to face Evan, who'd been pacing the room. "That's it."

He stopped mid-stride. "Okay, then. Let me shoot it over to Rusty and we're good to go."

Amber stood, and Evan took her place at the computer. He typed a few lines and, after a few clicks of the mouse, he was through. "Done."

They both heaved sighs of relief and stared at each other in silence for a moment.

"I feel like I don't know what to do with myself, now," Amber said.

"Yeah. A huge burden's been lifted from my shoulders."

Amber rolled her own shoulders. "I feel like the burden is still on mine."

"Poor sweetheart. Here." He got up, motioned for her to sit again, and positioned himself behind her. Then he began massaging her shoulders. "How's that?"

Her eyes closed, as she savored the feeling. "Mmm, heavenly."

"I've got an idea. Let's celebrate."

"How?"

He spun her around. "Pizza!"

"With anchovies?" Her stomach growled. They'd worked straight through dinner.

"You bet!" He pulled his cell phone out and made the call. After hanging up, he said, "It will be here in about forty-five minutes. Now where were we?"

"Right here." Amber tapped her shoulder and swiveled the chair so her back was to him.

"Oh, yeah." He resumed his sweet torture on her tight muscles and frayed nerves.

Soon his manipulations became slower, more sensual. His hands were no longer restricted to her shoulders but roamed to places that hadn't been touched in a very long time. Closing her eyes, she gave in to the sensations his touch provoked.

Evan turned the chair around so that Amber faced him. His eyes asked a question, and he held his hand out to her. Without hesitation, she took it. He pulled her up into his arms and trailed tender kisses from her lips to her ear and back again. Her knees weakened and she leaned against him. In one fluid movement, they lowered themselves to the floor.

She wanted this. She was wild for it to happen. Even though she'd told Evan she wanted to wait until they lived together. No more excuses. It was time.

Suddenly, she remembered and pushed him away. "Evan, we can't!"

"What? Why?"

"The pizza will be delivered soon."

Evan checked his watch. "We've got about half an hour." He waggled his eyebrows. "Wanna go for it?"

In answer, she pulled his head down to hers and gave him a long, passionate kiss.

"As always," he said, unbuttoning her blouse, "actions speak louder than words."

Within ninety minutes they were finishing up their pizza at the kitchen table. Evan had thrown on a sweatshirt and matching pants. Amber had donned the blue dress shirt he'd removed a short while ago.

She ate with gusto. It was now ten forty-five and she hadn't had a single crumb since before noon. As she drained the last of her Pepsi, her eyes met Evan's over the edge of her glass.

"You're staying the night, aren't you?" he asked.

"Absolutely." There was nowhere else she'd rather be. No worries about Melly, either. Having anticipated a long night of work, she'd arranged for Melly to sleep at her parents'.

Evan's playful gaze gave her goose bumps. "In that case," he said, pushing aside the pizza boxes and taking her hand, "care for seconds?"

CHAPTER 37

Amber woke feeling warm and secure in Evan's arms. Stretching lazily, she grinned to herself. Evan stirred, tightening his hold, inviting her to snuggle closer against him. Shifting within his embrace, she turned around to face him and breathed deeply of his male scent. His sleeping form reminded her of how she had always loved staring at him after a night of love-making, basking in the aura of their intimacy while she could still taste his kisses.

Things seemed perfect at the moment. But that would change soon, she reasoned, as she reached up and finger-combed his tousled hair. She knew he'd want her to move back home today, but there was still the matter of introducing him to Melly.

She shot up in the bed. Melly! Her baby would think she'd been abandoned if she didn't get over to her parents' house, pronto.

Evan lifted his head, his eyes heavy with sleep. "Whatsamatter?"

"I have to go." She untangled herself from the covers and scooted to the edge of the bed.

He caught her arm. "What's the rush?"

Amber gently pulled away. "I've got something to do." She dashed over to where her clothes lay in a neat pile on a bench at the foot of the bed. At one point last night, she'd collected them from the office floor and brought them up into the bedroom. She'd been stunned to see that, in their passion, she and Evan had flung their garments from north to south and east to west.

Evan rose up to lean on his elbow, resting his head against his fist. "Can't you do it later?"

"No," she said, wiggling into her slacks. She threw on her blouse, buttoned it haphazardly, then hoisted herself against the edge of the bed to place a brief kiss on Evan's lips. "We'll get together later. We need to talk."

"We'll do more than that." His eyes held a devilish gleam.

"I want to make up for lost time."

She giggled, feeling exactly as she did when they'd first wed: attractive, sexy, and young. Evan had always acted as though she were the most beautiful woman he'd ever seen. "I thought we'd done that last night," she said, heading out of the room.

"Not nearly." Evan's voice trailed after her.

She laughed out loud. "See you later."

* * *

As Amber pulled the minivan into her parents' driveway, her stomach clenched. She wondered if they could figure out what happened between her and Evan. Did she look like a woman who'd been made love to all night? Were her lips bruised? Swollen? She flipped down the sun visor and checked herself in the mirror. Nothing different *she* could see. She exited the car and hoped she could act natural.

Entering the house, she called out her arrival.

"I'll be right out," Ma called from the laundry room.

"Take your time."

Dad came down the hall from the family room with Melly sitting upon his broad shoulders, her little legs straddling his neck.

"Look a' me, Mommy!"

Amber smiled brightly, and spoke in that falsetto voice that most people used when talking to a toddler. "Oooh, I see! You're up so high!"

Ma rushed into the foyer. "Good morning, dear." She bent to kiss Amber's cheek. "We read the story. Oh, that man is such a snake!"

After last night, she'd almost forgotten about it.

Ma studied her for a few seconds while Amber squirmed under her scrutiny. "You look fabulous, this morning," she said, her gaze teasing. "Your eyes sparkle, your whole face is glowing. *Working* late into the night does wonders for you."

Mortified by Ma's openness, Amber blushed.

"For heaven's sake, Darla!" Dad said, dancing around in a circle, while Melly laughed. "Exercise some discretion, will you?"

Amber's face burned. Waving a hand, she said, "Forget that. There are more important things going on."

"Tell us," Ma said, perching herself on the sofa. Dad lowered Melly to the floor and sat next to Ma.

Amber sat too, barely able to contain her excitement.

Melly came over and climbed into her lap. "Today's the day I'm going to introduce Melly to Evan." She kissed her daughter's head. "Or, more likely, tonight."

Ma jumped up and clasped her hands together. "Oh, honey, that's wonderful!" She turned to Dad. "Isn't that wonderful, Ben?"

"Sure, but—"

"Oh, now you three can be a real family. I'm so happy!" Ma twirled around and plopped back down onto the sofa.

Dad scratched his head. "Yeah, but you know he won't take it well that Amber hid Melly from him all this time."

Ma looked over at him with a feigned look of anger. "Killjoy! Where's your faith?"

He spread his hands. "I'm just being practical."

Amber sided with her dad. Evan's reaction had been uppermost in her mind ever since she'd borne Melly. The thought scared her to pieces, for she'd be risking the happiness they'd just rediscovered. "You're right, Dad, but obviously it has to be done. I've waited too long, and the longer I wait, the harder it gets. I'm really afraid of what Evan will do. But Lord willing, whatever happens, it will all work out in the end."

Ma nodded hard a few times. "That's right, Amber. The Lord wouldn't have it any other way."

Amber, too, believed that was how God would want it. But would Evan listen to the Lord's guidance? If not, she didn't know if she could endure the heartache.

* * *

Once Amber left, Evan couldn't go back to sleep. After having her in bed with him all night, being there alone seemed unbearable. He couldn't face another night without her.

He had an idea: Instead of waiting for her call, he'd go to her apartment and invite her to move back home this day. And he wouldn't come back without her. He'd make it special, like a new marriage proposal. They could even have a little ceremony and burn the divorce papers as they renewed their vows.

His mind made up, Evan climbed out of bed and went to the bathroom to trim his goatee and shower. Afterward, he returned to the bedroom to make the bed. As he straightened the rumpled sheets, he smiled, remembering their passionate reunion. Just like it used to be. And after their two-year split, it still hadn't ebbed.

He wanted to look extra nice for this special visit with Amber, so he chose his clothing with care. After applying the cologne that seemed to drive her wild, he donned a pair of jeans he'd just had altered a few days ago. Next, he pulled on a sport shirt with green and dark blue pin stripes on a light blue background. He finished off with a navy blazer. After giving himself a confident nod in the mirror, he went to the night stand and retrieved the divorce papers he'd found the day the contents of Amber's purse had spilled onto the floor. He'd been waiting for some special way to signify that a divorce would never come to pass. A good way to do that would be the burning of the papers together, watching the flame dissolve them into ashes. He pushed the folded packet into the inside pocket of his blazer.

The drive over to Amber's took him past a florist. She might enjoy being wooed, he thought. On a whim, he swerved into the tiny parking lot. When he got inside, he searched for the roses, which he found in the refrigerated case.

"May I help you?" A tall, middle-aged woman with flaming red hair and sparkly eyes stood behind him.

"Yes, I'd like a dozen roses, please."

She slid open the glass door. "What color would you like?"

He scratched his head. "Hmm." He couldn't remember ever knowing whether Amber liked red, yellow, pink or white roses best. She would probably like any or all of them. "Give me a dozen of each."

With a broad smile, the sales woman responded, "Whoever these are for is a very lucky lady."

"Thank you, ma'am." Luck didn't enter into it. He knew he was blessed to have Amber again. Would Amber consider herself so?

He carried the shiny, oblong boxes out to the car, and placed them in the front passenger seat. His heart leaped as he drove off, knowing he came ever closer to that final step in their reunion.

Evan turned his Mustang into the parking lot of Amber's apartment building. As he drove through the line of parked cars, he didn't see Amber's Odyssey. Hadn't she arrived home, yet? Then he remembered her saying she had something to do. In his eagerness to see her again, he'd forgotten. Maybe she'd be home soon. He selected a parking spot a little farther down from the area where she would normally park, so he could see when she arrived. His anticipation of her surprise had him tapping out a beat on the steering wheel.

While waiting, Evan envisioned Amber's reaction to the

roses. Tears would likely trickle down her cheeks; she might kiss and hug him. Ah, he couldn't wait.

Soon he spotted her minivan pulling in. His heart pounded with excitement. He wanted to rush out and greet her, but decided to wait until she went inside, then show up at her door and make his grand presentation.

Amber zipped into a parking slot, but when she didn't exit the vehicle immediately, he wondered what could be taking so long. The tinted glass made it impossible for him to see what she was doing. He got out of his car as quietly as possible, intending to grab those awkward, elongated boxes. He softly pushed the door closed behind him, hoping Amber couldn't see him walk around the back of the car to the passenger side. While gathering the boxes, he heard Amber's back passenger door slide open. He looked up to see her easing herself down. Why she hadn't chosen a car she could get in and out of more easily, he couldn't fathom.

Chattering some kind of baby talk, Amber stood before the opening with arms raised. A small child appeared. *Hmm. Babysitting?*

He watched with interest as the child, a girl, snuggled into Amber's waiting arms. The motion seemed so natural. Then Amber hugged the cherubic little girl tightly and placed a few soft kisses upon her head.

Confusion ricocheted around his mind. Were those the actions of a common babysitter? He had nothing to compare them. No baby sitter had ever been that way with him as a child. He could only conclude that something significant existed between the two. The look that Amber had about her while interacting with this child, that aura, seemed . . . *motherly*.

Could this be Amber's child? He thought back to the countless times she'd had to stop at her folks' house after leaving him. Had they all been conspiring to make a fool of him? And if Amber had had a baby, whose was it?

Fury coursed through him. He slammed the door shut and charged toward her. "Would you care to tell me what's going on?" he shouted, as he stepped up to her. The child lifted her head from Amber's shoulder, peered at him with sleepy eyes and whimpered. Amber's gaze evidenced panic mixed with guilt. She rubbed the girl's back. "It's okay, Peaches." She glared at him, and if her eyes were weapons, he'd have been dead on the spot. "You're scaring her," she said. She pulled a tote bag from the minivan and shouldered it. "Let's go inside and talk without giving the neighbors a show."

When they reached Amber's apartment, she strode straight toward the hallway. "I'll be right back."

He stood there, fuming, unable to believe this was happening. Last night, everything seemed so perfect.

Amber returned to the living room. "I've put her down for a nap, so keep your voice down." She stood looking at him expectantly, all traces of guilt gone. Something else had replaced it, but he couldn't figure out what.

"Would you mind telling me who that child belongs to?"

Her body jerked back, and she looked stunned at his question. "Isn't that obvious?"

Was she whacked? He moved toward her and realized he still clutched the four flower shop boxes. He hurled them to the floor, where they crashed and opened on impact, spilling their contents in a colorful heap. "It's obvious she's yours, but who's the father?"

She stared at him in disbelief. "What? I—I can't believe you're asking that." Her brows furrowed and her expression turned stormy.

For a moment, the earth stopped spinning. Struggling for control, he stepped toward her. "What are you saying, Amber? Are you telling me I'm the father?" His voice began to rise.

"Sshh. You'll wake Melly."

Melly. That's what his mother used to be called; a variation of Melody. She was the only person, besides Amber, who ever really loved him. "How dare you keep this from me," he said in a dangerously quiet voice.

"I'm sorry," Amber said. "I didn't know how to tell you."

"You knew I wanted to get back together. Both you and your parents made a fool out of me. You should have told me, Amber."

Amber's fists flew to her hips. "How could I? You're against having children."

"That's not the point!" His voice thundered now, and he didn't care. This felt worse than if she'd literally plunged an iron stake through his heart. "All this time, playing me for a fool. And me! Acting like an idiot, trying to woo you back." He couldn't think, could barely see. Not knowing what to do, he tugged on the lapels of his blazer. The divorce papers crackled from the inside breast pocket. He reached in and retrieved them. Pulled out a pen, too. Laid them on the coffee table. Leaned down and scrawled his name on the appropriate line.

"No." Amber's voice floated to him as if from a distance. Evan didn't look at her. *Couldn't* look at her. He straightened up and flung the papers in her direction. Accompanied by Amber's soft sobs, he walked out of the apartment.

CHAPTER 38

For the last couple hours, Amber lay huddled on the floor in the very spot she'd been in when Evan walked out the door. Exhausted from crying, she felt there were no more tears left. Knowing Melly would be waking from her nap soon, she pulled herself out of her stupor and onto her feet. For the first time, she noticed the door had been left open. What if one of her neighbors had happened by? Trudging to the door to close it, she passed the flowers Evan had thrown on the floor. In all the ruckus, she'd barely noticed them. She crouched down and lifted one. Roses. Four different colors. Her heart melted. Bringing the delicate bloom to her nose, she thought about how he must have stopped and chosen these with such love. Laying a hand over her face, she shook her head. Why hadn't she listened to her parents and told Evan about Melly right away? More tears squeezed themselves out, trailing their wetness down her cheeks. Amber wiped them away with the backs of her hands.

Tenderly, she picked up the roses and carried them to the kitchen. She would not let this be the end. Though Evan had overreacted in his shock and anger, she knew that was just his way. Even so, he was a good man. She knew him like no one else. Knew the secret places of his heart that he'd revealed only to her. He could be as territorial as a lion, but he had a right to be. They'd given themselves to one another, never expecting their love to belong to anyone else.

After pulling several vases out of a lower cabinet, she began arranging the roses, wondering if Evan would ever forgive her. The offense of concealing the existence of his daughter garnered the worst kind of punishment. His signing that divorce agreement ranked high on the list of possibilities.

Last night, everything had come together perfectly. Evan had probably shown up this morning to ask her to move back home and had come early in his eagerness to see her again.

But why did he have the divorce papers with him?

Letting out a huge sigh, Amber placed the floral arrangements in various places around the living room. Today was an Armageddon of sorts. By now, hundreds of thousands of people had already read about Dr. Hines's deeds, but she hardly cared.

Yes, today was the beginning of the end. In more ways than one.

* * *

On Wednesday morning, Amber came awake to sunshine slicing through her closed eyelids. She couldn't open them, as they were crusted shut from dried tears. For the remainder of yesterday she fought the urge to cry, so as not to upset Melly. But at night, alone in the dark, all her pent-up anguish released itself, until she fell into an exhausted slumber just a few hours before waking time. In addition, at around 2:30 a.m., she'd heard a noise down in the parking lot, and had gotten out of bed to look out the window. There in the shadows, was a human form that seemed to be staring up at her. Gasping, she stepped back. After a few seconds, she chanced another peek, but the figure was gone.

Perhaps she'd imagined it.

Yawning and rubbing the flakes from her eyes, she turned onto her side and looked at the clock beside the bed. Six forty-five. Melly would be up soon. She needed to call her parents before that. She hadn't wanted to talk about it yesterday, but she'd better get it over with. They would be up, by now. Probably having breakfast and lively conversation together. She reached for the phone on the night stand and punched in their number.

When Ma answered, Amber attempted to sound normal. "Hi, Ma."

"Amber! Where have you been? We're dying to know what happened." Ma sounded excited, as if she expected to hear that she and Evan had spent all of Tuesday afternoon moving hers and Melly's things back to the house.

"I know, Ma, I'm sorry." She worked the muscles in her throat, but the words wouldn't come.

"Well?"

Tears pooled, as she struggled to speak. Then, the dam of her strength gave way, and the rapids of despair rushed through. Sobs racked her body.

"What's wrong, Amber?"

"Oh, Ma!" More tears. "Evan hates me."

"What? What happened?"

"When I got home from your house with Melly yesterday, Evan was waiting for me. He saw me with Melly before I had a chance to tell him."

"Oh, Honey. I'm so sorry."

"There was a big blowout. He had the divorce agreement with him, and he signed it before walking out."

"Divorce agreement? What divorce agreement?"

Uh-oh. In her misery, she'd forgotten that she never told Ma and Dad about filing for divorce. How could she explain to her parents why she'd done it? How could she tell them that she'd felt so ugly after kissing Dr. Hines, she had thought Evan would be better off without her? She couldn't. She took a deep breath. "It's a long story, Ma, but *I* filed for the divorce. I planned on asking Evan to sign the papers. Then things started going really well between us, and I changed my mind. But Evan found the papers one day when they fell out of my handbag. We argued and he took them with him when he left. He never said a word about them after that and things got good again. Until yesterday."

Ma's worried sigh filtered through the phone. "Oh, Amber, what a mess things have turned out to be. Dad and I will pray for you and Evan."

"Thanks, Ma."

"It will all work out. You'll see."

As she placed the phone on the night table, she hoped Ma was right. Chances seemed slim to her. But if, as the Bible promised, all things worked together for good to those who love God and are called according to His purpose, then the possibility had to exist.

* * *

As Amber poured milk into Melly's cereal, the phone rang. Dare she hope? She took it from beside her plate and checked. The tiny ID screen showed Evan's home number. Her heart leaped with joy. Without wasting even a nanosecond, she answered. "Hello, Evan."

"Hi." His voice lacked the usual warmth and her heart sank. "I'm calling for a couple reasons."

This wasn't what she'd pictured. "Okay."

"I wanted to tell you that after you told me about Rita's autopsy results, I called Uriah Washington and asked him to request further toxicology testing on her body."

This was the last thing she expected to hear. "Oh?"

"I remembered hearing about some drugs that could cause immediate heart attacks, or even death. Drugs any doctor would have easy access to. So I thought it should be checked out."

Melly tried to feed Amber a spoonful of her Cheerios and she shook her head, indicating she didn't want it. "Good idea," she said to Evan.

"We should be getting the results any day, now."

"He-ya, Mommy," Melly persisted, holding the spoon to Amber's mouth. For a brief second, Amber had the inclination to bolt from the table. But then she remembered she didn't have to do that anymore. It felt really good.

"Is that . . . her?"

Her? He couldn't even say his own daughter's name. "Yes, that's *Melly*, which is short for Melody, as you know."

"Yes, I do. I'm . . . grateful you named her after my mother." He paused and cleared his throat. "Ah, Amber, it seems so strange, your being there with a child, acting so naturally. I can't imagine it. I mean, I *can* imagine it, since you've always wanted children, but since I've never seen you interacting with a child of your own—I just can't picture it, because I . . . I missed it from the beginning."

Tears threatened and her throat tightened. "I'm so sorry, Evan."

He let out a long breath. "I know. But it's not all your fault. We've both made mistakes. I'm sorry for raising my voice to you. I was just angry. You know me, always flying off the handle without thinking."

She did know that about him. Had become used to it. If not, they'd have been divorced long ago. Probably would never have gotten married.

"Which brings me to the other reason I called. I'd like to visit . . . my daughter."

The tears that threatened earlier now spilled over, running down her cheeks. "Okay," she whispered.

"Mommy, o-tay?" Melly took her milk-dampened napkin and tried wiping Amber's face. Amber waved her hand away.

"Good. I'll be there around eleven."

She hung up and hugged Melly, sobbing happily. "Daddy's coming to see you!"

* * *

Throughout the time she took preparing Melly and herself for Evan's visit, Amber's anxiety level skyrocketed. Should she get dressed up? Or should she dress as she would for any normal day at home? She finally decided on something Evan had never seen her in. Not a dress, though. That would be too obvious at eleven in the morning. A pair of casual-chic black slacks and a powder blue cashmere sweater seemed a good choice. Then she carefully applied her make-up to hide any signs of lost sleep.

For Melly, she wanted to make it apparent that her little girl had dressed especially to meet her daddy for the first time. A frilly, pink dress with lace collar and cuffs, and puffy sleeves. After combing Melly's dark, baby-soft tresses into submission, she tried clipping back the sides with barrettes made of pink ribbon fashioned into fancy bows.

Melly yanked at them. "No!" She pulled one out. "Don't yike."

"Okay, Peaches. How about this?" Amber slid a pink elastic headband onto Melly's head and held a mirror in front of her.

Melly smiled at her reflection.

Amber sighed. Why her little girl liked one adornment over the other, she had no idea. Such were the ways of the female persuasion.

At ten forty-five, Melly sat in a corner of the sofa, flipping pages of a picture book they had just finished reading together. Amber paced the living room floor, her low-heeled pumps making muted padding sounds on the thick pile of the carpet.

Promptly at eleven, the doorbell chimed. Trying not to look too anxious, she straightened her sweater, took a deep breath and pulled open the door.

There stood Evan, holding a brightly wrapped package. His dark good looks never ceased to floor her.

"Hey." His voice still lacked its usual warmth.

"Hey. Come on in." She stepped aside.

He walked in as if he were on his way to the gallows and stopped a few feet from the couch. Melly looked up and stared at him. He stared back.

The moment seemed suspended in time. Even her heart stopped beating. She cleared her throat. "Go on, she won't bite."

Evan glanced at her, then closed the gap between him and Melly. He bent slightly to speak. "Hello, Munchkin."

Melly continued to stare. Amber held her breath. Why wouldn't Melly say something? Amber observed the tilt of her child's head and knew she was about to.

"Daddy?"

Both she and Evan drew in sharp breaths at the same

time.

He turned to look at Amber. "How did she know?"

Her mind briefly blanked out. And then it came to her. "I—I think it might be because I've been showing her your picture every night before bed."

A hint of softness crept into his eyes. "You have?"

She nodded. "Ever since the day she came home from the hospital." She tried to swallow the lump that formed in her throat as she recalled this. Melly hadn't understood, but she'd become familiar with the ritual. Apparently, it paid off.

Evan looked at Melly and let out a long, slow breath.

To Melly, Amber said, "Yes, sweetie, it's your daddy."

Evan must have remembered the package he held, stared at it for a few seconds, then placed the medium-sized, rectangular object on the sofa in front of his daughter. "Here you go. This is for you."

Melly giggled. "Pesent! Yook, Mommy!" She picked at a corner of the wrapping paper and pulled. When multicolored shreds lay heaped on the floor, Melly stared at the picture on the box.

"It's a computer," Evan told her.

She thrust it at him. "Open."

Amber gasped. "How do we ask for something, Melly?"

"Open, *peese*," she said with a huge nod on the last word, as if proud to know the answer.

Evan ripped open the box and had the toy out in a matter of seconds. Then, always one to be prepared, he reached into his coat pocket and pulled out a package of "C" batteries. After placing them in the proper compartment, he pushed the "On" button and the gadget sprang to life, the tinkle of a montage of cheerful notes streaming across the room.

"Ooooh," Melly sang out, staring at the colorful images on the screen.

"There's the stamp of approval," Amber said moving to sit next to her daughter. "You obviously made a good choice." She began pressing buttons on the "keyboard."

"I thought an educational toy would be best." He watched Melly following her mother's example by pushing several keys. "Are you sure she likes it?"

Amber motioned to Melly with her hand. "Can't you tell?" Then to Melly, she said, "Sweetie, what do you say when someone gives you something?"

She raised her dark, puppy eyes to Evan's. "Tank-y,

Daddy." Then she rose up on her knees and threw her little arms around his neck.

"Oomph!" Evan's hands went up, hesitated, then went lightly around Melly's back. Amber could tell he hadn't expected a hug. He probably never expected a positive reception from Melly, at all. But her increasing joy became shrouded in disappointment when Evan reciprocated with only a halfhearted embrace.

* * *

Evan sat next to Melly for a time, showing her how to use the toy computer. The screen displayed images of objects, animals, letters and numbers. He studied her as she reacted to each new feat of the gadget, oohing and aahing with delight. A cute little thing, he had to admit. His chest swelled with pride, as he realized she bore a close resemblance to himself. Regret again pinched his gut at the accusation he'd made to Amber, yesterday. He sneaked a glance at her. His heart snagged, as he watched her sitting on the other side of Melly, head bent close and making excited comments of her own. She didn't deserve what he'd said. Still, keeping him in the dark about their child sliced deep.

Amber's phone ringing pulled him out of his meditations. He listened as she greeted Maggie.

"Oh, I've nearly forgotten! Picketers? And TV cameras?" She paused to listen while reaching for the remote on the coffee table. "Okay, Mags, I'm turning the TV on now. Thanks. 'Bye."

Amber flung the phone down on the couch. "I can't believe I forgot about what might happen because of today's story in the paper," she said flipping a few channels. She stopped at a local station showing breaking news. Both Evan and Amber stilled to watch. A female reporter stood outside the Cedarview Women's Center reporting on the situation. The noise was cacophonous, as angry demonstrators chanted in the background. Their exact words got lost in the melee of sounds because, just as on Amber's first day at the facility, there appeared to be two separate groups. Apparently, one represented pro-lifers, and the other represented pro-choicers. Just like her first day there. A couple police cars stood in the parking lot at odd angles

"For security reasons, police are escorting employees from the building, but Dr Hines, the proprietor of Cedarview Women's Center, has not yet made an appearance," the attractive Asian reporter said.

"I don't need to see anymore." Amber turned to Evan. "Do you?"

He shook his head. "No. Our job is done, and I want to move on as soon as possible."

Amber switched off the TV. "I'll go make us all some lunch."

* * *

By the end of the meal, Melly's eyes began to droop.

"I'd better put her in for a nap," Amber said. "This has been a big day for her." She took Melly's hand and led her out of the kitchen. "Come on, sweetie. Time for a nap." Melly went along without complaint, rubbing an eye with her little fist.

To kill time while he waited for Amber, Evan cleared off the table, then rinsed and stacked the dishes in the washer. He returned to the living room.

As he sat on the couch, a sweet fragrance drifted to his nostrils. He looked around and noticed, for the first time, the roses he'd thrown on the floor the other day were arranged in vases in various places around the apartment. That Amber had salvaged and kept them touched his heart. But he still couldn't bring himself to fully forgive her, yet.

Amber appeared and stood awkwardly for a moment, her gaze not meeting his. "Well, I'd better go clean up in the kitchen."

Evan pushed himself off the couch. "I've already done that."

"Oh. How sweet of you. Thanks."

He waved a dismissive hand without answering. He wasn't feeling very sweet toward her, at the moment.

They remained in place, silent again, each staring off in different directions. Finally, Amber said, "Well, I guess the clinic's closed down, at least for the day. A small accomplishment, but still . . ."

He nodded. "Mmm."

Amber sighed. "I just wish I hadn't been so deceitful. I'm feeling sort of ugly about it."

Bitterness settled on his tongue. What about how she'd treated him? Keeping Melly's existence from him. "That butcher's actions killed your sister. He's been lying to everyone for years, and you feel bad about lying to *him*?"

Her lips pressed into a thin line. "Evan, don't start. That's not what I meant. I was referring to my spiritual condition."

As if he'd been splashed in the face with a bucket of cold water, he came to his senses. Man, this woman drove him crazy.

"I'm sorry."

"Forget it." She turned and headed out of the room.

Now he'd gone and made things worse. The Angel Gabriel should come down and strike him dumb. Would he never learn to curb his tongue?

All at once, his insides were bursting with emotion. Familiar emotions he hadn't felt in a long time. He stood alone in the living room, sorting them out. Yeah, he was still angry that Amber had hidden Melly from him, but he loved her more than ever. What's more, he'd already begun to love his daughter, and was proud to be her father.

He knew exactly what he needed to do.

CHAPTER 39

After putting on a pot of coffee, Amber came back to the living room, but Evan wasn't there. Where did he go? Heading down the hallway to check on Melly, she wondered if he could be in the bathroom. Melly's bedroom door was ajar. Peeking in, her breath caught at the sight that met her eyes: Evan stood at the side of Melly's bunny-shaped bed, gazing down at her. Amber couldn't see his expression, because his back was to her, head bent toward Melly's sleeping form.

Amber stood there a few moments and watched, as he reached out and gently smoothed a strand of hair off Melly's cheek. Her throat ached from fighting back her tears. She wouldn't interrupt this precious moment.

As she started back toward the living room, she heard, "Psst!" He was right there behind her. "I'm sorry. I just wanted to see her before I go," he whispered.

"You're going?" She spoke above a whisper, and used every ounce of resolve not to pout. "I just made coffee. Won't you stay and have some?"

"No."

Amber turned away as she entered the living room, so he couldn't see her disappointment.

"I have to get back to the paper," he continued, voice at a normal level now. "But before I go, we need to talk about something."

"What is it?"

"I want you and Melly to come home. Tonight."

Her heart twittered. "But I thought you . . . we . . ." This time, she lost the battle against her tears, and they sprung to her eyes.

His voice hardened slightly. "Don't mistake this for something it's not. I just think it's best for Melly if we're all together in the same house as soon as possible. And with everything that's going on, it will be safer." He paused and stared at her. "We'll work on the rest as time passes."

"I understand." He'd thrown her a crumb, and it tasted so

good. She'd work hard to earn the whole cake.

"I want you to take the rest of today to pack as much stuff as you can; then you and Melly come home tonight. Tomorrow morning, I'll come back with a couple guys and a truck to pick up the rest."

At times, she had complained when he took charge. But then there were those moments, like now, when she was glad to surrender completely. "Whatever you say," she told him, trying to suppress a smile.

Evan opened the door. "Keep this locked," he said, before walking out.

* * *

By three-thirty that afternoon, Amber felt wilted. The day had been eventful, and there was more to come. She swiped the hair from her forehead with her forearm. Melly hadn't awakened from her nap yet, so she figured soaking in a hot bath would relax her.

She went to Melly's bedroom door and quietly pushed it open a crack, just to make sure. Still asleep, but she'd better hurry. After softly pulling it closed again, she headed for the bathroom, only to be stopped by the doorbell.

Who could that be?

It rang again. Because she didn't want anything to awaken Melly, she scampered to answer, but the bell rang a third time. Pounding immediately followed. "Who is it?" she snapped.

"It's me."

She froze. *Dr. Hines.* Weren't the FBI supposed to be watching him?

"Amber?"

What should she do? She scrounged for an excuse. "I—I'm not feeling well, Al. How about if you go home and call me on the phone?"

"I can't. Reporters and protesters are milling around outside my house. I promise I won't stay long." She heard shuffling through the door, as if he were changing his position.

"Really, I—I can't."

"Please, Amber. I have nowhere else to go. I thought maybe you could give me a quick bite to eat. I haven't eaten all day."

For lack of anything to say, other than a flat-out "no," she remained silent.

"Please," he said again. "You're the only one . . ." His

voice came out in a moan.

She sighed and leaned her head against the door. He sounded so forlorn. She had ruined his practice. Basically, his whole life.

"I'm begging you, Amber."

Although he snagged at her heart, she just couldn't. Evan would kill her. "Please, Doc, just go home."

He must have heard the hitch in her voice. "Are you afraid of me, Amber? C'mon, it's me. You know me. I would never hurt you. There's no reason to be afraid." His downtrodden tone from a minute ago had changed to almost jovial.

This could be true. She remembered the hostage situation at the center, and how he offered his life for hers. But he'd just demonstrated again how volatile he could be. She knew the joviality was fake.

"Doc, if you don't leave, I'll have to call the police." Pressing her back against the door, she closed her eyes and prayed he would go away.

"Okay. How about if you just crack the door with the chain on and hand me some food through the little space? I'll go away and find someplace to sit and eat it."

"Promise?"

"Promise. And you know me. I'm a man of my word."

That was true. As far as she knew, he had always been up front with her. Maybe it wouldn't hurt just to open the door with the chain and hand him something. "Hold on," she said, and went to the kitchen. She removed an apple, a half-used brick of cheddar cheese, some fried chicken, and a can of Pepsi from the refrigerator and laid them on the counter. Then she opened the bread box and tore off a hunk of crusty Italian bread. From a lower cabinet, she pulled a lunch bag from a package and placed all of the items in there. At the last minute she went to the cupboard, found a pack of cheese-peanut butter crackers and threw them in with the other food. As Amber reached the door, she prayed she was doing the right thing. A feeling of doom enveloped her, but she shrugged it off. This seemed to be the only way to make him leave. She unlocked the deadbolt, checked that the chain was latched and pulled the door open to its limits. She handed the sack through the small space. "Here y—"

All at once, Amber found herself flung backward amid splinters of wood. Smacking against an end table, she landed in a sitting position on the floor. Disoriented, she watched in a haze as Dr. Hines stepped over the threshold and pushed the door closed.

Like a death knell, she heard the deadbolt driven home.

CHAPTER 40

Evan surfed the channels of the TV in his office, searching for any news about the clinic. Nothing. He clicked it off, just as the phone rang. "Evan Blake, here."

"Evan, Uriah. Listen, the new toxicology report came in. It's bad."

Evan sat forward in his chair. "What is it?"

"Tubocurarine chloride, better known as Tubarine. It was found in the victim's body."

He rubbed a finger behind his ear. "What does that mean?"

"This is a substance that medical personnel commonly use as a homicidal poison. It's a muscle relaxant that when given in large amounts causes respiratory failure. So there you have it. Your suspicions about the doctor were right on the money. We'll have to bring him in for questioning."

A breath whooshed from Evan's lungs. "Wow. I didn't expect it to be this cut and dry. And Amber's been . . ." Visions of his wife being with that monster flitted through his mind, while beads of moisture formed on the back of his neck. "You know, Amber overheard Rita and Hines talking together the last night anyone saw Rita. It was after the clinic closed. By what they said, she thought they were going to get together. Looks now like quite the opposite."

"When we have him here, we could probably hold him on suspicion."

Relief washed through him. "Good. I'm going to call Amber and warn her. She needs to be extra careful, now that we know what he's capable of."

CHAPTER 41

The hairs at the base of Amber's neck stood on end.

She and Melly were locked in here with him. What was he planning?

"You disappoint me, Amber."

"What do you mean?" she asked, looking up at him from the floor.

He shrugged. "I thought you were more intelligent than to fall for my act. To open the door even a crack." He extended a hand to help her up. "Are you hurt?"

She didn't take his hand, and she deliberately avoided answering his question. She didn't want to give him the satisfaction of knowing he could hurt her. Wincing as she rose, she said, "I didn't think you were a liar. You've never lied to me in the past." He stood close and the air between them felt oppressive. She inched a few feet away from him. "How did you . . .?"

He raised an eyebrow. "Get away from the feds you sicced on me?"

No surprise he figured that out.

"Simple. They're such idiots, thinking they had all points of entry covered. I have another, quite obscure one. I slipped out there, crossed through a neighbor's yard, walked to a convenience store, and used my cell phone to call a taxi." He spoke as if he'd had experience dealing with law enforcement officials before.

"Why did you come here?"

"I'll get to that in a moment. First I have a few questions." He pulled something from the pocket of his jacket. A torn-off piece of newspaper. He unfolded it. She knew without looking it was the article from *The Tri-County Informer*. "How could you do this to me?" He waved the paper in front of her. "I treated you like a queen. I trusted you. Told you things I'd never told anyone. I *cared* for you."

Her tongue felt like sandpaper. She swallowed hard. "It was . . . just my job."

"Just your job? This is my life! Everything I've accomplished, have been trying to accomplish, is ruined. And this headline: 'A Good Doctor Goes Bad.' Why? I'm *not* bad."

"Please lower your voice, Doc." She had to get him out of here before he woke Melly. "Look, I'm sorry. I—I started out wanting to get back at you for the death of my twin sister twelve years ago. Other than that, I'm a reporter and I was just doing my job."

He looked at her in puzzlement. "Your sister?"

"Yes. You performed an abortion, and . . . she died."

He shot her a frown. "Amber, that wasn't my fault. It happens all the time. Women who agree to abortions know the risks."

"This is my sister we're talking about, Doc."

Waving a dismissive hand, he said, "Forget that now. Who's this?" He pointed at the byline where Evan's name was printed together with hers. A tiny headshot of them together, smiling blissfully out at the rest of the world accompanied the article. "This Evan Blake? Is he your husband? Please don't tell me you're married."

She hesitated, looked away. She wouldn't even discuss Evan with him. But for the first time she could see what a coldhearted man he really was.

"I can't believe it! The way you acted toward me. The kisses. All of it was a lie?"

Maybe he'd calm down if she told him what was going on at the time. How she felt. "We were separated. As I got to know you, I found that I liked you. It wasn't always an act."

He stared down at her, as if trying to make a decision. Finally, he said, "Well, that's of some comfort." He sighed resignedly. "Nevertheless, you've betrayed me." He reached into his pocket again. "And now—"

The phone rang.

Before she could even move to answer it, he said, "Don't!"

She turned toward the end table where she'd left the phone. "I have to. If it's Evan, he'll expect me to answer." She gestured around the room. "As you can see by all the boxes, I'm moving back home tonight."

She reached for the ringing phone.

"Daddy?"

With her hand an inch from the receiver, Amber froze in place.

"Daddy here?"

Amber spun around and strode toward Melly. She felt an urgency to gather her child into her arms. "No, baby, Daddy's not here."

Dr. Hines beat her to it and swept Melly up. The forcefulness of the sudden action caused a short squeal to escape Melly's lips.

Amber's heart bounced in her chest as she watched Melly's reaction. Complete shock froze her miniature features, as she gaped at the strange face so close to hers. Then her baby squirmed, trying desperately to free herself, but Dr. Hines tightened his hold. His expression became darker and angrier. He raised his voice to speak over Melly's bawling. "The surprises just keep coming." He shook his head. "The woman I fell for wasn't the real you, at all."

"Please. Give her to me."

Struggling to hold onto Melly with one arm, he reached into his pocket with his free hand. He pulled out a hypodermic syringe, uncapped it with his teeth, and spit the cap out the side of his mouth. Then he pointed the needle against Melly's arm.

"Stop!" Her voice shrilled. "What *is* that?"

"Just a little muscle relaxant. In high doses, it causes respiratory failure." He looked down at Melly with a demonic smile. "It will work much faster on this little one than it did on Rita." He pinned Amber with a glare. "I was going to use this on you, but I think it'll hurt you more if I use it on your child."

CHAPTER 42

When Amber didn't answer his call and her voicemail switched on, Evan hung up, waited five minutes and tried again. Still no answer on either her home or cell phones. Where could she be? Out somewhere? She was supposed to be home packing. If she'd gone on an errand, or taken Melly out for a walk, she would at least answer the cell.

Something was not right.

He jumped off his chair, snatched up his cell phone and raced out the door.

On the way to Amber's he tried both her numbers again. Nothing. He kept at it for the duration of the drive. If a cop wanted to stop him for being on the phone while driving, all the better. He'd make them chase him all the way to Amber's.

After catching every red light on the way, Evan finally arrived at Amber's apartment building. He noticed Hines's car, as he tore out of the Mustang and dashed into the building. His heart rate increased two-fold. Even with his short legs, the stairs would be quicker than waiting for the elevator, so he raced to them and began climbing.

God, please keep Amber safe.

Winded, he finally arrived at the third floor and crashed through the door leading to the hallway. He sped down the long passageway, then turned the corner, finally arriving at Amber's unit. His heart rate and rapid breathing created too much noise to hear anything going on inside. He waited for them to subside before resting his ear against the door.

Through the thick wood, he heard a male voice. Hines. Somehow he'd gotten inside. There was crying and screaming. A child. Melly! What was that monster doing to his little girl? His fist went up, ready to pound the door, but he stopped short. Revealing his presence could jeopardize the lives of the two people he loved most.

Moisture formed on the back of his neck as he stood there, helpless, wondering what he could do.

Think, Blake, think!

If only there was a way to get inside without the doctor knowing. Then he could use the element of surprise. That would—then it came to him like the snap of a finger. He remembered Amber mentioning that her bedroom often felt too warm, and she'd have to crack open the window to cool the room down. He prayed that was the case now.

While rushing back to the stairwell, he pulled out his phone and dialed Uriah's cell number.

When the detective answered his call, Evan quickly explained the circumstances. "Uriah, the guy's in the apartment, right now. Melly's crying, and I'm worried."

"Hold up. Who's Melly?"

In his haste, he'd forgotten Uriah didn't know what had been going on between him and Amber. "My daughter. Long story. I'll explain sometime, but we need to get some officers here."

"Okay, my friend. Stay calm. I'll see that they get there."

Evan pushed through the front door of the building, out into the brisk, late afternoon air. "And please ask them not to burst on the scene with flashing lights and wailing sirens. We don't know the situation."

"Don't worry, we'll handle it. What's the address?"

Evan gave it to him as he rounded the back of the building. "Will you also alert the FBI for me? And listen, Uriah. I won't be waiting outside to meet any of them. I'm going to see if I can get into the apartment through a window off the fire escape. I'll leave it open for your men."

"Evan, no! Wait for help. You could be putting your own life on the line."

"Doesn't matter. I've got to take that chance." Flipping the phone closed, he realized how much he really meant that. Without Amber and Melly, he may as well be dead himself.

He stood under the fire escape, wanting to throw a tantrum of the worst kind. The stairs were too high for him to reach and pull down.

Now what? Frantic, he looked around for something to stand on. Huge trash bins and parked cars. Forget the bins, they were much too high. But if he could get a car under the ladder, he could climb onto the hood to reach it.

He needed to go back and pull his own car around. Cursing, he sprinted for the parking lot at the front of the building.

As he ran, he railed at God for letting this happen; for not making him average-sized, so he could get where he wanted to go faster, and not waste time looking for things to stand on.

He finally reached the Mustang, hopped inside, started it and sped out of the space. Good thing no one had been walking in the lot at the time, since he'd hardly used any caution. He zipped around to the back lot with squealing wheels, and stopped short of the fire escape ladder. Then he jumped out of the car and climbed onto the hood, using the bumper as a step-up. This brought him to the fourth rung. Looking up, it seemed a daunting ascent. Determined, he applied foot to metal.

After the endless climb, he reached Amber's window. Relief washed over him at the sight of the tiny space between window and sill. Quickly he pulled out his car key to pry away the screen. When it came free, he gently set it down, slid the window up higher and slipped inside.

CHAPTER 43

"So Evan was right. You did kill Rita. You were probably the one making those crank phone calls, too."

His eyebrows drew together in puzzlement. "Crank phone calls?" Then his face lit as if he'd become enlightened. "Oh, that was Rita. She told me the night I killed her she'd been doing that. I told her it was childish behavior."

Melly's crying had continued through the conversation. "Please," Amber pleaded, "I'm the one who caused all this. Let her go." Amber stretched her arm out, half expecting him to immediately acquiesce.

Dr. Hines shook his head. "No. When I dashed over here, I had no idea what I would do. I brought this 'magic potion' just in case." He looked down at Melly as she struggled in his hold. "But then I saw this one and couldn't pass up the opportunity to punish you, just as you're punishing me."

"How am I punishing you?"

His gaze hardened on Amber. "I finally found something I could do in my son's honor. A way to help cure children of Duchenne dystrophy in his name. You've destroyed that. You've taken him from me a second time." His voice became rigid. "Now you'll see what it's like to lose a child."

Oh, Lord, help me, here! I couldn't live without Melly. "I thought you cared about life, Doc." She had to keep him talking until she thought of a way to get Melly away from him. "Isn't that the whole point of donating the parts and fetuses to research?" She hoped he didn't detect the shakiness of her voice.

"The whole point was to make up for what I couldn't do to save my son."

Amber's heart squeezed. Here was this murderer threatening to kill her baby, and she could feel compassion for him. She had to be deranged. "Doc," she said gently. "Al, there was nothing you or anyone could do. The disease he had takes the life of everyone who contracts it."

He seemed to look right through her. His face squinched with anguish, and she could barely hear him above Melly. "But I was a top doctor. I saved so many lives. Surely, I could have done *something*."

"No. No one could." She chanced a step toward him.

"Stop! Don't come any closer."

Melly screeched and squirmed in his arms. Couldn't any of the neighbors hear? Amber couldn't breathe for fear that Melly's thrashing about would cause that needle to enter her arm unintentionally.

Dr. Hines struggled with her and squeezed her into a tighter position. "Quiet!" he yelled into her ear.

Melly stilled instantly. Mouth agape and eyes wide, she stared at Dr. Hines's face, convulsing from stifled sobs. The little dark ponytail at the top of her head quivered with the action. Seconds ticked by. Finally, she let out a long, loud wail which preceded another round of fresh tears. Amber's baby girl turned to look at her, water-sparkled eyes asking why she just stood there and didn't come take her away from the bad man.

Seeing Dr. Hines's frustration as he wrestled with Melly, Amber thought she'd better do something fast. But what?

She took another step forward, hoping he didn't notice. "Al, what do you want from me?"

"Back off, for one thing," he said through his teeth.

Darn! "Okay, but tell me what I can do to help you."

He glared at her. "I want my life back. My dignity. My good reputation. I don't think you can do that."

Her mind frantically searched for a way to get her baby away from this lunatic.

Suddenly, Melly stopped fighting and stilled. Her wailing became quiet sobs. Her body had gone limp and, eyes half closed, her head hung back, like a rag doll. Amber couldn't tell what happened, and wanted to freak out on the doctor. She would have, if he didn't have that needle pressed against her baby's side. Her blood boiled, and it took all she had to keep from attacking him like a bear protecting its cub. "Al, let me put her to bed, then we can figure something out."

"No."

"This is not honoring to your son. You're sullying his good name with your actions."

He shot her an ironic look. "Amber, I'm not stupid. All you want to do is save your child. Might as well save your breath, instead."

Dear God, help! I'm grasping at straws, here. Give me something!

Her heart hadn't stopped pounding from the moment he rang the doorbell. If she didn't do something fast, she'd have a massive coronary on the spot. "You think I hate you, but I don't. What I said before was true. I did like you, once I got to know you."

Dr. Hines shook his head sadly. "None of that matters anymore, Amber. The damage is done. Unless you can perform a miracle and make it all go away, the center is finished."

"Maybe I *can* do something." A blatant lie. "Let me think. But in the meantime, give me my child, so I can put her down to nap. She'll go back to sleep and we can talk it out undisturbed." She held out her empty arms, aching to receive her daughter.

All of a sudden, she noticed the complete silence. Dr. Hines seemed to notice, too. Melly had cried herself to sleep. But every few seconds, she hiccupped and quivered as a result of her prolonged fit. Her head still hung backward, and Amber worried about her neck.

Oh, she longed to cradle her baby against her.

"Well, will you look at that? Your little girl has fallen asleep in my arms." His lips settled into a satisfied smile. "Now, tell me what you have in mind."

CHAPTER 44

Evan tiptoed around the edge of Amber's bedroom. He had no idea where Hines was positioned in the living room and didn't want to risk being seen through the open doorway. Plastering himself against the wall by the opening, he listened.

"Your argument is with me, Doctor. Deal with me and leave her out of it." Amber's voice was shrill. Evan could tell she was about to snap. Or maybe she already had.

"Oh, so it's back to 'Doctor' now. A few minutes ago you called me Al."

Evan had never heard Hines's voice in person before. Now that he had, the monster no longer remained a vague figure flitting through the halls of his imagination. He had seen the doctor from a distance that night he followed Amber and Hines home from the restaurant, but the voice lent completeness to the picture. Only now the picture differed greatly from the one Evan had imagined. He had always thought Hines's voice would be a deep baritone. But no, it sounded more like the doctor spoke around a lump in his throat. All along, Evan had been secretly jealous of Hines's height, but the man's voice sure cut him down to size.

"What would you like me to call you?" Amber asked.

He could think of a few choice words.

Slowly he poked his head around the doorjamb. Neither Amber nor the Mad Doctor were within his view.

"It doesn't matter. The end result will be the same."

Was that a note of remorse he detected in Hines's tone? Maybe there was still hope.

"Please." Amber had broken into tears. "Just give me my baby. I'll do anything you want."

He had to do something. Where were the police? Pressed against the wall, he inched his way down the tiny, darkened hallway.

"Anything?" Hines asked, sounding interested.

"Yes," Amber answered, still tearful.

Amber, Amber, hold on. I'm coming, Sweetheart. Don't

do anything rash!

Evan came to the end of the hall and peeked around the corner. Amber was hidden from his view by the hulking doctor, whose back faced him. In his arms looked to be an unconscious Melly. He couldn't see her face, but her head and limbs hung limp. What had that monster done to their little girl? She couldn't be . . .

Rage coursed through him. His hands instinctively curled into fists.

"First tell me how you came to know what we've been doing at the center." Hines said. "Only someone who works there could have brought you the story. Who was it?"

Don't say a word, Sweetheart. He'll probably pop Maggie off too.

His Amber remained silent. *Good Girl.*

"Okay, then. If that's the way you want it." Hines's shifted Melly in his arms and looked down at her. Evan couldn't see what the doctor did with his other hand.

"Stop!" Amber screeched.

Moisture broke out on Evan's forehead, as he resisted the urge to storm out there. He leaned back against the wall and closed his eyes in an effort to restrain himself. Now there's an idea. He could charge the doctor, but if he had a gun or some other weapon, Melly could be harmed. The guy was a skyscraper, so Evan couldn't see past Hines's back to what his hands were doing. Maybe if he showed himself that would take the focus off Melly. It could buy them time until either the police or feds got there, or he thought of some way to get their little girl away from Hines.

"Okay, okay! I'll tell you." Amber said.

Hines stayed silent and still.

"I—I already knew about it."

"That has to be a lie." Impatience crept into Hines's voice.

"I mean I've been there before. Years ago."

"I gave you an abortion?" Evan saw the back of his head shake. "No. I would remember you."

"Not me. My twin sister. Remember? I mentioned it earlier." Her voice cracked. Evan could see where she was going with this, but would it bring her the satisfaction she sought?

"I guess it didn't register. But if she looked like you, same height and all, I would remember."

"She wasn't the same height. She was an average-sized person."

Evan saw Hines's free arm drop and spied the hypodermic needle. *What on earth?* And then he remembered how Rita died.

"Was?" Hines asked.

The doctor seemed to forget about the needle, and Evan figured now would be the time to act. But what if he fouled up? Someone he loved could get seriously hurt. Or worse. He had to try, though, and believe the Lord would protect them all. Maybe the least that would happen is the doctor would drop Melly and she'd end up with a bump on her head.

"As I said before, after you . . . Afterward, she died."

Even though he couldn't see her, Evan knew tears rolled down her cheeks. Sidestepping along the wall, he turned the corner that brought him out into the living room.

Hines said nothing, his back as rigid as a stone statue. The arm that hung still held that needle.

It's now or never, Blake.

He rushed toward the doctor.

CHAPTER 45

It happened so fast. At first, Amber didn't know what was going on. In her peripheral vision, she thought she noticed movement beyond Dr. Hines. She dared not focus on it, because she felt certain Evan had just crept by. Her knight in shining armor. How did he get in here? How did he even know? But Dr. Hines blocked her view. Maybe in her desperation she had imagined him.

Until she heard a Tarzan-like call. In a split second, she knew she'd better be ready to catch Melly. Amber plunged forward.

"What the—?" Dr. Hines's self-assurance morphed into shock. His body bucked, but he remained on his feet as the hand holding the needle was pulled and twisted behind him. His hold on Melly loosened, and Amber tried wrenching her away, almost succeeding. But Hines tightened his grasp again.

So close . . . "Give her to me!" Melly woke up and started crying.

He didn't reply. Evan kept him busy trying not to lose the needle.

With that thought, deep concern pierced her heart. "Evan, be careful! That stuff is deadly," she yelled, as she tried prying Melly from Dr. Hines's arms. "It's what he used to kill Rita."

"I know." Evan grunted and struggled to free the syringe from the doctor's grasp.

With both hands occupied, Dr. Hines twisted and battled them with his body. "This is preposterous!"

"Ow!" Evan's cry came from behind the doctor.

Amber couldn't see. "Evan, what happened?"

"The needle stuck me."

She sucked in a breath. *No, God, no!*

Hines laughed, but his satisfaction was short-lived.

"Don't worry, though, the plunger didn't move."

If she had the time, she would breathe a sigh of relief, but through it all the three of them still wrestled. Long minutes passed. Melly's screams became whimpers that blended with their panting and deep guttural sounds, forming a chaotic chorus of desperation.

Suddenly, Dr. Hines howled and the syringe dropped to the carpet. Evan kicked it out of the way and continued to keep the doctor's arm twisted behind his back. But with a mighty tug, he pulled it free. Evan sprawled to the floor.

Amber still worked to release Melly. Until she felt something hard press against her temple. She froze.

"That's right. A gun. I didn't want to do it this way. Too messy and undignified. But you give me no choice." He stared down at her, his eyes as cold as the weapon he held to her head. "Now back off."

Fresh tears sprung to her eyes as she did so, while he kept the gun trained on her. "Please. Do what you want to me, but don't hurt my baby." Melly had quieted again, as if knowing her silence were crucial to the outcome of this debacle.

In an instant, Dr. Hines moved the gun away from her head and pointed it out to the side. "I wouldn't try that, Blake. Now come over here and stand where I can keep an eye on you."

Amber had only seen movement out of the corner of her eye but guessed that Evan had probably moved to pick up the hypodermic needle that had been hurled across the floor minutes ago. He came up beside her and took her hand, giving it a reassuring squeeze. Dr. Hines sidestepped until he reached the syringe. Switching the gun to the same hand with which he held Melly, and keeping it trained on Amber and Evan, he bent down to retrieve the deadly needle. He slipped it into his pocket, then switched the gun back. "Now then." He returned to where they stood.

"What are you going to do?" Evan asked. "What have you got to gain by killing three more people? You'll be the first to be suspected. It's all over, Hines. Just let us go."

"Yes, it's all over, but at least I'll have the satisfaction of snuffing out the lives of the two people who are responsible."

"Why don't you let Amber and Melly go? Just deal with me."

"Oh, I'll deal with you, all right. Both of you will suffer while watching someone you love being destroyed. Just like I suffered when that horrible disease destroyed my son."

Amber spoke up tentatively. "We had nothing to do with what happened to your son."

His eyes bore into hers. The joviality and kindness she

once found in his handsome features were no longer there. "No, but now you've stolen from me the only thing I had left to give him. I created a legacy, and you've crushed it with your printed words." His features crumbled with despair. "I loved you, Amber. You've hurt me to the very center of my being."

"I'm sorry, Doctor." And she was, for his son's sake. "But keeping late-term aborted fetuses alive in tanks for the purpose of harvesting their organs is unethical and immoral."

Amber thought she heard sirens in the distance, and she wondered if Evan had called the police before he'd come. She snuck a glance at him. His lips pursed slightly for a microsecond. She could guess why. Several times, he'd voiced his frustration that they always used their sirens to hail their arrival, even in situations where the element of surprise would work best.

The sirens quickly faded. Evan shot her a look of despair.

Dr. Hines seemed not to have noticed the sirens at all. "Unethical and immoral? Who appointed you as God?" Melly began to cry and squirm, again, reaching her arms toward her parents. Dr. Hines shook her. "Stop it!" She only cried and squirmed harder.

Amber started to move toward the doctor, but Evan's grip held her in place. She could feel him tense beside her. "If you hurt my daughter, Hines," he said, "I'll—"

"What? What will you do, Blake, while I stand here with this gun and a lethal drug that could kill any one of you at a moment's notice?" His lips fixed into a satisfied smile.

Evan's hand tightened around hers, and Amber knew his other one had balled into a fist. Her heart ached for him, and she gave his arm a reassuring rub.

Please, Lord. Evan and Melly have just found one another. They can't lose each other now.

"Trust me," Evan said. "You won't get away with this. The police are coming. I spoke with them before I got here."

Dr. Hines laughed. "Well, where are they then? What's taking them so long? Do you think I believe you? Besides, as I said, it doesn't matter anymore. My own life is over. There's nothing left for me."

A spark of hope dashed through Amber as a thought came to her. "What about Jasmine? You still have her, and she loves you. I'm sure she wouldn't want you to give up."

"Jas can see that the research goes on without me. I'm just a burden to her, anyway."

"That can't be true. The two of you seem to be very

close."

Dr. Hines shrugged. "She'll get over it." His hand tightened on the gun.

CHAPTER 46

Though he tried not to show it, Evan was in a panic. Hines was right. Where were the police? Maybe Uriah couldn't convince them to send anyone.

"Enough talk," Hines said, reaching into his pocket.

The gun barrel sagged. The police still hadn't arrived, so it was up to Evan to save them. He sized up the situation, and made a quick decision.

Hines pulled out the needle and, with amazing dexterity, one-handedly brought it into position. With thumb poised on the plunger, he pushed the deadly tip against Melly's shoulder. Amber screamed. Evan held her back.

What if his plan had the opposite effect? The impact could force the needle into Melly's tender flesh.

"Take a good look. Once I administer this drug, it will take immediate effect. You'll never see her alive again." Hines looked down at Melly as he pushed the needle through her clothes. She yelped, and Evan's blood roared in his ears. Dr. Hines began to apply pressure to the plunger.

Now!

He sprinted toward Hines and yelled, "Amber, get Melly," hoping she understood what he wanted her to do.

The distance was short and his target now loomed before him. He couldn't afford to miss. Evan swung his foot at Hines's kneecap with all his might.

Hines's face crumpled as he howled in pain. His eyes glazed over and his knee gave out. His body dipped toward the floor and the needle followed suit. Melly slid to the carpet with a soft thud before Amber could catch her. His little girl screamed in fury, but he was glad to hear it. Amber swept Melly into her arms, and they moved out of his line of vision. He grabbed Hines's gun hand and bent it back. Good. They were both out of harm's way. The doctor howled again, but didn't let go. They grappled.

Hines's red face became demonic, as he glared at Evan at close range. "You haven't got a chance, Blake. I'm bigger and stronger. Give up!"

"Never!" He fought to twist the gun free. With one hand on the weapon, Evan jabbed two fingers into Hines's eye. Hines howled again.

A shot rang out.

Both men stilled. The sudden silence hung like a heavy curtain that divided this second in time from the previous.

Then he heard her voice.

"Evan?"

The two of them turned as one to see Amber collapse onto the floor.

CHAPTER 47

What happened?

Amber lay there in a haze, the pain too great to do anything more. Had she been shot? Was she dying? Already dead? As if from a distance, she heard voices. Masculine voices.

"Amber!" That was Evan.

"Hold it, police!" Vaguely familiar, but she couldn't bother to think about who spoke.

Suddenly, she felt warmth, as a strong but gentle hand swept the hair from her forehead. "You're going to be all right, my love. I promise." Evan again, beside her this time. She tried telling him not to worry, but her mouth couldn't form the words. His hands searched her body. "Where are you hurt?"

All she could do was moan.

"Oh, God, blood! Uriah, call an ambulance."

Oh, Uriah was here. Good.

"They're on their way."

"Hang on, baby, they're coming.

"You have the right to remain silent. Anything you say can and will be used against you in a court of law." Uriah's voice sounded very far away.

"Mommy? Daddy?"

Melly! The pain was too great, stealing her breath away. Gradually, the haze darkened, all shimmers of light gone.

"Mommy's going to be fine, Munchkin." Evan's words floated around her, garbling.

Don't go away! I need you. Come back!

She felt herself being lifted.

Evan spoke again, but the ocean's waves roaring in her ears drowned him out.

Then, total blackness.

CHAPTER 48

"I'm sorry, Evan," Detective Uriah Washington said. "Things should never have turned out this way."

"You're right, they shouldn't have. No wonder people have no confidence in the local police force. No wonder they ask 'Where are the cops when you need 'em?' What took you so long to get there?"

From a chair next to the hospital bed, Amber watched the two men in amusement. Evan's face was void of its usual cocky grin, and his tone still carried the anger he'd been voicing for two days, since it had fallen to the two of them to save their little family. But she knew it wasn't a personal affront toward Uriah, nor did their friend take it that way.

"Hey, you did just as good your own self. I keep saying you got to be workin' for us." Uriah flashed a bright smile. "And what about the feds? They took even longer to get there."

"Please, Evan, it's no big deal," Amber said. "I'm fine. Let's thank the Lord the bullet wasn't buried too deeply into my thigh. Besides, the police couldn't help that there was a major accident on the freeway. At least Uriah was able to get there."

He turned to her, and his eyes softened. She could read his love for her written in them. "I just don't want to lose you again. I was so scared."

Their gazes held and tears threatened.

"Here's Mommy and Daddy," Ma sang out as she entered the room carrying Melly. Dad followed, clutching a handful of ribbons attached to colorful Mylar balloons.

"Mommy!" Ma had barely set Melly down before she ran to Amber's arms.

"Hello, Peaches." Amber wrapped her baby in a tight embrace.

The Sharps and Uriah exchanged salutations, then Uriah said, "I'd best be going."

Evan offered his hand. "I'm sorry I've been so grouchy. I really am grateful you came for us."

Uriah shook his hand and clapped him on the shoulder. "No problem, my man. You have a right to be grouchy with all you've been through." He nodded to Amber and winked before walking out of the room.

Dad took Melly by the hand and ushered Ma to the door. "We'll bring the car around front."

"Thanks. I'm ready to get out of here." The mixed odors of antiseptic and sickness alone nauseated Amber.

After her folks left, a nurse came into the room with a wheelchair. Evan grabbed Amber's jacket and purse off the bed then took her arm to help her out of the chair. "Take it easy, now."

She reached for the miniature footed cane the doctor had special-ordered to suit her height and leaned her weight into it. "So do you think the outcome of the story was worth the price we paid?"

Sighing, he placed his hand on the small of her back and guided her careful steps. "I don't know, Amber. I'm thinking we need to quit doing undercover investigating now that we have Melly to consider." He helped her onto the seat of the wheelchair and took the cane from her.

She smiled at him. "You know what? I'm thinking you're right."

He looked at her in surprise. "Really?"

She nodded. "Even though we won in the end and Dr. Hines will be in jail for a very long time, the trafficking he participated in will still go on. Part of it through his sister." The nurse pushed Amber down the hallway.

"Yeah, but the FBI will be watching her, so it's only a matter of time."

"I feel like we almost lost our lives for very little, though."

They arrived at the elevator and Evan pushed the down button. Surprisingly, the door opened immediately, and they entered. "Yeah, I still can't believe some of the things going on that skirt the edges of the law," he said, shaking his head. "And whatever happened to those babies Hines kept?"

Tears welled up at the mere mention of those tiny souls. This was the hardest part—knowing she couldn't do a thing about them. She'd never forget the sight of them being kept alive in those containers Rita had called "chambers."

Amber rubbed the moist blur from her eyes. "My guess is he somehow got them to Jasmine, who then quickly dispersed them among her clients." She paused for a moment. "Evan, I want to apologize for all of the heartache I've caused you over the past two years. I should never have left you. I should have just trusted in the Lord. Rested in Him. And then, not to tell you about Melly was irresponsible of me. I'm sorry." Tears spilled down her cheeks, and the nurse thrust a tissue in front of her face. She'd almost forgotten the woman was there.

The elevator stopped on the ground floor with a thud and Amber felt that strange bounce of her body.

Evan cleared his throat. "Amber, no need to keep beating yourself up over it. You weren't completely at fault. I should have been more sensitive to your needs as a woman. And I should have asked the Lord to change my heart."

Everyone remained quiet, as though lost in their own thoughts. The nurse continued to push her until they reached the large, glass double doors. Amber saw Dad's car parked just outside. The doors slid open with a swish. Ma and Dad were already seated in the front seat, and Melly was buckled into her car seat.

"Wait right there," Evan said. Dad popped open the trunk from inside the car. Evan threw Amber's things inside, and crammed the Mylar balloons down before slamming the lid shut. While the nurse steadied the chair, he helped her off the seat. A sharp pain shot through her thigh and she stumbled.

Evan steadied her. "It's okay, I've got you," he said softly.

She stopped and gazed into his chocolate eyes. "You certainly do."

He chuckled, wrapped an arm around her shoulder, and kissed her temple. "C'mon, Mrs. Blake. Let's go home."

THE END

Other Books from Sword of the Spirit Publishing

2008

All the Voices of the Wind by Donald James Parker
The Bulldog Compact by Donald James Parker
Reforming the Potter's Clay by Donald James Parker
All the Stillness of the Wind by Donald James Parker
All the Fury of the Wind by Donald James Parker
More Than Dust in the Wind by Donald James Parker
Angels of Interstate 29 by Donald James Parker

2009

Love Waits by Donald James Parker
Homeless Like Me by Donald James Parker

2010

Against the Twilight by Donald James Parker
Finding My Heavenly Father by Jeff Reuter
Never Without Hope by Michelle Sutton
Reaching the Next Generation of Kids for Christ by Robert C. Heath

2011

Silver Wind by Donald James Parker
He's So In Love With You by Robert C. Heath
Their Separate Ways by Michelle Sutton
Silver Wind Pow-wow by Donald James Parker
Will the Real Christianity Please Stand Up by Donald James Parker
The 21st Century Delusion by Daniel Narvaez

Made in the USA
Monee, IL
07 July 2026